D0796293

Storied Stone

Storied Stone

Indian Rock Art in the
Black Hills Country

Linea Sundstrom

University of Oklahoma Press : Norman

ALSO BY LINEA SUNDSTROM
Rock Art of Western South Dakota (Vermillion, S.Dak., 1984)
Rock Art of the Southern Black Hills: A Contextual Approach (New York, 1990)

LIBRARY OF CONGRESS CATALOGING-IN-PUBLICATION DATA
Sundstrom, Linea.
  Storied stone: Indian rock art in the Black Hills country / Linea Sundstrom
      p. cm.
  Includes bibliographical references and index.
    ISBN 0–8061–3562–X (hc. : alk. paper) — ISBN 0–8061–3596–4 (pbk. :
alk. paper)
    1. Indians of North America—South Dakota—Antiquities. 2. Indians
of North America—Black Hills Region (S.D. and Wyo.)—Antiquities.
3. Petroglyphs—Black Hills Region (S.D. and Wyo.) 4. Picture-writing—
Black Hills Region (S.D. and Wyo.) 5. Black Hills (S.D. and Wyo.)—
Antiquities. I. Title

E78.S63S87 2004
978.3'901—dc21

                                                        2003051389

Designed by Ellen Beeler

The paper in this book meets the guidelines for permanence and durability of
the Committee on Production Guidelines for Book Longevity of the Council
on Library Resources. ♾

Copyright © 2004 by Linea Sundstrom. Published by the University of
Oklahoma Press, Norman, Publishing Division of the University. All rights
reserved. Manufactured in the U.S.A.

All photographs are copyright Linea Sundstrom or Glen Fredlund unless otherwise noted. All drawings are copyright Linea Sundstrom unless otherwise
noted.

1 2 3 4 5 6 7 8 9 10

Contents

Preface

The Lakota people have a proverb: *We are known by the tracks we leave behind.* Leaving tracks—whether pyramids, skyscrapers, or simple tipi rings—is a universal human experience. The desire to understand the tracks left behind by others is only slightly less universal. A sudden encounter with the traces of an earlier sojourner strikes a note of wonder in most people. Who passed this way before us? What made them laugh, cry, despair, rejoice, or pause in silent reflection? Who left these tracks, and why?

Rock art—the paintings and engravings on cliffs and in rocky overhangs or caves—is a kind of track that seems to speak to everyone. Today, all over the world one can buy rock art T-shirts, mugs, refrigerator magnets, jewelry, place mats, lamps, CD holders, coats, hats, ties, pencil holders, sofa pillows, mouse pads, and paperweights (fig. 1). Modern culture's fascination with rock art is not purely aesthetic. Instead, people are riveted by these images because they seem to evoke a timeless realm of material simplicity and spiritual richness. The rock art perhaps reminds us of what we as a culture have lost in our quest to acquire more. And it contains an element of mystery, because its makers seem to be forever gone. Like fossils, rock art takes us back to a world we never knew.

The reality, of course, is not so simple. The peoples who made rock art are still with us. In many cases, they *are* us. Many of our ancestors created rock art, somewhere in the world. Some of us are so removed from our ancestors that we hardly know

them. Others, however, have kept real connections intact through ceremonies, oral traditions, and pilgrimages to sacred or historic places. In North America, despite centuries of deliberate attempts to remove native peoples from their traditional homelands, religions, and ways of life, native traditions have tenaciously persisted. Many people are unwilling to abandon the ideas and environments that define their existence and that will define the existence of their children and grandchildren.

My interest in rock art developed slowly. Growing up in the Black Hills, I knew from childhood that there were "Indian writings" around. Sometimes I noticed strange markings on the cliffs along dusty back roads. But they were just part of the background noise, as it were. It was not until I started college as an anthropology major and began to visit rock art sites in the Pacific Northwest that I wanted to go back and learn more about these places.

In 1980, as a young college graduate, I received a grant from the South Dakota Historic Preservation Office to record and enumerate the rock art sites in the southern Black Hills (fig. 2). I needed a field assistant, and by a great stroke of luck, a graduate student named Cherie Haury appeared. Cherie was smart, witty, determined, and tough as buffalo hide. After three months of scaling up and down cliffs, hiking for countless miles in labyrinthine terrain, and interviewing dozens of landowners, I was hooked on rock art research. If Cherie wasn't, she never showed it. It was

Figure 1. This petroglyph (left) was modified to create a design acceptable to today's T-shirt purchasers (right). Whoopup Canyon, Wyoming.

the hottest, driest summer since the dust bowl days. The heat was not just miserable, it was dangerous. With a full load of cameras, notebooks, first-aid kit, and other field gear, it was difficult to carry enough water to last half a day in that heat. Sometimes a half-day hike turned into a full day, and the water ran out. Concern about sparking a fire in the tinder-dry grass meant walking miles to reach places normally accessible by automobile. The rattlesnakes were hot and thirsty, too, and sought shade by the dozens in the very rocks we were trying to photograph.

But what rocks they were! Some were covered with intricate swirling designs, something between road maps and mazes. Some had scores of tiny, perfect deer and antelope pursued by tiny hunters meticulously pecked into the smooth cliffs. Some had red or black paintings of fantastic creatures. Some had footprints or handprints as deeply engraved into the stone as impressions in soft mud. Other designs were engraved so lightly that they entirely disappeared from view in direct sunlight. Since there *was* nothing but direct sunlight that summer, we found these only when our own shadows happened to fall across the rock and the petroglyphs popped into view. Some paintings were in painfully narrow crevices; others were on cliffs shining like billboards in the bright sun. We found ourselves surrounded by one of the largest and most diverse collections of rock art on the continent.

It was immediately clear that several distinct kinds of rock art dotted the Black Hills. Some of it seemed very old, and some was obviously more recent. But how to explain carvings on sheer cliffs 20 or 30 feet above the ground surface? As we began to find places where one kind of rock art overlay another, it became clear that rock art had been made in the Black Hills for a long time indeed, and probably by many different groups. How did these observations fit with archaeologists' rapidly expanding knowledge of the prehistory of the Black Hills? This was only the first of many questions the rock art raised.

Perhaps the strongest impression I received during those weeks of clambering up and down the canyons was that this rock art was not mere doodling. It had meaning. It was too elaborate, too labor intensive, too beautifully made, and too thematically striking to have been an idle pursuit. This seemingly subjective first impression has since been borne out by ethnographic and archaeological research. Thus began a long and alternately rewarding and frustrating inquiry. What was the meaning of this art? Who made it? When? And most elusive of all, why?

In my doctoral dissertation, completed in 1989, I attempted to answer these questions by looking at the rock art in its total physical, temporal, spatial, and cultural contexts, insofar as I could reconstruct these. This approach was an amalgam of archaeological and art historical methodology. Like much of archaeology, it was a mix of science and humanities. At that time, science had failed to produce a reliable method for dating rock art, and this limited my ability to draw conclusions. Progress has since been made in this area, but the vast majority of rock art in the Black Hills country is still undatable except relative to other rock art. This does not mean, however, that its meaning is completely lost to us. Clues in the rock art itself and in the archaeology and oral traditions of the cultures within which it was produced help to reveal its meaning. No one will ever achieve a complete understanding of the rock art

Figure 2. Rock art survey in Red Canyon, southern Black Hills, August 1980. (Photo by Joe Alan Artz; reproduced with permission.)

of the Black Hills country. What happened in the past is rarely provable in the scientific sense of the word. Instead, like a historian, I have tried to bring together the various clues to tell the story of the rock art as completely and accurately as possible. Other voices may tell the story differently.

My dissertation, published in 1990 as *Rock Art of the Southern Black Hills: A Contextual Approach,* is now out of print, although still available in many libraries. An earlier report on the 1980 survey published by the South Dakota Archaeological Society is also out of print. Rather than merely reprinting these earlier books, I wanted to write a new book that would focus on the most fascinating aspect of the rock art of the Black Hills and Cave Hills: its meaning and significance as part of the larger world of the Plains Indians. This book includes many ideas from the earlier publications but also much new data from subsequent rock art surveys in 1992, 1993, and 1997–2002, along with the results of new analyses of rock art done for various articles and presented papers.

So many people have given me assistance and advice over the years that is a daunting task to list them all. My deepest thanks go out to these people and to any others I may have inadvertently omitted: Peg Ahlness, the late Robert Alex, Arthur Amiotte, Robert Aramant, Joe Artz, Mike and Margaret Bergstrom, Charlotte Black Elk, Renee Boen, Jim Brozowski, Anthony Buchner, William Buckles, Jeffrey Buechler, Stuart Conner, Tim Cowan, Mike Cowdrey, Carol Diaz-Granados Duncan, Shirley and Jennings Floden, Michael Fosha, Julie Francis, Chris Fulton, Jennifer Galindo, David Gebhard, Mavis and John Greer, Joseph Gullion, Robert Hall, Adrien Hannus, Linda Hasselstrom, James Haug, Cherie Haury, Phil Henry, George Hey, Everett Hill, Mary Hopkins, Paul Horsted, David Hovde, Dayton Hyde, Alfred Johnson, Alice Kehoe, James Keyser, Halcyon LaPoint, Kerry Lippincott, Larry Loendorf, Ron McCoy, Helen Michaelis, Mr. and Mrs. Alex Mitch, Brian Molyneaux, Anta Montet-White, Jon Muller, Talli Nauman, Margaret and Jerry Nelson, Gabriele Nowatczyk, Linda Olson, Richard Ott, Ben Rhodd, Camille Riner, Lance Rom, Steve Ruple, Karl Schlesier, Helen Schuster, John Slay, Signe Snortland, Robert Squier, Jack Steinbring, Louis Stevens, Andrea Stone, Jessie Sundstrom, Alice Tratebas, Michael Turney, and Karen Zimmerman. I have special thanks for my husband, Glen Fredlund, who got hooked, too, and has made my research all the more fun and rewarding.

Storied Stone

The Black Hills Country and Its People

The mountains and tablelands of western South Dakota and northeastern Wyoming are places of spectacular beauty and harshness. They lie within the northern Great Plains (fig. 1.1), a region of sun and wind, bitterly cold winters, killing blizzards, and sometimes relentless droughts. Despite these hazards, the region teems with life. The vast tracts of grassland are capable of supporting millions of bison or cattle. Deer, mountain sheep, and pronghorn antelope thrive in the broken, brushy country of the western plains. Plants such as prairie turnip, chokecherry, and saskatoon berry provide additional food for humans. The broad floodplains of the Missouri, Platte, and other rivers are natural garden beds for a variety of hardy cultigens. To those equipped for the often extreme climate, the Great Plains offer a tremendous range of resources.

The Natural Environment

The towering white cliffs and green valleys of the Black Hills and the wooded buttes and barren badlands of the Cave Hills stand in stark contrast to the surrounding plains (fig. 1.2). To its original inhabitants, the Black Hills country was a storehouse of water, timber, game, tool stone, and shelter. The wooded valleys and draws provided shelter from winter blizzards and gave shade and fresh water during the parched days of late summer. The Black Hills and buttelands were more than a resource bank, however. To the historic Kiowa, Naishan Dene (Kiowa Apache), Arapaho, Cheyenne, Crow, and Lakota people they were a homeland, dotted with sacred places such as Bear Butte and Bears' Lodge Butte, known today as Devils Tower (fig. 1.3).[1] The Mandans, Hidatsas, and Poncas, who dwelled in farming villages along the Missouri River, ventured westward into the Black Hills and butte country to hunt, trap eagles, and pray for visions.[2]

The Black Hills are a heart-shaped mountain range extending about 100 miles north to south and 60 miles east to west.[3] They rise 7,242 feet above sea level at Harney Peak, the highest elevation east of the Rockies. As the Black Hills were thrust upward, rock layers were exposed in a series of concentric rings. The ancient granites forming Harney Peak and the central Black Hills are among the oldest rocks exposed anywhere on the continent. Millions of years of erosion removed two-thirds of the Black Hills' height and softened and rounded the peaks. This central core is surrounded by a wide ring of limestone that forms sheer white cliffs overlooking high, grassy meadows (fig. 1.4). Outside this dissected limestone plateau, a layer of relatively soft shales and sandstones has eroded into a broad lowland that completely encircles the higher mountains. This feature is called the Red Valley for the striking purple to brick-red color of its rocks and soil. An older name for the feature, the Racetrack, refers to a Cheyenne and Lakota story about a great race held there between all two-legged and all four-legged creatures, which established order in the universe.[4]

Outside the Racetrack lies a ring of hard sandstones, eroded into a maze of high, narrow canyons (fig. 1.5). This ring is cut in places by deep gaps formed by streams draining the interior Black Hills. The largest and best known of these is the Buffalo Gap, for thousands of years a gateway for people and bison entering and leaving the interior Black Hills.[5] The Cheyenne River drains all but the western extremity of the Black Hills. Its northern and southern branches embrace the mountains like two arms reaching around from the east.

To the north of the Black Hills lies a vast tableland dotted by buttes and mesas. It is drained by tributaries of the Little Missouri, Grand, and Moreau Rivers. The higher buttes tower like fortresses above the dry, rolling plains. The largest two, known as the Slim Buttes and the Cave Hills (fig. 1.6), are flat, sandstone-capped mesas covering 67 and 22 square miles, respectively. The softer sandstones of the Slim Buttes have eroded into barren badlands around the edges of the mesa. The Cave Hills sandstones erode more slowly, allowing the formation of wooded and brushy valleys below high, sheer cliffs. Numerous caves and rockshelters perched among the sandstone cliffs give the Cave Hills its name (fig. 1.7).

Figure 1.1. The northern Great Plains, showing the locations of the Black Hills and north Cave Hills in western South Dakota and northeastern Wyoming.

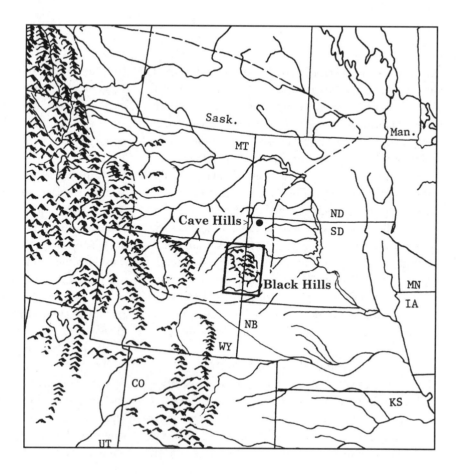

Figure 1.2. View of the rocky peaks of the central Black Hills from Harney Peak.

Historical Background

As one of the last places in the United States to feel the imprint of Euro-American society, the Black Hills country lay clouded in mystery to outsiders until the last quarter of the nineteenth century. Held inviolate by the 1868 Fort Laramie Treaty and securely defended by the Lakotas and northern Cheyennes to whom it was home, the Black Hills country lay unmapped, unexplored, and unexploited by the hand of white America. Rumors of gold lured some adventurers into the territory, but few came out again. The Black Hills were the meat source, winter shelter, and holy sanctuary of the Indians. Their pursuit of trespassers was swift and thorough.[6]

In June 1874, a brazen young cavalry officer forever changed the face of the Black Hills country. Lieu-tenant Colonel George Armstrong Custer, with an entourage of soldiers, Indian scouts, reporters, and scientists more than 1,000 strong, entered the sacred lands of the Lakotas on what was purported to be a reconnaissance to locate good fort sites.[7] His real mission was to investigate rumors of gold. The long-awaited announcement of gold in the Black Hills hit the front pages of the eastern newspapers by late July. A flood of white miners swept through the Black Hills country, effectively ending more than 13,000 years of Indian control of the area.

Those 13,000 years had witnessed a slow procession of distinctive native cultures.[8] With changing environmental conditions, migrations, and new technologies, one life-way gradually yielded to another. Mammoth hunters gave way to bison hunters; the spear

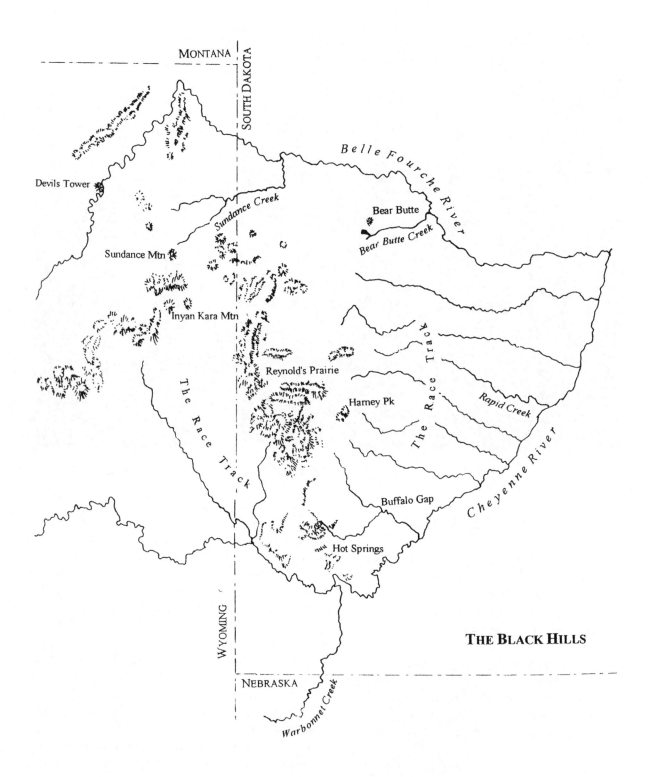

Figure 1.3. The Black Hills, showing locations of some sacred sites.

Figure 1.4. View of lower French Creek. Flat, grassy meadows and high cliffs are typical of the Limestone Plateau zone of the Black Hills.

Figure 1.5. Crane Creek rockshelter, in the ring of eroded sandstones outside the Racetrack. This rockshelter in the western Black Hills Hogback was used prehistorically as a temporary dwelling place. It contains rock art from several different periods.

Figure 1.6. View of the Cave Hills from site 39HN150.

Figure 1.7. This natural arch in the north Cave Hills marks the location
of a contact-era Indian petroglyph, site 39HN49.

and dart thrower gave way to bow and arrow and finally the gun; groups with ties to the western basins made way for newcomers from the eastern prairies and woodlands (Table 1.1). Through the centuries, people literally left their marks, in the form of petroglyphs and paintings, on the rocky canyons and caves of the Black Hills country. In this way, they unknowingly provided the future a window to the past.

Archaeologists measure the rate of decay of certain carbons found in organic materials in order to date artifacts and sites. Because this radioactive carbon breaks down at a continuous rate, measuring the amount of decay gives a good estimate for the age of such things as charcoal, wood, and bone. New information has shown that at the older end of the scale, radiocarbon dates may be as much as 2,000 years more recent than calendar years.[9] At the end of the last ice age, the amount of carbon in the atmosphere was different from amounts in later periods, affecting the rate of decay of organic carbons. A radiocarbon date of 11,700 years ago probably means the material dated is about 13,500 calendar years of age. This means that the human occupation of the Black Hills may cover a period of more than 13,000 years. On the more recent end of the scale, radiocarbon and calendar years are in better agreement. Because archaeologists are still working on the exact correction needed for the older dates, such dates are given here in radiocarbon years, not calendar years. Table 1.2 shows the approximate conversion from radiocarbon years before the present (pegged at 1950) to calendar years, based on current information.

The Paleoindian Period

The earliest Indians so far identified in the Great Plains were the Paleoindians. These people lived at the end of the late ice age and the beginning of the most recent geological period, the Holocene. The early Paleoindians probably were new arrivals from Siberia via the Bering land bridge and the newly opened interglacial corridor leading from Alaska to the northern Great Plains. They may have been proceeded by earlier human migrants from Europe and Asia who came via the ice-free corridor, the Pacific coastline, or a route that skirted the great glaciers in the north Atlantic. Evidence for earlier migrations is scant but increasingly convincing.[10] The Paleoindian period extends from about 11,500 to 7,500 radiocarbon years ago and includes the Clovis, Goshen, Folsom, and Plano (Late Paleoindian) archaeological complexes.

The earliest inhabitants of the Black Hills country probably were the people recognized by archaeologists as the Clovis and Goshen cultures. If there were earlier Black Hills dwellers, they left no trace that archaeologists can identify today. Here and elsewhere throughout western North America, Clovis peoples were wandering hunters of now-extinct animals—giant bison, mammoths, and camels. Clovis spear points are masterpieces of chipped stone workmanship. Apart from hunting methods and diet, little is known of Clovis life. Still unknown are the people's means of shelter, dress, communication, and worship. The accidental discovery of a Clovis-age skeleton in Montana in the 1970s offered a glimpse of Clovis beliefs: the body of an infant had been covered with red pigment and laid to rest with a set of finely crafted tools.[11] Archaeologists hypothesize that small, family-based groups wandered the plains in pursuit of big game.

Whatever the details of their lives, Clovis peoples were highly successful in their adaptations to life on the North American continent at the end of the last ice age. Clovis sites date between 11,500 and 10,600 radiocarbon years ago. The Clovis complex apparently ended with the extinction of the mammoth and other ice-age animals about 10,000 years ago.

No Clovis sites have been excavated in the Black Hills country, but Clovis spear points have been found in a few places. A mammoth kill site was excavated in the White River Badlands, just east of the Black Hills,[12] and Clovis points were found in the Powder River Basin, just west of the Black Hills.[13] A small Clovis-age deposit formed the lowest portion of the Agate Basin site, immediately southwest of the Black Hills.[14]

More definite evidence for use of the Black Hills country comes from a slightly later culture represented archaeologically by the Goshen complex. Goshen overlaps Clovis in time and seems to be an offshoot of it. Like sites of the Clovis complex, Goshen sites indicate an emphasis on large game hunting. Little else is known of Goshen life-ways. The Jim Pitts site in the western Black Hills had a Goshen layer at the bottom.[15] Goshen spear points were found there,

TABLE 1.1
GENERALIZED CHRONOLOGY OF CULTURES IN THE
BLACK HILLS REGION, WITH ASSOCIATED ARTIFACTS

Years before Present	Period	Typical Artifacts	Life-way
50–140	Historic	Euro-American items	Farming and ranching, mining, logging, light industry
140–240	Postcontact	Metal arrow points, glass beads, and other trade goods	Bison hunting; fur and hide trade; horse herding; winter camps in foothills; probably less use of the interior Black Hills except for resource gathering
240–1500	Late Prehistoric and Plains Village	Stone arrow points and Middle Missouri Tradition pottery	Earthlodge villages on major rivers; farming along major rivers; bison hunting and plant gathering on plains; tipi camps dispersed in winter with large gatherings in summer; camps and resource gathering throughout the Black Hills
1500–2500	Late Archaic	Stone atlatl dart points and cord-marked pottery	Communal bison hunting; deer, mountain sheep, and antelope hunting and plant gathering; camps and hunting sites in Black Hills; camps and plant food processing in foothills
2500–5000	Middle Archaic	Stone atlatl dart points	Hunting of many kinds of game and plant gathering, some communal hunts; camps and hunting sites in Black Hills; camps and plant food processing in foothills; possible use of pit-house dwellings
5000–7500	Early Archaic	Stone atlatl dart points	Hunting and gathering of many kinds of plants and animals; cooperative bison hunts; camps in rockshelters in foothills
7500–10,000	Plano	Large, leaf-shaped stone dart or spear points	Cooperative game hunting; plant gathering and hunting of other game; use of portable shelters; camps throughout Black Hills
10,000–10,900	Folsom	Deeply fluted stone dart or spear points	Cooperative bison hunts on plains; some plant food gathering; probably used foothills for camps and hunts
10,600–11,500	Clovis/Goshen	Fluted or plain leaf-shaped dart or spear points	Hunting mammoth, bison, and other game; camps and hunts in Red Valley and foothills; other use of Black Hills is not known

TABLE 1.2
DATES OF ARCHAEOLOGICAL PERIODS AND COMPLEXES IN THE BLACK HILLS

Period	Radiocarbon Years before Present	Calendar Years
Historic	50–150	1850–1940 C.E.
Contact era	150–250	1750–1850 C.E.
Late Prehistoric and Plains Village	250–1,500	500–1750 C.E.
Late Archaic	1,500–2,500	500 B.C.E.–500 C.E.
Middle Archaic	2,500–5,000	500–3000 B.C.E.
Early Archaic	5,000–7,500	3000–6000 B.C.E.
Plano	7,500–10,000	6000–11,500 B.C.E.
Folsom	10,000–10,900	9500–11,000 B.C.E.
Goshen/Clovis	10,600–11,500	10,500–11,500 B.C.E.

together with fragmented bison bones and stone butchering tools. This was probably a place where bison were brought for butchering after a communal hunt. A reported Goshen site near the Cave Hills has not yet been investigated by archaeologists.

Following the transition to modern climatic conditions and the extinction of mammoths, the Folsom complex replaced Clovis and Goshen on the northwestern plains and elsewhere in North America. At the edge of the Black Hills, the Agate Basin site contained Folsom material dated 10,665 to 10,780 radiocarbon years ago. The Folsom levels at Agate Basin contained animal bone, hearths, red ocher, and artifacts including a bone awl or projectile point fragment, two Folsom projectile points, and several scrapers, flake tools, and bifaces.[16] Most of the bone scrap was from bison, but rabbit, pronghorn, and canid (dog, coyote, or wolf) bone was also present.

One Folsom level at Agate Basin also contained the remains of two possible structures. The better defined of these was a circular area about three meters in diameter marked by a change in soil color and texture. This feature contained a hearth and a concentration of flakes and stone tools. Among the artifacts were several bone needle fragments, stone projectile point preforms, and antler tools used in making the projectile points. Just outside its perimeter was a bison

rib stuck into the underlying sediments like a peg. An identical bison rib "peg" was found alongside the second possible structure. These structures were thought to be for special activities such as ceremonies or equipment storage rather than living quarters.

This level also contained large amounts of red ocher, as well as fluted and unfluted Folsom points, scrapers, gravers, serrated flakes, flake and blade tools, stone knives, cobble tools, anvils, hammerstones, abrading stones probably used in hide processing, and a grinding slab used to pulverize red ocher. Several finely incised bison ribs were also found in this level.[17]

Several small Folsom sites have been found in the northwestern Black Hills. A Folsom site in the western foothills was identified as a bison hunting overlook. Situated on a prominent butte on the Cheyenne–Belle Fourche divide in northeastern Wyoming, this site contained a small number of stone tools and flakes. Another possible Folsom component in the northwestern Black Hills, site 48CK840, consisted entirely of redeposited stone artifacts. These included a utilized flake, a retouched flake, a scraper, a hammerstone, a core, and a stone knife, as well as an unfluted projectile point that could be either Goshen or Folsom. A third site in the northwestern Black Hills, 48CK1317, contained a Folsom projectile point, a point base with a channel scar on one side, and several knives, scrapers, and pieces of fire-cracked rock.[18]

The trend toward more diverse use of animal and plant resources was even more marked in the Plano period, the last Paleoindian cultural tradition. Plano includes several distinct archaeological complexes. From early to late Plano, these are Agate Basin, Hell Gap, Alberta, Cody/Scottsbluff-Eden, Frederick, Lusk, Angostura, and James Allen. Dates from Plano sites range from about 10,000 to 7,500 radiocarbon years ago. The various complexes overlap one another in time and space.

Three Plano sites have been excavated in the general vicinity of the Black Hills: the Hudson-Meng bison kill, about 50 miles south of the southern Hogback; the Long (or Angostura) site, just outside the southern Hogback; and upper components of the Agate Basin site, in the southwestern foothills.[19] The Jim Pitts site in the southwestern Black Hills also contained Plano levels.[20]

Late Paleoindian projectile points have been found throughout the interior Black Hills as well. These are most common at large sites in high-altitude meadows occupied over hundreds or thousands of years.[21] Fewer Plano sites have been found along the edges of the Black Hills. These foothills sites may represent the warm-season habitations of small groups of hunters from the surrounding plains.[22] It is not known whether any Late Paleoindian groups occupied the Black Hills year-round.

Throughout the northwestern plains, Plano peoples were bison hunters (fig. 1.8). They sometimes used natural features as bison traps and jump-offs, leaving large concentrations of bison bone for archaeologists to find.[23] At the same time, they began to use a great diversity of resources, especially in mountainous areas. Some cooperative hunts were focused on mountain sheep or pronghorn, and remains of deer, elk, pronghorn, and smaller animals occur along with remains of bison in Plano sites.[24] Undoubtedly, late Paleoindians used plant resources as well, including prickly pear cacti and seedy plants.[25] Some Plano sites appear to contain the remains of shelters, perhaps similar to the hide tipi.[26] It appears that group size and overall population density increased during this period. Cultures also seem to have become more diverse. Mountain dwellers began to follow a pattern of using many kinds of food resources. Plains dwellers continued to focus on bison hunting. People may have followed both patterns in intermediate areas like the Black Hills and Cave Hills.

Figure 1.8. Bison nursery herd, Wind Cave National Park. The Black Hills country provides excellent bison habitat that may have attracted Paleoindian groups to the area.

The Archaic Period

The retreat of the great glaciers about 8,000 years ago signaled the end of the most recent ice age and the beginning of a climate pattern more like today's. During the ice age, wet and cool conditions persisted year-round. Afterward, the climate became warmer, and precipitation decreased. Increased seasonality meant that many resources were available for shorter periods of the year. People needed to develop more diverse means of obtaining food to take advantage of seasonal availability of resources. They also began to develop more regular patterns of movement, because plants ripened and animals migrated into particular areas with the seasons. People needed to learn ways of storing food in order to survive the lean times of winter cold and summer drought. Resource differences between areas became more pronounced. Groups became increasingly localized, developing specialized knowledge of a local territory that ensured their survival in increasingly extreme climates. Competition for resource-rich areas may have increased at this time. These changes marked the end of the Paleoindian period and foreshadowed the developments of the Archaic period, which would extend for the next 6,000 years.

The period just after the end of the ice age, about 8,000 to 5,000 years ago, was a time of prolonged drought in many parts of western North America.[27] Archaeologists term this the Early Archaic period. Relatively few archaeological sites date to this time. Perhaps human populations decreased because the dry climate supported fewer game animals and food plants. Or perhaps climatic conditions led to the destruction of the archaeological sites dating to this period. For now, archaeologists are unable to tell which of these possibilities is more likely. Perhaps both factors contributed to the scarcity of sites.[28] Bison decreased in size during this transitional period but continued to provide much of human subsistence.

Early Archaic sites in the Black Hills country indicate two kinds of activities. Some sites contain a wide variety of animal bones and plant remains. One example is the Beaver Creek site in the southern Black Hills. This streamside rockshelter contained deer and small mammal bone and seeds, together with Early Archaic artifacts.[29] The Victoria Creek, Boulder Creek

Rockshelter, 48CK1387, Red Canyon Rockshelter, Buster Hill, and Blaine sites provide additional evidence for the use of both large and small game and plant foods during the Early Archaic (fig. 1.9).[30] These sites suggest that local groups were using a variety of wild food resources.

Other Early Archaic sites, in contrast, indicate that some groups still specialized in large-scale bison hunting. The Hawken site in the northern Black Hills is the remains of a bison kill area. Bison were driven up into a narrow arroyo and killed by hunters wielding dart throwers.[31] The Hawken site led some archaeologists to speculate that the Black Hills were a refuge for bison and humans during the great drought. The Licking Bison site just south of the Cave Hills is another Early Archaic bison kill. It contained piles of bison bone with the skulls carefully placed in a circle atop the other bones. Found among these bones were projectile points similar to those found at the Hawken site.[32] Apart from these two sites, there is little archaeological evidence to support the idea of a refuge area. As in the rest of the Great Plains, the number of archaeological sites in the Black Hills country plummeted during the Early Archaic.[33]

Perhaps large bison drives, like those represented by the Hawken and Licking Bison sites, were confined to certain seasons or to especially wet years. Perhaps local groups alternated between specialized bison hunting and more diverse hunting and gathering lifeways. Perhaps some groups hunted bison while others relied on smaller game and plants. The diverse subsistence pattern resembles life-ways known archaeologically and historically from the Great Basin and other arid parts of the West. The use of pit houses for shelter and food storage during this period also resembles a western basin pattern.[34] Perhaps dryland-adapted peoples from the western basins expanded their ranges into the Black Hills country during this period. These possibilities continue to be subjects of debate and inquiry in plains archaeology.[35]

The next period, termed the Middle Archaic, was something of a heyday in the prehistoric Black Hills country. Middle Archaic sites are numerous.[36] They indicate a frugal, efficient, and highly diverse subsistence pattern. Although the Hawken III site indicates that a tradition of communal bison hunting persisted

Figure 1.9. Atlatl dart points dating to the Early and Middle Archaic periods. Andoni site, 39PN326, central Black Hills. These mountain-foothills projectile types contrast with the corner-notched dart points typical of large bison kill sites in the open plains.

to some degree in the Black Hills Middle Archaic, most sites contain a mixture of bison, deer, and small animal remains.[37] By now, production of pemmican—dried meat and berries preserved in rendered fat—was a major seasonal activity. Food resources included all sorts of large and small game, prickly pear cactus, wild onions, goosefoot and other seedy plants, various kinds of berries, and even Mormon crickets.[38] Small Middle Archaic groups were able to stay in one place for the winter. Sites dating to this period often contain evidence that people stored food and tools for later use. Sites also show signs of reuse over periods of hundreds or thousands of years. This indicates a regular pattern of seasonal movement. Groups planned their movements to coincide with resource availability. In the Black Hills, small groups may have followed ripening berries up into the higher elevations in summer, returning to the foothills in autumn as game animals sought shelter in the lower elevations.

Excavated Middle Archaic sites in the Black Hills country include periodically reused open-air campsites with numerous hearth and pit features and diverse food remains. Sites displaying this pattern include Lightning Spring, McKean, Lissolo Cave, 48CK13, 49CK46, Deerfield, Ditch Creek, Battle Creek, Jim Pitts, George Hey, Oatman Spring, and Buck Spring.[39] The McKean and George Hey sites may contain the remains of pit houses, suggesting cold-season use, but other sites appear to have been warm-season camps. The Hermosa Tipi Ring site may indicate use of tipi-like shelters during the Middle Archaic period, but the age of the site is not certain.[40] The Beaver Creek, Boulder Creek, Mule Creek, Belle, and Red Canyon rockshelters contained evidence for repeated use by groups consuming deer, bison, small animals, shellfish, seeds, and wild plums.[41] Some Middle Archaic sites in foothills locations contain large numbers of stone-filled pit hearths and are thought to have been frequently revisited places where roots or other plant foods were processed for winter storage. Examples are the Gant, 39CU271, and Harbison sites.[42] Other sites appear to have been short-term camps where people made dart throwers (atlatls) and darts for hunting forays.[43] Higher altitude spring-side sites in the Black Hills frequently contain Middle Archaic levels. In fact, except for the smallest hunting camps, nearly all Middle Archaic sites in the Black Hills country also contain material dating to earlier or later periods, especially the Late Archaic. Overall, Middle Archaic peoples in the Black Hills country seem to have developed a highly efficient pattern of meshing their seasonal travels with familiar places and resources.

A few burial sites suggest a complex ritual life during Middle Archaic times. The Sidney Burial site in northwestern Nebraska contained the bones of a teenage boy and an infant that had been buried in a pit capped with slabs of rock. Several items had been placed with the bodies, including a large stone knife, a raven wing (perhaps a fan), mussel shells, and powdered red ocher. Several pendants of amazonite (a turquoise-like stone) and a perforated turtle carapace probably were personal ornaments.[44] Other Middle Archaic burials from southern Saskatchewan also contained mussel shell, bird bones, powdered ocher, and stone slabs. Some of the northern sites contained copper as well. Although no clear picture emerges of Middle Archaic beliefs, shell, turtles, blue stone, and copper are emblems of water and the underworld in native North American religions. Other Middle Archaic burials from the northern plains, including those from the McKean site in the northwestern Black

Hills, provide the earliest evidence for "bundle" burial. Bodies were placed on burial platforms or in trees for one or two years, after which the bones were collected, neatly bundled, and buried in pits.

During the Late Archaic period, the climate was similar to today's. An increase in moisture promoted lush growth of grasses throughout the northern plains. Bison populations increased. Bison again became the mainstay for food and other necessities. To the west of the Black Hills, communal bison kill sites are associated with the Yonkee and Pelican Lake cultures.[45] In the Black Hills foothills, Yonkee sites contain a variety of food remains, hearths, and circles of stones probably used as tipi weights.[46] Projectile points typical of the Pelican Lake culture are found throughout the Black Hills. Both groups were hunter-gatherers, following a regular, seasonal pattern of movement throughout their homeland. Many Late Archaic sites show evidence of reuse over decades, centuries, or millennia (fig. 1.10).

Later in the Late Archaic period, a new pattern of life appeared in the Black Hills country. The culture known as Besant entered the area from the north or east.[47] Besant people seem to have lived sometimes in settlements along the Missouri River and sometimes in dispersed hunting camps on the plains to the west

Figure 1.10. Excavations at the Summit Spring site (39HN569), east of the Cave Hills, revealed a series of Late and Middle Archaic occupations.

of the river. They built elaborate, highly sophisticated bison-trapping structures. Bison were taken in large numbers in these corral traps.[48] Besant and other Late Archaic cultures also renewed the ancient practice of driving bison herds over cliffs. In their eastern range, Besant people constructed burial mounds that sometimes contain complete bison skeletons or arrangements of bison skulls around the perimeter. In the west, circles of bison skulls are sometimes found at Besant bison-trapping sites. Although the exact form of the Besant complex will never be known, it is clear that bison were central to Besant existence on both a practical and a spiritual level. Stone circles at western Besant sites indicate the use of tipis, and both eastern and western sites contain pottery.

In the eastern plains, the Woodland period largely coincides with the Late Archaic of the western plains. Woodland culture was characterized by small settlements along the major streams, supported by mixed hunting and gathering and perhaps a small amount of gardening. Woodland people made distinctive pottery and constructed burial mounds. Woodland pottery is found in the western plains as well, but the relationship between the Woodland and Late Archaic archaeological complexes is poorly understood. In the Black Hills, a few sites have yielded stone tools typical of Besant sites and pottery generally related to eastern Woodland types, but the relationship between these is unclear. Late Archaic sites in the Black Hills indicate small groups engaged in hunting and tool production. Overall, the Late Archaic groups seem to have been more bison focused and to have used the Black Hills only for occasional resource gathering. At the same time, some local groups continued the Middle Archaic pattern of intense use of a wide variety of resources. Late Archaic levels of the Red Canyon Rockshelter, site 48WE320, and the McKean site are similar to Middle Archaic levels, with evidence for pemmican making, seed and root roasting, and consumption of large and small animals.[49] The Late Archaic–Woodland period was thus a time of both change and continuity in the Black Hills country.

The Late Prehistoric Period

About 2,000 years ago a new technology reached the northern plains and Black Hills country. The bow and arrow appeared and quickly replaced the older dart and dart-thrower weapon system.[50] With the longer range and greater accuracy of the bow, people continued to increase their reliance on animal foods. This period, called the late prehistoric, was a time of cultural diversity in the northern plains. Along the Missouri River, the ancestors of the Mandans, Hidatsas, and Arikaras built large, fortified farming villages, beginning about 900 C.E. They planted corn, beans, squash, tobacco, and other crops in the spring. After the first weeding, most of the able-bodied villagers left to hunt bison in the western plains and hills. In the autumn they returned to the villages in time to gather in the crops and prepare winter stores of dried bison meat and corn. Some villagers may have lived full-time in or near the Black Hills until a period of drought from 1300 to 1600 C.E. forced them to concentrate their settlements closer to the ever-reliable Missouri.[51]

These village farmers shared the Black Hills country with hunter-gatherers. The hunting groups moved around from place to place, using the foothills for shelter in winter and venturing into the open plains and higher mountains in summer. They made their living primarily by hunting bison, but they took many other foods as well, including deer, mountain sheep, pronghorn, and wild plants. These hunter-gatherers probably lived in skin shelters something like the historic tipi (fig. 1.11). Like their later counterparts, these groups may have come together in late spring for ceremonies and trade fairs.

Several types of late prehistoric sites have been excavated in the Black Hills. These include tipi camps;[52] a pit trap into which bison herds were driven (fig. 1.12);[53] and settlements and temporary camps used by middle Missouri village dwellers.[54] Surface collections suggest use of the interior Black Hills for camps and use of the foothills zone for various kinds of tool making and resource gathering.[55] Several hundred circles of tipi stones in the vicinity of Tepee and Hell Canyons in the southern Black Hills probably date to the late prehistoric.[56] These indicate use of the area for winter camps. Such tipi camp sites are found throughout the Black Hills country.

The Postcontact Period

By the end of the late prehistoric period, people in the Black Hills country were feeling the effects of Euro-American encroachment. The Dakota alliance had

Figure 1.11. This ring of stones probably marks the location of a late prehistoric tipi, site 39HN186, in the north Cave Hills. A petroglyph overlooks the tipi ring site.

Figure 1.12. Late prehistoric and contact-era groups drove bison into this huge sinkhole on several occasions. Vore site, 48CK302, northwestern Black Hills.

shifted its territory westward under pressure from the better-armed Ojibwa alliance. By the middle of the eighteenth century, horses and guns began to appear on the northern plains. Devastating epidemics of European and Asian diseases reached the Plains Indians even before material items made their appearance. These factors laid the groundwork for a shift in political alliances, territories, trade patterns, warfare, and social structure.[57]

The first Lakota (western Dakota) bands reached the Black Hills by about 1775, the last in a succession of immigrants. Ponca groups from north-central Nebraska may have briefly occupied the Black Hills in the early eighteenth century but had left by about 1735. The allied Crows, Kiowas, and Naishan Dene (Kiowa Apaches) remained in the Black Hills country until the end of the eighteenth century, joined at some point by the Arapahos and Cheyennes. Although Cheyennes, Arapahos, and Kiowas were still camped around the edges of the Black Hills when Lewis and Clark reached the Missouri villages in 1804, the Lakotas pushed the Kiowas and closely allied Naishan Dene out of the Black Hills country over the next two decades.[58] Their Crow allies were driven west into the Powder River basin soon afterward. By the mid-1800s, the Lakotas and northern Cheyennes and Arapahos had joined in a powerful military alliance and were in the process of driving the Crows from the rich hunting grounds of the Powder River basin and the Pawnees from the North Platte River.[59] All of these groups were highly mobile, using horses and dogs to carry their tipis and household goods from camp to camp (fig. 1.13).

Competition for hides and furs for the burgeoning fur trade provoked further intertribal rivalries.[60] Although warfare on the northern plains was a constant concern, it seldom resulted in the loss of more than a few dozen lives during any battle season. At its

Figure 1.13. Two tipis are visible among the confused array of incised lines on this rock art panel from site 39FA7 in the southern Black Hills. Indian groups living in the Black Hills during the postcontact period dwelled in tipis like these. (Scale bar shows 30 cm.)

most violent, perhaps a hundred women, children, and old people might be slain at once during raids on farming villages along the Missouri and Platte Rivers. But such events were rare, and the plains certainly never witnessed the kind of bloodletting that stained the battlefields of the divided United States. The Civil War diverted U.S. military forces away from the western frontier. When the war ended, idle soldiers readily found work among the units moving west to subdue the Indian threat to white settlement on the western frontier.

For another decade, the Lakota-Cheyenne alliance would win a series of victories over U.S. forces and effectively seal off most of their territory to American expansion, despite the discovery of gold in the Black Hills and Montana.[61] In 1876, news of the defeat of Custer's forces at the Battle of the Little Bighorn interrupted the great American Centennial celebrations and focused attention on the western frontier. For the Indians, the Little Bighorn victory was a short-lived boon. An enraged American public demanded that both food rations and the guns by which Indians obtained their own food be denied to all Lakota and Cheyenne people. Starvation, not military conquest, forced their surrender in the months following the Battle of the Little Bighorn. With the great bison herds gone and treaty rations rescinded, the last of the Lakota and Cheyenne warriors were quickly forced into submission by an angry America. Most of their people were already confined to reservations by this time. The Ghost Dance uprising and Wounded Knee massacre in 1890 marked the end of armed resistance to U.S. dominance.[62] The free life had ended a few years earlier with the surrender of Sitting Bull, the last of the Lakotas to hold out against the U.S. military.

The Rock Art Sequence

Rock art has been a part of life in the Black Hills for thousands of years. The glaring graffiti and scrawlings of recent years are merely the top layer. Mentally peel them back and you will find names and dates carefully inscribed by early cavalrymen, prospectors, and ranchers. Peeling those back reveals the vivid rock art of the Indians' horse days. Guns, hatchets, and wagons all appear in this rock art, in the context of traditional Indian scenes of the warrior life. The same scenes minus the horses and metal trade goods make up the next older layer. These warriors carry large body shields and lances or bows. A complex interweaving of animal tracks, abraded grooves, mythical figures, and images from dreams and visions, all incised into the sandstone cliffs and rockshelters, make up the next layer. Intermixed are painted images of animals, weapons, highly schematized symbols, and mythical creatures. Below this are even older layers consisting of designs painstakingly pecked or pounded into the rocky surfaces. Strange, abstract designs made up of a dizzying array of spirals, waves, concentric circles, crosses, and zigzags form one layer. Below these are carefully pecked designs of humans, animals, and hunting gear. This oldest Black Hills rock art dates well back into the Archaic period and perhaps extends as far back as the late Paleoindian period. A few painted designs belong to the Archaic period as well.

Several kinds of observations help to place different kinds of rock art in time (Table 1.3). One important clue to the age of rock art in the Black Hills country is superimposition—the order in which paintings or petroglyphs were placed over other, earlier ones. Another is the amount of weathering apparent on the petroglyphs and paintings. The position of rock art relative to the current ground surface is yet another clue to its age. Usually, the older rock art is stranded high above the current surface, while the more recent work is closer to eye level. This indicates that in many places, ground level dropped because of erosion. Other rock exposures of different ages may occur virtually side by side. This happens when part of a rockshelter or cliff spalls away, leaving a fresh surface exposed next to the older one. Taken together, these clues can be used to construct a sequence of rock art styles in the Black Hills country.[63]

Pecked naturalistic rock art is frequently superimposed by abstract pecked designs, which in turn are often superimposed by various kinds of incised petroglyphs. These three kinds of rock art follow a uniform pattern in weathering, age of the rock surfaces on which they occur, and distance above the current ground level. The Pecked Realistic style is consistently oldest, followed by Pecked Abstract and then the various incised and ground rock art styles. Painted rock art occurs both before Pecked Abstract and during the period when incised rock art was made. Some painted art is older than some incised rock art, but the reverse is also true. Similarly, abraded grooves are older than some, but not all, incised rock art.

Pecked rock art was made by pounding the rock surface directly with another rock or with a stone or bone chisel. Nearly all of the pecked rock art in the Black Hills dates to the Archaic period. Although exact dates are unknown, it appears most likely that the Pecked Realistic hunting scenes date to the Early and Middle Archaic, whereas the Pecked Abstract panels date to the Middle and Late Archaic. Incised rock art was made by cutting through the rock surface with a sharp bone or stone stylus. Ground rock art is also cut into the rock surface, by a combination of incising

Table 1.3
CLUES TO THE RELATIVE AGES OF BLACK HILLS ROCK ART STYLES AT SELECTED SITES

Site	Relative Order of Rock Art Styles	Indicator
39FA79	Lightly Incised over Incised	Superimposition
39CU91	Grooves over Incised	Age of rock exposure
39FA6	Grooves over Incised	Superimposition
39CU91	Incised over grooves	Superimposition
39FA75	Incised over grooves	Superimposition
39FA683	Incised over grooves	Superimposition
39HN17	Incised over grooves	Superimposition
39HN17	Incised over grooves	Age of rock exposure
39HN17	Incised Track-Vulva-Groove over Incised Ceremonial	Superimposition
39HN17	Incised Track-Vulva-Groove over Incised Ceremonial	Age of rock exposure
39FA819	Incised over red painted	Superimposition
39FA316	Incised over black painted	Superimposition
39FA316	Pecked circle over black painted	Superimposition
39FA819	Painted Realistic over red painted	Superimposition
39FA819	Red painted over black painted	Superimposition
39FA819	Red painted and incised over black	Age of rock exposure
39FA88	Red painted over black painted	Superimposition
39FA316	Red painted over black painted	Superimposition
39FA1190	Red painted lines over abraded groove	Superimposition
39FA1190	Black painted lines over red painted lines	Superimposition
Crane Creek	Incised and ground over pecked	Relative weathering
39FA7	Incised over pecked	Superimposition
Crane Creek	Incised over pecked	Superimposition
39FA79	Incised over indistinct pecked	Superimposition
39FA677	Incised and abraded grooves over indistinct pecked	Superimposition
39FA1190	Incised over indistinct pecked	Superimposition

Table 1.3 continued

Site	Relative Order of Rock Art Styles	Indicator
39FA88	Red painted over indistinct pecked	Superimposition
39FA7	Shield-bearing warrior over pecked human head	Superimposition
39FA243	Painted Abstract over Pecked Abstract	Age of rock exposure
39FA7	Incised over Pecked Abstract	Age of rock exposure
39FA73	Incised over Pecked Abstract	Age of rock exposure
39FA395	Incised over Pecked Abstract	Age of rock exposure
39PN438	Incised over Pecked Abstract	Age of rock exposure
39FA58	Incised over Pecked Abstract	Superimposition
39FA75	Incised over Pecked Abstract	Superimposition
39FA79	Incised over Pecked Abstract	Superimposition
39FA1154	Incised over Pecked Abstract	Age of rock exposure
39FA1048	Incised over Pecked Abstract	Superimposition
39PN438	Grooves over Pecked Abstract	Age of rock exposure
39FA75	Grooves over Pecked Abstract	Superimposition
39FA554	Grooves over Pecked Abstract	Superimposition
39FA6	Grooves over Pecked Abstract	Superimposition
39FA680	Grooves over Pecked Abstract	Relative weathering
Oil Creek II	Incised over Pecked Realistic	Relative weathering
39FA79	Incised over Pecked Realistic	Superimposition
39FA6	Incised over Pecked Realistic	Superimposition
39PN438	Incised and grooves over Pecked Realistic	Age of rock exposure
39PN438	Grooves over Pecked Realistic	Superimposition
39FA6	Grooves over Pecked Realistic	Superimposition
39FA446	Abraded areas over Pecked Realistic	Superimposition
39FA1190	Abraded areas and Incised over Pecked Realistic	Superimposition
Oil Creek II	Incised and painted styles over Pecked Realistic	Age of rock exposure
39FA395	Pecked Abstract over Pecked Realistic	Age of rock exposure
39FA439	Pecked Abstract over Pecked Realistic	Relative weathering
39FA79	Pecked Abstract over Pecked Realistic	Superimposition
39FA89	Pecked Abstract over Pecked Realistic	Superimposition
39FA1048	Pecked Abstract over Painted Geometric	Superimposition
39FA316	Pecked over painted	Superimposition

Note: "Over" means that the first kind of rock art is superimposed over the second or that the first occurs on a more recent surface or exhibits less weathering.

and abrading the surface with bone or stone tools. Most of the incised and ground rock art dates to the late prehistoric period, as does much of the painted rock art. Generally, black painted animals and arrows are the oldest of these, followed by red painted animals (fig. 1.14), the mythic creatures of the Painted Realistic style, and incised petroglyphs. Within the incised category, it appears that Track-Vulva-Groove style rock art (chapter 8) persisted for the entire late prehistoric period. Warrior art (chapter 9), including first the shield-bearing warrior or ceremonial style and later the biographical style, overlaps Track-Vulva-Groove art in time but lasted into the postcontact period. Many other kinds of incised rock art can be found in the Black Hills country, but no clear patterns emerge regarding their relative ages.

Medicine Creek Cave in the northwestern foothills of the Black Hills contains hundreds of petroglyphs, all estimated to date within the last 2,000 years. Because the cave began to fill with sediment during this period, the ages of various petroglyphs can be estimated according to their height above the floor of

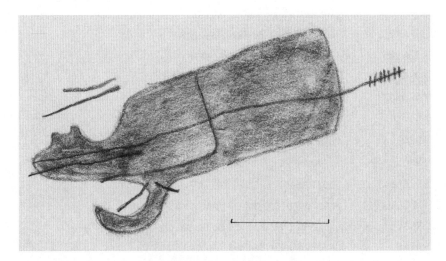

Figure 1.14. In this painted rock art from site 39FA819, a southern Black Hills rockshelter, red designs superimpose black ones. In the panel at top, the bear is black, and the arrow and other lines that seem to penetrate the animal are red. In the panel at bottom, the rabbit-eared figure, the spear point, the arrow or dart that crosses the deer, and the line at upper left are red; the deer, the fragmentary bear at left, and the broomlike figure are black. (Scale bars show 15 cm.)

the cave. The topmost petroglyphs are estimated to be most recent, because they likely were made only when sediment deposition had raised the floor of the cave to its pre-excavation level. Many older petroglyphs were completely covered by sediment until the cave was excavated in the 1940s. A study of the site showed that some kinds of rock art, including the Track-Vulva-Groove style and a series of finely incised human heads, continued to be made throughout the period when people used the cave. A series of pecked bison heads, by contrast, seems to represent a short-lived intrusion about halfway through the span of occupa-tion. A series of incised mountain sheep heads is gen-erally the same age as the early incised human heads, but these did not continue to be made for as long as the human heads. Overall, Medicine Creek Cave shows that many kinds of rock art were made over the last two millennia, with various types and motifs over-lapping in time.[64]

These clues to the relative ages of Black Hills rock art mean that particular rock art styles can be roughly correlated with particular archaeological or historic periods (fig. 1.15). This, in turn, provides a context for exploring the meaning of the rock art.

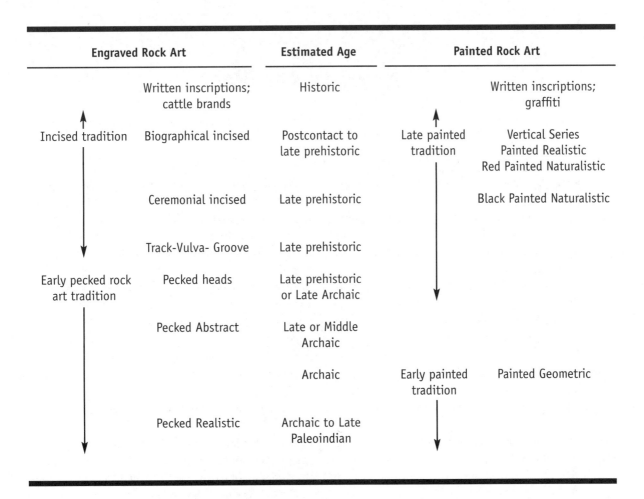

Figure 1.15. Chronological sequence of Black Hills and Cave Hills rock art styles.

Windows to the Past

Archaeologists and art historians refer to markings, paintings, etchings, and carvings made on cliffs and in caves and overhangs as *rock art*. This term encompasses virtually all intentional modifications made to rock surfaces. Although "art" may not be the best term for markings that might have been made for purposes other than aesthetics, the term is widely accepted among researchers. Other terms, such as petroglyph and pictograph, have also been used for particular kinds of rock art. *Pictograph* generally means painted rock art. Since pictograph more accurately refers to an element in picture writing, the term may be confusing when applied broadly to all painted rock art. Here I use the term *painting* instead. *Petroglyph* refers to carved rock art—incised, ground, scratched, or pecked. A pictograph or painting is made by adding pigment to the rock surface, whereas a petroglyph results from the removal of some of the rock surface (fig. 2.1).

Like much of the rest of archaeology, rock art studies are as much educated guesswork as science. Rock art, like other kinds of artifacts, is more akin to historical documents than to laboratory specimens (fig. 2.2). Historical research is a matter of collecting relevant information in the form of documents, photographs, drawings, maps, and oral accounts, placing them in an accurate historical context, and interpreting their meaning in a way consistent with other information. History is more a matter of interpretation than deduction. It is impossible to prove what happened in the past in the same way that, for example, a chemical reaction can be proved. The past cannot be replicated like a laboratory experiment. Instead, the historian writes the story that best accounts for the information available at the time. This story is subject to review and revision as new information becomes available.

American rock art research is still a young field. Rock art was largely ignored by Americanists until recently. Two factors combined to relegate rock art to the realm of book covers and T-shirts. The first was the difficulty of dating it and tying it to other archaeological remains. The second was the failure of researchers to devise a comprehensive theory of its origin and meaning. Over time, students of rock art have proposed first one, then another grand theory. First, hunting magic was embraced as *the* explanation for American rock art. Then, archaeoastronomy came

Figure 2.1. This panel from site 39FA1048 contains a mixture of modern graffiti and incised, pecked, and red painted rock art. The abstract pecked designs cut into the older red painted design, and the incised lines and vulva forms superimpose the pecked rock art. Modern names and initials cut through all three types of prehistoric rock art.

Figure 2.2. This pecked rock art tells the story of a bison hunt. Site 39FA94, southern Black Hills.

on the scene, and suddenly every site was viewed as a potential observatory. Most recently, shamanism has been called on to explain all sorts of rock art. There is a grain of truth to each of these theories. Certainly ancient Americans hunted, watched the sky, and had spiritual experiences. They probably expressed some of these activities graphically. The problem is that no single theory can account for the vastly diverse collection of images that make up American Indian rock art. Instead of ignoring or minimizing the rock art that doesn't fit the theory, researchers need to develop theories that more realistically account for all the rock art.

In addition, the grand theories are limiting in terms of gaining a real understanding of the rock art. To label a set of rock art "shamanic" tells us little of its role within the larger culture.[1] All cultures have religions, and all religions involve trance, vision, belief in unseen worlds, and the idea that some individuals can transport themselves spiritually into these other realms

through prayer, fasting, physical ordeals, sensory deprivation, or use of mind-altering substances. Virtually all cultures have spiritually based healers, whether they are called shamans, witch doctors, priests, or therapists. The difference between a Native American petroglyph of a winged "shaman" and a medieval European fresco of an angel is a matter of the observer's perspective, not some absolute division between shamanic and Western religions (fig. 2.3). The visions of Joan of Arc reflected the culture of fifteenth-century France, just as those of Sitting Bull reflected the culture of nineteenth-century northern Plains Indians, but they were otherwise similar in seeming to come from an outside source and in providing divine guidance to a people confused and wounded by larger political forces. Praying to St. Anthony to help one find a lost object is not substantially different from praying to a rock medicine for the same purpose, nor is a guardian angel or patron saint entirely different from a spirit helper. Absent Western bias, virtually all

Figure 2.3. Precontact-era American Indians, like medieval Europeans, sometimes drew people with halolike rings or rays around their heads. Site 39FA7, southern Black Hills. (Scale bar shows 30 cm.)

religious art contains elements that can be considered "shamanic," especially in the way individuals use religion in daily life.

Because of these limitations, many researchers today have abandoned the grand theories in favor of analyzing particular sets of rock art within their larger cultural context. They use clues from archaeology and from the cultural traditions of the descendants of those who created the rock art to help reconstruct this context.

Dates and Cultural Links

Determining who made a body of rock art is one of the greatest challenges facing researchers. Unlike other kinds of archaeological sites, rock art rarely contains material that can be confidently linked to a particular group. Rock art is also difficult to date.[2] Even if datable material is found in excavations at a rock art site, there is usually no guarantee that these materials were left behind at the same time the rock art was made. They could be earlier or later. Attempts to date pecked or incised rock art directly, by measuring chemical changes in the rock surface, have not yet proved reliable. Painted rock art has been successfully dated when organic materials such as charcoal or blood were used in the paint. Then archaeologists can use radiocarbon dating to estimate the age of the pigment. Sometimes organic materials such as wasps' nests have been deposited over rock art. These can be dated through radiocarbon and other methods to provide a minimum age for the art. Unfortunately, few rock art sites can be dated this way. Rarely, pieces of pigment or paint brushes are found in archaeological deposits below rock art panels. Their minimum age can be determined from their association with other dated archaeological material, or it may be possible to date them directly if they contain organic materials. Occasionally, a rock art panel is covered by undisturbed archaeological deposits. Since the rock art must have been made before the other deposits were laid down, datable material within the sediments can provide a minimum age for the rock art. Few such sites exist, however, largely because most such deposits have been removed or disturbed by looters.

Deciding when and by whom rock art was made is usually a matter of detective work. Archaeologists use clues from the positions of paintings and petroglyphs in relation to the ground surface and to one another in order to tell which kind of rock art was made first and which was made later. If the ground surface is slowly eroding, then higher rock art will be older than lower rock art. Conversely, if the surface is building up, then older rock art will be at the bottom of the rock surface, perhaps even buried under the aggrading sediments. Designs superimposed over other rock art must be later than the designs they overlie. Sometimes the distribution of a certain kind of rock art coincides with the distribution of a particular group whose historic or ancient territory is known to anthropologists, suggesting that those people made the rock art.

Sometimes the things depicted in the rock art provide clues (figs. 2.4, 2.5). Rock art showing atlatls (spear throwers), for example, is earlier than that showing bows and arrows. Rock art showing horses must date within the last 250 years. Sometimes shields, lodges, or personal costumes shown in rock art can be matched with particular groups. The amount of weathering evident on a rock art panel may be a clue to its antiquity, but this depends on the type of rock used and its degree of exposure to the elements. Archaeologists consider all these factors in hypothesizing the age or affiliation of a rock art panel, always alert that new data may change their estimates.

Rock Art as Information

Rock art has both pluses and minuses as archaeological data. It provides kinds of information unavailable elsewhere. It often gives insight into the nontechnological aspects of culture that are poorly represented in other kinds of artifacts. At the same time, the lack of a reliable means of dating rock art has made it difficult to tie the images to defined prehistoric cultures. This sometimes leaves rock art "floating" in prehistoric space.

Despite these limitations, interest in rock art research has increased sharply in the last two or three decades. The number of scholarly publications on rock art has jumped as researchers gain confidence in new ways to analyze and interpret it. Today's researchers will not have the final say. Instead, they will be the pioneers in a movement toward ever better understanding of rock art. New dating methods are

Figure 2.4. Drawing of rock art showing a horse-drawn wagon, bow and arrow, and human. Site 39FA58, southern Black Hills. The panel probably dates around 1830, when traders first entered the area with wagons. (Scale bar shows 20 cm.)

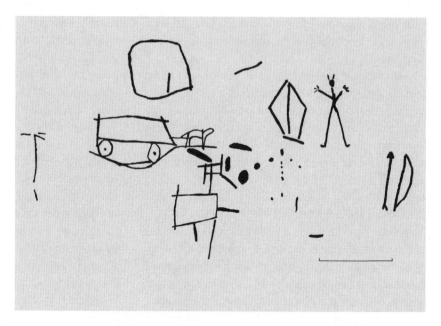

Figure 2.5. These early hunting scenes from Stone Quarry Canyon (upper and lower left), Whoopup Canyon (upper right), and Long Mountain (lower right) in the southern Black Hills include depictions of atlatls, or spear throwers, that provide clues to the images' dates. (Upper scale bars show 30 cm; lower shows 20 cm.)

being developed that will eventually allow researchers to place rock art firmly within the archaeological time line. More and more, rock art will be recognized as an important, perhaps essential, piece of the archaeological puzzle.

Context and Rock Art

The interpretations of rock art presented here rely on an understanding of the many contexts in which the art was originally made.[3] Rock art has a physical context, including the immediate site surroundings, the specific geographical area in which it occurs, and the larger territory in which similar carvings or paintings can be found. Seldom does a rock art style occur in isolation. Instead, a style will exhibit similarities to rock art or other kinds of art found in a broader region. These similarities provide important clues to the age and origin of the rock art. Sometimes rock art is found at particular kinds of places, such as at springs, along trails, or in passes (fig. 2.6). This may be a clue to its meaning or use. Rock art has a temporal context as well. A particular style will have a definite life span. It will develop, mature, and eventually be replaced by other styles. These transitions may be gradual or abrupt, but no style lasts forever. The nature of the transition from one style to another may reveal whether cultural change was sudden or gradual. It may tell whether the same group continued to occupy an area or was replaced by newcomers.

Rock art also has a cultural context. Individual expressions are limited by the cultural milieu. No two panels of rock art are the same, but some clearly can be grouped together on the basis of shared characteristics (fig. 2.7). It is often easy to recognize the culture in which art was produced. Indeed, this is the basis of much of art history. Medieval European art forms a

Figure 2.6. Site 39FA7, adjacent to an old trail running along the Cheyenne River, contains older rock art high above the current ground surface (upper right quadrant of photo) and younger rock art partially buried by terrace deposits (rock surface next to person in photo and inside the cave at left center).

Figure 2.7. This rock art is typical of the Pecked Abstract style of the southern Black Hills. The style is easily recognized from the interconnected abstract elements, the horizontal orientation, and the wide, pecked lines forming the design. Site 39FA1032 overlooks the Cheyenne River.

recognizable body. So does colonial Mexican art and 1930s American public art. The more the researcher knows about the larger culture, the more closely he or she can delve into the meaning and significance of a body of art, including rock art. In the case of prehistoric cultures for which other information is limited, such interpretation is more difficult and can never be perfect or complete. It can, however, help to flesh out other kinds of information about the culture.

Some objects shown in rock art may have been intended as metaphors.[4] A deer might represent a particular trance state or a shaman's ability to transform into an animal, rather than being simply a deer. The meaning of such metaphor is specific to the culture within which it was produced, and it can be lost when the culture dies out. This makes the accurate interpretation of old rock art difficult.

At the same time, powerful ideas have great staying power. The ideas that nourish a culture tend to survive it as new peoples borrow from their predecessors. Sometimes the remnants of an older culture can be discerned among the threads of a new one. For example, many modern Christmas traditions can be traced back to the pagan rites of the early Roman Empire. This means that traces of an image's original meaning can be found in the traditions of later people. A bison skull found in a Folsom-age site in Oklahoma was painted with lightning symbols,[5] perhaps expressing a connection between the sound of thunder and the rumbling of an approaching bison herd. This idea is often expressed in historic Plains Indian art.[6] When old ideas have been carried over into new contexts, the present is a window to the past.

Explorations

Non-Indian newcomers to the Black Hills country quickly developed a fascination with the rock art that dotted the territory. The 1874 Black Hills expedition led by George Armstrong Custer was among the first well-recorded incursions into the Lakota lands of the western Dakotas and eastern Wyoming. Custer diverted the expedition to visit a sacred cave described by his Lakota-Arikara scout, Goose. Newspaper correspondents accompanying the expedition provided colorful descriptions of the rock art adorning the rockshelter, thereafter known as Ludlow Cave, after Custer's chief engineer.[1] Custer himself and a few of his men also wrote of the strange carvings.[2]

Early Studies of Black Hills Rock Art

More formal rock art research in the northern Great Plains began in the 1880s. Anthropologists and natural historians began recording Indian rock art and legends related to it. In 1886–87, Theodore Haynes Lewis noted the existence of several incised boulders in the eastern portion of what is now South Dakota.[3] This was part of his ambitious effort to record archaeological remains throughout the north-central United States. The boulders were incised with footprint or bird-track designs. Lewis learned of a Dakota myth explaining that the tracks had been made by the thunder being when it landed at that place. In 1916, Marie McLaughlin published a collection of Lakota myths and legends. One story, "The Mysterious Butte," referred to a sacred cave containing rock art.[4] Collected from Lakota elders residing at Standing Rock Agency in the 1880s, this story could refer to Ludlow Cave in the Cave Hills, to Medicine Creek Cave in the Black Hills, or to sacred sites in a general sense (fig. 3.1).

The noted ethnologist and archaeologist George F. Will recorded a wide variety of archaeological remains in northwestern South Dakota in 1908.[5] These included rock art and boulder effigies (stone alignments) in the Cave Hills area. Will's work on rock art was limited to descriptions of petroglyphs in and near Ludlow Cave. He collected two pieces of rock art for the Peabody Museum at Harvard University. These panels contained incised and painted depictions of shields. The same year, Harlan I. Smith was scouting archaeological sites in Wyoming for the American Museum of Natural History. He described a rockshelter in the southwestern Black Hills that contained incised petroglyphs (fig. 3.2).[6]

In the 1930s, two projects were undertaken to record rock art in South Dakota. The first was a cursory survey of high plains rock art. E. B. Renaud of the University of Denver oversaw this project and completed much of the survey himself (fig. 3.3).[7] At Renaud's request, a local amateur archaeologist, L. W. Buker, briefly described the principal rock art sites in the southern Black Hills. Buker published this infor-

mation in *American Antiquity* in 1937.[8] He recognized the occurrence of several distinct styles of rock art in the southern Black Hills and correctly surmised that these were of different ages. In concluding their reports, Buker and Renaud called for further analysis of the rock art sites, including the establishment of a relative chronology of styles. Their comments were not to be heeded for another half century.

Another member of the Buker family took a less dispassionate view of Black Hills rock art. During the

Figure 3.1. This drawing of the "Mysterious Butte" cave from Marie McLaughlin's *Myths and Legends of the Sioux* (1916) contains a thunderbird shield (dark circle at center), a human or spirit, and many animal tracks— all motifs found at Ludlow Cave. It also depicts a bear paw and heads of mountain sheep, bison, and deer such as those found at Medicine Creek Cave, and a horse similar to one in the north Cave Hills. Note the arrow, bow, pipe, and other items scattered around the floor of the cave. Medicine Creek Cave and Ludlow Cave contained hundreds of arrow points remaining from arrow offerings. The drawing suggests that the storyteller was familiar with these or other rock art sites.

1930s and 1940s, Frank Buker advocated grand theories about it. Informed mainly by his imagination, these theories held that the area had been a "crossroads of civilization" visited by Coronado, Franciscan monks, Tsin Dynasty Chinese, Mongols, Jewish rabbis from Ninevah, and Eskimos, among others. He published these theories in booklet form.[9] Frank Buker's work was of little scientific or historic value, but he doggedly tried to generate professional interest in studying and preserving the rock art sites. To some extent, he succeeded. At Buker's invitation, Aleš Hrdlička of the United States National Museum visited some of the southern Black Hills rock art sites. Hrdlička, one of the preeminent anthropologists of his day, pronounced the rock art to be the work of the ancestors of modern Indians. Undaunted, Buker took Hrdlička's comments as confirmation of his theories.[10]

Buker aroused interest in one group of rock art sites near Edgemont, South Dakota. Local citizens approached U.S. Forest Service officials with a proposal for an automobile tour route including many of the rock art sites. The proposal was not acted on.

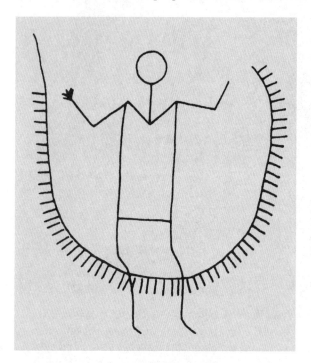

Figure 3.2. Sketch of incised petroglyph on Oil Creek, Wyoming, in the southwestern Black Hills. (From a photograph by Harlan I. Smith, 1908.)

Buker's correspondence with Forest Service personnel bemoaned the disturbance of many sites precipitated by this flurry of interest. Unauthorized digging during this period badly damaged many of the site deposits in the area. Lack of funding and the unavailability of federal archaeologists to evaluate the sites meant that little could be done to preserve them.[11]

The second project of the 1930s was a federal Works Project Administration (WPA) endeavor.[12] As part of archaeological investigations of 14 rockshelters in the southern Black Hills, crews recorded several rock art panels. Unfortunately, no detailed report of the fieldwork was ever completed, and nearly all the field records pertaining to rock art were lost.[13]

In 1941, W. H. Over, director of the University of South Dakota Museum in Vermillion, published a monograph entitled *Indian Picture Writing in South Dakota*. Over was a self-educated naturalist with a strong interest in local antiquities. He vigorously promoted professional archaeological research in South Dakota, especially in the middle Missouri area. Many consider Over the father of South Dakota archaeology (fig. 3.4).

Over's monograph was the first and only attempt at a comprehensive study of South Dakota rock art until 1992. He assembled it from material he had collected during the previous 30 years. Much of his information was received from local informants rather than gathered firsthand. Consequently, much of it is inaccurate. The study is also uneven in its coverage of various parts of the state. Nevertheless, it remained the most oft-cited source of information on South Dakota rock art until 1980. Over described and illustrated some 27 rock art sites scattered across South Dakota. In addition, he discussed and illustrated 10 boulder alignments. The purpose of the monograph was to record the known rock art of the state and to promote its preservation through public education. In earlier publications, Over had mentioned the occurrence of petroglyphs and painted rock art in the Flint Hill vicinity of the southern Black Hills and at Ludlow Cave in the north Cave Hills.[14]

Over discounted several popular theories about the origins of the rock art. These included ideas that Spanish explorers, Pueblo Indians, and Aztecs had created the carvings and paintings. Instead, he suggested

Figure 3.3. Sketches of rock art from three sites in the southern Black Hills, reproduced from E. B. Renaud's 1936 report. (Upper left and right, lower center, site 39FA321; lower left, 39FA88; lower right, 39FA94. Variable scales.)

Figure 3.4. H. E. Lee and W. H. Over (on right) preparing to camp in Red Canyon during a rock art recording expedition, 1925. (Courtesy W. H. Over Museum; reproduced with permission.)

that at least some of the rock art was made by Cheyenne Indians, operating within a general Algonkian
art tradition. In this, Over displayed a remarkable ability to sort through competing theories to arrive at the
most plausible and logical alternative. He accomplished this despite a lack of formal training in archaeology or anthropology. Over also recognized that the
boulder petroglyphs typical of the eastern part of
South Dakota were essentially different from most of
the petroglyphs found in the Black Hills and Cave
Hills. He correctly surmised that the two types had
been made by different cultural groups. He also recognized that at least some of the rock art represented
religious symbols and pictographic notations. He did
not, however, believe that efforts to interpret this rock
art could succeed. Over also noted that the pecked
animals in the Black Hills did not include horses and
thus must be prehistoric.

Later Approaches to Black Hills Rock Art

From 1947 through 1980, a large number of South
Dakota rock art sites were included in archaeological
projects done in advance of mineral exploration,
highway construction, reservoir projects, and federal
timber sales. In the late 1940s, projects carried out as
part of the Smithsonian Institution River Basin
Surveys in the Angostura Reservoir area led to the discovery of several small rock art sites near the Cheyenne River. Little archaeological work involving rock
art was done in the 1950s and 1960s.[15] But passage of
the Historic Preservation Act of 1966, the National
Environmental Policy Act of 1969, and complemen-
tary state legislation in 1975 meant that construction
and development projects involving federal or state
land or funds would now have to be preceded by
archaeological surveys. The newly formed South
Dakota Archaeological Research Center in Rapid City
and the federal Tennessee Valley Authority conducted
archaeological surveys related to mineral exploration
(mainly uranium prospecting) in the southern Black
Hills. Several rock art sites were recorded and evaluated during these projects and others administered by
the Black Hills National Forest.[16] A 1980 project on
Forest Service land in the southern Black Hills focused
on providing a detailed record of several rock art sites
in a uranium exploration area.[17] Additional rock art

sites were recorded during timber sale surveys and
other projects conducted by or for the Black Hills
National Forest.[18]

In addition to publishing reports on these projects, the South Dakota Archaeological Research Center
collected photographs and sketches of area rock art
sites.[19] Many of these came from the collection of the
late John George Day, an amateur archaeologist.

In 1965, Black Hills National Forest personnel
requested help from the South Dakota Historic Preservation Office in evaluating southern Black Hills rock
art to determine its eligibility for listing as a National
Historic Landmark. Apparently, the request was never
answered. A few years later, local residents again proposed a plan for automobile tours of the rock art sites.
Their proposal sparked another attempt to evaluate
and provide special protection for the sites on Forest
Service land. Between 1970 and 1974, various preservation actions were discussed. On the basis of these
discussions, Forest Service personnel decided to post
signs at the sites and to limit access by leaving the road
to the main concentration of sites in disrepair. The
signs briefly explained that the sites were protected by
federal preservation laws. At the same time, Black Hills
National Forest personnel prepared a National
Register of Historic Places nomination for one group
of rock art sites. The South Dakota Historic Preservation board of directors approved this nomination in
1973, but the nomination was never submitted to the
National Park Service for final approval.[20]

In 1980, I received a grant from the South Dakota
Historic Preservation Office to inventory rock art
in the South Dakota portion of the southern Black
Hills.[21] My assistant and I recorded 54 rock art sites,
which I nominated to the National Register of Historic
Places as a thematic group. All 54 sites were declared
eligible for inclusion in the National Register, but only
those on private property were listed at the time.

Another major rock art recording project was also
completed in 1980—a survey of Cave Hills rock art in
Custer National Forest. James D. Keyser conducted
this effort as part of an inventory of archaeological
resources in the north Cave Hills. During the course
of the project, Keyser and his assistant recorded 42
rock art sites.[22] These contained incised or abraded
depictions of humans, horses, bison, tracks, vulvas,

snakes, shields, and weapons. Some nonrepresentational rock art was found as well. The rock art comprised several styles. Keyser proposed specific dates and cultural affiliations for each style and suggested functions for the rock art. Some probably recorded and reinforced the maker's personal powers and accomplishments. Other kinds of rock art were probably used in rituals. Like the southern Black Hills project, the Cave Hills project demonstrated that rock art could help show how past people had lived.

Together, Keyser's and my reports were reissued in 1984 by the South Dakota Archaeological Society.[23] Probably the most significant finding included in the dual report was that the various styles occurred in a definite chronological sequence. The most recent styles dated to the early postcontact and historic periods. The exact age of the oldest styles was unknown, but an age of more than 2,000 years was strongly suggested for the oldest rock art. This upset conventional wisdom about the rock art, which held that all of it

Figure 3.5. Rock art specialists Alice Tratebas and Linda Olson use a reflector and ladder to photograph rock art at Whoopup Canyon, Wyoming, 2001. Tratebas is the figure holding the reflector.

was relatively recent. By establishing even rough dates for the southern Black Hills rock art, archaeologists could start to tie it to particular periods and cultures. This greatly increased its archaeological value.

In 1989, I completed a doctoral dissertation on southern Black Hills rock art.[24] In it, I drew together various kinds of information to explore the age, cultural affiliation, function, and symbolic significance of each of the main styles of rock art present in the area. I included comparisons with rock art from other areas and information intrinsic to the southern Black Hills, and I attempted to use rock art to suggest how the Black Hills had been perceived by various prehistoric and protohistoric groups. I also used the rock art to flesh out the view of prehistoric life-ways provided by other kinds of archaeological data.

Alice Tratebas, of the Wyoming Bureau of Land Management, began an intensive study of the Whoopup Canyon site in Wyoming in the late 1980s. Her work included detailed recording of the dozens of petroglyph panels lining the canyon walls, limited excavations below the panels, and statistical analyses of the images shown in the rock art. Tratebas also attempted to date the rock art using experimental dating techniques. She called attention to the richness of the Black Hills rock art and renewed attempts to preserve the Whoopup Canyon petroglyphs (fig. 3.5).

In 1991, the Black Hills National Forest initiated a program to complete National Register listing of eligible rock art sites on Forest Service land. As part of this initiative, the Black Hills National Forest and the South Dakota Historic Preservation Office jointly sponsored a statewide rock art survey in 1992. Members of the 1992 project attempted to compile a complete inventory of rock art sites in the state, to classify these by style, and to determine the age, cultural affiliation, and archaeological significance of each style. Sites were evaluated for National Register

Figure 3.6. The author points out features of site 39HN17 to Passport in Time volunteers at Custer National Forest, 1998, before they begin surveying the area for unrecorded rock art sites.

Figure 3.7. Rock art recording specialist Linda Olson prepares to trace a petroglyph panel directly onto archival plastic at site 48CK1544, 1999. This technique requires extensive knowledge of rock art and the microgeology of rock surfaces, as well as artistic skill.

status, and all previously unlisted eligible sites were nominated for inclusion in the register. The project report detailed the results of the survey, made recommendations for the management of all rock art in the state, and addressed a series of research questions.[25] The report revisited some of the theories presented in earlier studies. These were refined, corrected, or confirmed as new data dictated. The 1992 project resulted in the nomination of about 100 sites to the National Register.

In 1995, Custer National Forest and the South Dakota Historic Preservation Office sponsored an additional archaeological survey in the north and south Cave Hills. It resulted in the discovery of six additional rock art sites. Small surveys in 1997–2002 led to the discovery of 69 more rock art sites in the Cave Hills (fig. 3.6).[26] In 1999, the archaeologist Lawrence L. Loendorf conducted a project to record and analyze several panels of incised rock art at site 48CK1544 in the northwestern foothills of the Black Hills, funded by the Wyoming Department of Transportation (fig. 3.7).[27] The same year, an additional rock art site was found in the northern Black Hills during a timber sale survey; another had been recorded in that area in 1997.[28] Forest Service–sponsored projects in 2001–2 revealed seven more rock art sites in the southern Black Hills.[29]

Research on rock art in the Black Hills country is ongoing. Certainly, sites will continue to be discovered on public and private land alike. Much remains to be learned concerning when, by whom, and for what purposes the rock art was made.

Plains Indians and Rock Art

Archaeologists, naturalists, and nineteenth-century explorers were not the first to discover rock art in the Black Hills country. Indians who occupied the region historically knew about places where markings could be seen on the cliffs and in the rockshelters. To them, rock art sites were powerful places. They recognized some rock art as records of warriors' brave acts. Like the pictographs that decorated the Indians' robes and tipi liners, these images reinforced the reputations of respected men and warned away intruders. Most rock art, however, appeared to have been left behind long before by unknown people or spirits. Each time a person visited one of these places, he or she was apt to see something different. Today's researchers experience this phenomenon as well, as their field notes verify. Depending on the time of day, the weather, and the viewer's alertness, researchers frequently find previously unseen rock art at previously studied sites. The strange markings probably were as much a source of interest and wonder to the Indians who encountered them long ago as they are to researchers today.

As one Lakota folklorist put it, referring to his people's beliefs: "The Indian knew about the hiero-glyphic stone writing in Red Canyon and elsewhere in the Black Hills. He said that ancient peoples of considerable intelligence made the writings. Their meaning? He did not worry about it because unexplainable things belong only to Taku Wakan [Holy Mystery], and only after death can full knowledge of all life's mysteries be revealed."[1]

Rock Art as Oracle

Most northern Plains Indian belief systems include specific traditions about the significance and meaning of rock art (figs. 4.1, 4.2). In these traditions, rock art is often thought to carry messages from the spirit world. After prayer and fasting, religious specialists can interpret the meaning of these messages.[2] Because the rock itself is believed to have a living spirit, rock art is a direct interface between humans and supernatural beings. Among many northern plains groups, rock art is a means of foretelling the future. Historically it was consulted to predict the outcome of a hunt or war expedition, for example. Rock art can also be a means of channeling the power of a spirit into an individual. In some places, such as the red pipestone quarries in eastern Minnesota, rock art marks places of great spiritual significance. An agent to the Brule Lakota in 1869–70 noted that "a curiously formed rock or stone found on the prairie was always a shrine of worship, covered with rude figures of wild animals, and with medicine sacks and trifling ornaments hidden in its crevices."[3]

In his 1889 book *Indian Sign Language,* William Philo Clark observed that rock art sites were a focus of religious activity among Plains Indians:

Images are carved on the sandstone rocks by some of the medicine men, and the kind and groupings of the figures are suggested to them in a dream or vision. They sometimes repair to the rocks, and remain seated and lying on top for four nights and days fasting,—neither water nor food during this time,—and if blessed with a vision of some special remedy to cure disease, or the location of the camps of their enemies, and if afterwards by a happy use of the remedy satisfac-

Figure 4.1. On the basis of historic Plains Indian art objects, this incised petroglyph from site 39CU90 in the eastern Black Hills can be readily identified as a thunder being, symbolizing the powerful spirits of the sky realm and the ability to overcome one's enemies. The figure is about 15 centimeters tall.

tory results ensue, or the war expedition is successful, the images receive a rude worship; and in some cases sacrifices and gifts are made to them long afterwards as the Indians pass by. A famous rock of this kind is located on Painted Rock Creek, near the Big Horn Mountains, a stream emptying into the Big Horn River. The fissures of the rock and the ground near its base are strewn with beads, bits of clothing, etc.,—gifts or sacrifices for good luck.[4]

The Lakota people who occupied the Black Hills during the late eighteenth and the nineteenth century maintained strong traditions that rock art could reveal information about the future.[5] The Oglala holy man Nicholas Black Elk told of Lakota use of rock art in the Black Hills: "There is a place in the Black Hills, also on the Little Big Horn, a bank of solid rock where there are inscriptions that only a medicine man can read. It is a mystery. There is one in the Black Hills that only a medicine man can read. We don't know who wrote it, but a medicine man can decode it and get the meaning. We would camp and when we would come back there would be more writing."[6]

In 1934, the Lakota chief and elder White Bull recalled his people's belief in the power of rock art to foretell events:

In some places, there were sign rocks that told what was going to happen. If some of your people were going to be killed by enemies, in a few days, the rock would show a sign that your people would be shot with an arrow and the very same thing would happen in a few days. And if you were to have plenty of meat the rock would show some poles with enough meat on them to break the poles and in a few days the buffalo would come and everybody would kill enough to have

Figure 4.2. Historic traditions indicate that this horned lizard or turtle may have been a symbol of long life, tenacity, and the powers of the underground realm. The lizard is about 10 centimeters long.

plenty of meat. After this sign had been seen, it would be polished off. I do not know how the signs appeared or who polished the sign off smooth. This rock had a sign for every important thing that was going to happen to our people.[7]

Another Lakota elder had heard similar stories of Black Hills rock art and its mysterious power to foretell the future. He indicated that his people made regular pilgrimages to this place:

Up there in the Black Hills somewhere, I don't know where, a long time ago there was a piece of rock—a bank or something—the people went there every year. Every year there would be a different picture on the rock. Nobody knew who put the picture on the rock, but if there is going to be a war within the next year, there will be a picture of people laying there. That shows that there is going to be a war. If they go there and see pictures of buffalo and pictures of drying racks where they hang the meat to dry, if they see that, then they'll have a good year. Plenty to eat.[8]

The Medicine Rock, now at Gettysburg, South Dakota, was also used to tell the future.[9] A place called the Mysterious Butte or Holy Butte was another place where Lakotas received signs about their future.[10] This might have been Ludlow Cave in northwestern South Dakota, Medicine Creek Cave in northeastern Wyoming, or some other cave covered with petroglyphs. Lakotas and northern Cheyennes believe that a petroglyph on Deer Medicine Rock in eastern Montana appeared there just before the Custer fight and predicted the great victory that was to come.[11] Interestingly, the Arikara scouts accompanying the Seventh Cavalry on its way to the Little Bighorn also interpreted rock art on Rosebud Creek as predicting a great Lakota victory.[12] Images that appeared on cliffs after holy men fasted and prayed near them foretold success or failure in warfare or hunting.[13] The Mandans and Hidatsas had an "oracle stone" on which messages about the future appeared in the form of inscriptions or drawings.[14] Blackfeet war parties sought signs of the outcome of their raids at Writing-On-Stone in southern Alberta.[15] The

Yankton Dakotas had an oracle stone or council stone near the James River. It was covered with mysterious designs thought to predict the future.[16]

Rock Art Sites as Spiritual Places

Rock art sites were also traditionally considered places where power could be obtained from spirits residing there (fig. 4.3). Plains Indians frequently left offerings at rock art sites—a practice documented historically or archaeologically at sites including the pipestone quarries in Minnesota;[17] Vermilion Springs and Writing-On-Stone in Alberta;[18] the Swift Current and Herschel petroglyphs in Saskatchewan[19]; the Malta Medicine Rock,[20] the Marias Medicine Rock[21] and the Simanton Hills site in northern Montana;[22] Deer Medicine Rock in southern Montana;[23] Painted Rocks near the Bighorn Mountains[24] and another site by the same name near the Powder River;[25] Ludlow Cave in northwestern South Dakota;[26] Medicine Creek Cave in the northern Black Hills;[27] the Gettysburg Medicine Rock;[28] the Mandan Medicine Rock in North Dakota;[29] Thunder Bird's Track Rock in northeastern South Dakota;[30] and a site near the Missouri River in South Dakota still visited as part of Lakota Sun Dance rituals.

According to Arthur Amiotte, in a 1987 article about the Lakota Sun Dance,

a Northern Lakota tradition calls for visitation to an ancient site where there are petroglyphs, sacred markings on rock. The intercessors leave during one of the breaks in the ceremony and go to the sacred place. There offerings are made to the sacred markings. The designs are memorized, brought back, and replicated on the earth altar [in the Sun Dance enclosure]. Oddly enough, it is not unusual to find that a certain kind of transformation does take place even today. Year after year the visitation to the sacred site reveals to us that the marks do change, and in each year they are in turn brought back and replicated on the sacred altar. Following the Sun Dance proper, the shamans gather in the purification lodge—the sweat lodge —and interpret those markings in terms of the potential message that they might have for the people during the forthcoming year.[31]

Figure 4.3. This panel from Medicine Creek Cave in the northwestern Black Hills contains an elaborately carved bear paw (upper center) along with smaller bear paws, bison tracks, vulvas, and grooves. Many northern plains groups associated the bear with the healing arts, because of its knowledge of plants, and with women's sexuality and motherhood, because it dwells in caves and fiercely defends its young. (Photo by Phil Henry; reproduced with permission.)

Other rock art marks places in the landscape where mythical events took place. A boulder carved with intermingled tracks of animals, men, women, and children on a high hill overlooking the Heart River in North Dakota was the place where, according to Arikara tradition, people and animals long ago took refuge from a great flood.[32] The Hidatsas related stories of Old Woman Who Never Dies sending heroic young men to Pictured Rock near the Missouri River to pray and receive power to help them in their undertakings.[33] She also watched over a group of seven other stones—one with carvings on it—which were said to be the bodies of slain enemies.[34] Another rock near the Missouri River bore the footprint of the culture hero who led the Hidatsas to their new homeland.[35] The Crees told of a Little People who gave them large boulders carved with the ribs, eyes, and horns of bison where they could pray and leave offerings to ensure success in hunting.[36] Blackfeet people attributed the markings at Writing-On-Stone in southern Alberta, Canada, to spirit beings dwelling in a lodge-shaped butte there.[37] Petroglyphs on boulders in the eastern Dakotas were believed to be the work of water spirits, thunder beings, or the mysterious female spirit known as Double Woman.[38]

Some rock art, such as the Crazy Horse petroglyph on Reno Creek, Montana, is believed to record visions (fig. 4.4).[39] The Poncas traditionally made petroglyphs in response to visions. They say that many of the petroglyph boulders dotting the Missouri River country are records of successful vision quests.[40] Visions were sometimes sought in the rock art itself. Battiste Good's account of a vision he received in the Black Hills in 1856 provides another example.[41] In describing his vision, Good stated that he saw "prints of a man's hands and horse's hoofs on the rocks." This is clearly a reference to petroglyphs. Writing-On-Stone in southern Alberta and sites in northern Wyoming are hypothesized to have been vision quest sites at which rock art recorded especially powerful visions.[42] The Wind River Shoshones and the Kootenais have traditionally held strong beliefs that rock art sites were ideal places to seek visions.[43]

The oral history of the Poncas, a Missouri River village tribe, gives rock art an important role in marking the migrations of the people. As the Poncas gradu-

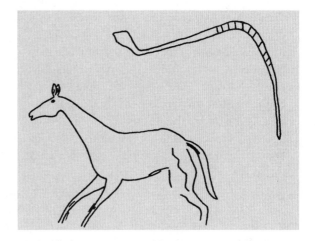

Figure 4.4. According to Cheyenne and Lakota oral history, this petroglyph near Reno Creek in eastern Montana was made by the Oglala leader Crazy Horse to record a vision experience.

ally made their way west from the Ohio Valley, the holy men began to mark their trail on big boulders. The first of these markings were made at the sacred pipestone quarries in Minnesota. Designs were carved into the rocks, with natural fissures and protrusions incorporated into the images. This made the designs difficult for others to discern, but they could readily be seen by the few Poncas who had knowledge of them. In 1928, Peter Le Claire was given the task of writing down his people's oral history. The Ponca elder historian named Mi-Ojin-ha-the told Le Claire of the locations of some of these petroglyphs, which served as trail markers, historical monuments, and places of prayer.[44]

The Sacred Nature of Rock Art

Whether rock art was accidentally discovered or was made by supplicants or religious practitioners, Plains Indians have traditionally regarded most of it as inherently sacred. A narrative collected from Crow's Heart, a Mandan-Hidatsa warrior, in 1931 suggests that his people distinguished between secular rock art, comprising records of events, and sacred rock art, thought to be messages from the spirits. His remarks indicate that not all rock art sites were sacred places:

In early days war parties going north when they came to this side of the cliff [High Hill With

Picture Writing, near the Souris River] would draw pictures of events that had happened. If they killed an enemy they drew a picture of a man lying down, if they took horses they would draw horses' hoofs. . . . Westward you come to a flat country with a knoll on top of which is picture writing made by the spirits. That country is known as the Stone-with-picture-writing. Nobody knows who makes the pictures, so they think it is the gods.[45]

Archaeological investigations at rock art sites on the northern plains have shown that such places have been used as shrines for centuries. Items that may have been left as offerings at several northern plains rock art

sites date as far back as 2,000 to 1,500 years ago.[46] Other rock art sites contain historic trade goods such as metal knives and guns, showing that these shrines continued to be used in the postcontact era. Some sites continue to be used as shrines today.[47] Items left as offerings include beads, tobacco, bone ornaments, stone pipes, feathers, arrowheads, pots or pottery sherds, brass rings and bracelets, cloth, coins, guns, hatchets, and kettles (fig. 4.5). These items were considered desirable to the spirits. They reflect the worshiper's attitude of reverence and personal sacrifice.

To many American Indians today, places with rock art are not archaeological sites or relics—quaint but fading reminders of the past. They are living, powerful, holy places. They are part of a vital and

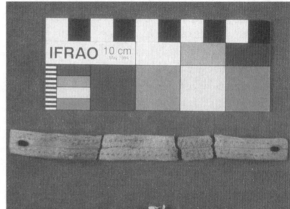
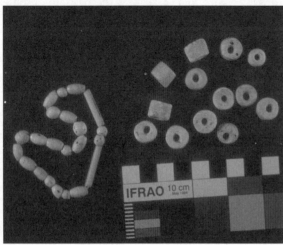
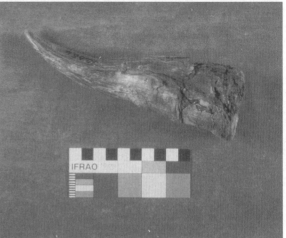

Figure 4.5. Among the hundreds of items left as offerings in Ludlow Cave were these points from complete arrows (A), an incised leather bracelet (B), strings of beads (C), and a reshaped bison horn (D).

Figure 4.6. According to Cheyenne and Lakota mythology, the portion of the Black Hills known as the Red Valley or Racetrack was the setting for a great race between the Two-Legged and the Four-Legged nations. One can speculate that the hundreds of petroglyphs of running animals and humans in the sandstones that line the Red Valley served to reinforce the belief that this was the setting of the ancient story.

growing religious tradition, strongly rooted in the past but still blossoming today. To these people, rock art sites are windows not just to the past but also to the present and future. They are places where a person can still seek help through fasting, prayer, sacrifice, and contemplation. They are also places where children and the spiritually immature can be taught religious ideals. As interest in native religious traditions has seen a revival in recent years, rock art sites have been sought out as intact, tangible symbols of tradi-tional religious concepts (fig. 4.6). These places of great mystery speak to today's Indians much as they did in the past: as portals to the spirit world. Many rock art sites were forgotten in the upheaval of the early reservation period, but others have continued to be visited and revered even through the most disrup-tive times. The continuity of these traditions—some-times over a span of a thousand years or more—is powerful testimony to the importance of these places in Indian belief systems, past and present.

5

Ancient Hunters and the Idea of Transformation

The outer edge of the Black Hills is formed by a high ring of hard sandstones. This ring is cut through in about a dozen places by streams that drain the interior mountains. These form narrow, steep canyons providing natural passes into and out of the Black Hills. In the southern Black Hills, tan, gold, crimson, and rust-colored cliffs rise high above the narrow canyon floors, creating a landscape more like that of the U.S. Southwest than the Rocky Mountains or northern grasslands. These canyonlands are the setting for the oldest rock art found in the Black Hills country.

Pecked Realistic Rock Art

Pecked Realistic rock art comprises complex, detailed pictures of humans, animals, and hunting implements. Some are individual images, but most are scenes with more than one figure. Cooperative hunts and rituals related to hunting are the subjects of most of these scenes. Nearly all of the designs show people, animals, or things—hence the term *realistic*. The designs were made by pecking away the dark outer surface of the rock, probably with a stone or bone chisel and a stone hammer, to reveal the lighter rock

underneath (fig. 5.1). The designs were carefully planned, then skillfully pecked into the rock by artisans. The resulting panels are busy yet delicate in their depiction of early human life in the Black Hills.

The exact age of Pecked Realistic rock art is unknown. It may be among the oldest rock art anywhere in the Americas. Attempts to date the art using experimental chemical dating methods yielded dates of 11,500 to 2,000 radiocarbon years before the present.[1] (Recent research on atmospheric radiocarbon suggests the correct calendar range would be about 13,000 to 2,000 years ago.)[2] The accuracy of these dates has since been called into question,[3] but no one doubts that this rock art is among the oldest on the continent.

Pecked Realistic is certainly the oldest rock art in the Black Hills. Where it occurs together with other styles of rock art, the Pecked Realistic is always "at the bottom"—that is, the other art is carved or painted over it (fig. 5.2). Also, much of the Pecked Realistic rock art is stranded high above the current ground surface (fig. 5.3). This shows that the carvings were made before a major drop in surface elevation in the

Figure 5.1. Pecked Realistic–style rock art was made by pecking the rock surface using a stone hammer or hammer-and-chisel combination. Detail of panel from Whoopup Canyon, Wyoming. Animal at center is about 20 centimeters wide.

canyon. This change may have occurred as regional water tables dropped in response to changing climate, leading to erosion of the dirt and rocks forming the canyon bottoms. A mix of heavily weathered and newer-appearing panels shows that Pecked Realistic rock art was made for a very long time—perhaps several thousand years. A chemical patina has formed over some of the petroglyphs, returning them to the same dark brown or black of the surrounding rock.

Major climate changes took place about 10,000, 7,000, and 5,000 radiocarbon years ago in the Black Hills.[4] The stranding of the rock art probably followed one of these changes, but we cannot say which one until more research is done. The earliest date is unlikely, because the rock art does not depict mammoths or other ice-age animals. The last of these animals went extinct about 10,500 radiocarbon years ago. Either of the other dates could reasonably mark the beginning of the erosional period that left the rock art stranded high above the surface. It appears that Pecked Realistic rock art was made for thousands of years, because it shows various degrees of weathering

Figure 5.2. Careful examination of this panel from site 39FA79 reveals a series of Pecked Realistic figures under the incised lines. In the close-up view at bottom, a deer's head and antlers are visible at upper left, and legs at lower left. The extreme weathering of the pecked rock art probably resulted in part from scouring by sand dunes that migrated along the cliff face, alternately covering and exposing the rock face.

Figure 5.3. The stranding of old rock art is seen in this photo of site 39FA1336. Older, pecked rock art is visible at the top of the photo, and later incised designs cover the rock at the bottom of the photo. The two overlap in the middle. (Ruler shows 10 cm intervals.)

and repatination and occurs both very high and very low on cliff faces. This indicates that the rock art continued to be made as the landscape slowly changed shape. No reported scientific excavations have been completed at any Pecked Realistic sites. Good localities for excavation are difficult to find, because in most cases sediments beneath the panels have been removed by erosion.

The pictures themselves offer important clues to the age of Pecked Realistic rock art. They feature detailed images of hunting tools, including spear or dart throwers (atlatls) and large nets (figs. 5.4, 5.5). Spear throwers began to be replaced by bows and arrows in this area about 2,000 years ago.[5] Depictions of bows and arrows are lacking entirely, so the most recent Pecked Realistic rock art must be at least 2,000 years old. Only one game-hunting net has been pre-

served in the archaeological record of the northern plains. This net, found in a cave in the Absaroka Mountains of north-central Wyoming, was large enough for ensnaring deer or mountain sheep. Three sharpened stakes were attached to the net as supports, and it would have looked something like an elongated tennis net when erected for use. It was radiocarbon dated to 8,800 radiocarbon years,[6] or about 9,700 calendar years, before the present.

Taken together, these clues indicate that Pecked Realistic rock art was made throughout much of the Archaic period, from about 10,000 to 2,000 years ago. This rock art may have been made during the later part of the preceding Paleoindian period, too, but it probably does not extend back into the early Paleoindian period. A more exact date for this rock art awaits development of better dating methods.

Figure 5.4. This drawing of a pecked panel from Whoopup Canyon, Wyoming, shows a deer hunter with a spear or spear thrower. (Scale bar shows 30 cm.)

Figure 5.5. This hunting scene is unusual in depicting a herd of bison on the right side of the panel. The left side is more typical in showing deer. The looped lines seem to represent large hunting nets or other temporary enclosures into which the animals were driven. The meaning of the crosses is unclear, but one can speculate that they might be shaman's poles, as indicated by both archaeological finds and historical accounts of animal drives. (Scale bar shows 30 cm.)

Archaic Life as Seen through Pecked Realistic Rock Art

Pecked Realistic rock art provides an important window into Archaic life in the Black Hills (fig. 5.6). Although it does not match exactly the early rock art from other parts of North America, it shows a strong resemblance to early petroglyphs from the Great Basin and other areas in and west of the Rockies (fig. 5.7).[7] This suggests a western connection for the people who created the rock art—a link echoed in other archaeological material dating to the Early and Middle Archaic periods. These Black Hills sites and their contents bear strong resemblances to sites and material from the Great Basin. This western influence probably reached the Black Hills via the western Bighorn Mountains and other portions of the eastern Rockies.

Pecked Realistic rock art reveals much about Archaic life-ways in the Black Hills country. Many panels are hunting scenes (figs. 5.8, 5.9). Men, women, and even children are depicted driving small herds of deer into large enclosures, most likely formed by stand-nets, represented by looped lines (figs. 5.10, 5.11). Hunters with spears, clubs, or dart throwers kill the enclosed animals. The picture provided by the rock art matches that drawn from ethnographic accounts, which were summarized by George Frison when he described the game net found in the Absaroka Mountains:

A net . . . is designed to entangle its prey when stretched across an area through which [the animals] normally travel. Animals can also be driven

Figure 5.6. Five humans, two with distinctive headgear, are visible in this hunting scene from site 39FA681. Two are holding semicircular objects of unknown function. (Scale bar shows 30 cm.)

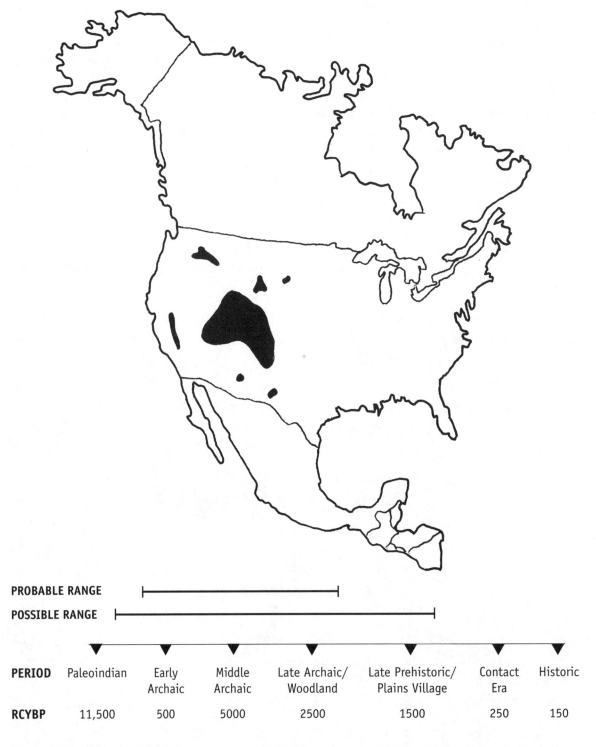

Figure 5.7. Distribution in the western United States of rock art with solidly pecked animals and humans in hunting and other action scenes. The time line shows the probable and possible ranges of dates for Pecked Realistic rock art in the Black Hills.

into the net. The animals lose their footing, become disoriented, and while struggling to free themselves, are vulnerable to hunters stationed at the net who are armed with clubs. In this situation the arrow, dart, or thrusting spear was neither necessary nor even the most efficient method of dispatching the animals, although ethnographically all of these weapons were used in conjunction with net hunting.[8]

Most of the animals shown are deer, but pronghorn, mountain sheep, elk, and a few bison are included in some panels. Dogs are often shown at the edges of the herds, as if helping to drive the prey into the enclosures (fig. 5.12). Although dog or dog-wolf hybrid bones are often found in Paleoindian and Early Archaic bison kill sites, this rock art provides the ear-

liest definite evidence of the use of dogs in animal drives.

The rock art also shows that ceremonial activities were important parts of early hunting practices. Several panels show people in special costumes (fig. 5.13). Some of these costumes appear to imitate deer or other animals, but others are less easily interpreted. On several panels, lines of costumed men appear to be performing a dance or ceremony. On others, the costumed men are shown at the edge of the animal drive. Although other kinds of clothing are not shown in the rock art, a distinctive hairstyle appears on one male figure (see fig. 1). He wears his hair in two braids, much like the historic Lakota and Cheyenne Indians did. Men are clearly nude or nearly so in many of the petroglyphs, but whether this shows actual hunting attire or is meant to indicate gender is unknown. One

Figure 5.8. Costumed humans appear at the upper edge of this deer-hunting scene from Whoopup Canyon, Wyoming. (Scale bar shows 30 cm.)

Figure 5.9. Another panel from Whoopup Canyon includes several deer and five humans with horned or eared headgear. (Scale bar shows 30 cm.)

Figure 5.10. Only a small fragment has survived of this pecked panel from site 39FA688 in the southern Black Hills. It shows two deer heading toward a hunting net (looped line at upper right). (Scale bar shows 30 cm.)

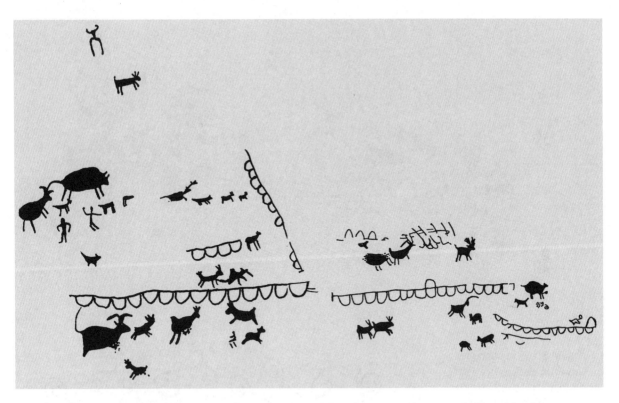

Figure 5.11. Two hunters, at far left, drive a line of deer into an enclosure probably made of large stand-nets (looped lines) in this panel from Whoopup Canyon. The object at upper left may be an animal skull placed atop a stand. The large animals just above the humans, at lower left, and at right center appear to have been added to the scene later. Deer at upper left is 30 cm long.

Figure 5.12. A line of hunters runs through the deer, pronghorn, and mountain sheep shown in this panel from site 39FA99, while a pack of dogs apparently helps contain the game at bottom center. Note the mountain lion at upper center. (Scale bar shows 30 cm.

Figure 5.14. Implements shown in Pecked Realistic rock art in the southern Black Hills: (a) spiral-shaped objects perhaps used as goads; (b) possible throwing sticks; (c) hand-held hoops of unknown use; (d) staffs, spears, or clubs; (e) atlatls; (f) spears or atlatls; (g, h) unidentified items shown among animals in hunting scenes; (i) goads; (j) possible rabbit snare.

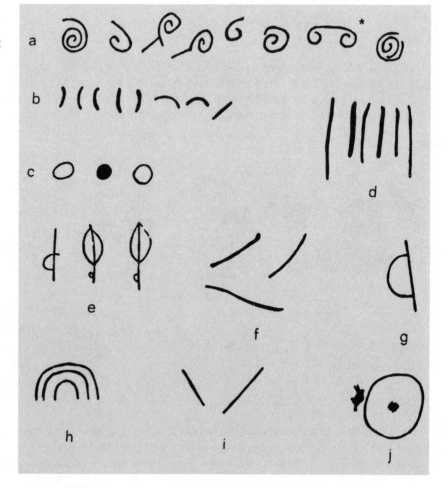

Figure 5.13 (above and top left). These four panels appear like a frieze stranded high above the bottom of Stone Quarry Canyon at site 39FA395. They form a single, complex hunting scene, now broken by vertical strips of eroded rock. Humans in eared or horned headgear stand near the "loop-line" net enclosure in the third panel from the left. Note also the man and the pregnant woman at the upper center of the second panel from left and two large atlatls (spear throwers) adjacent to the looped lines in the second and fourth panels.

panel at the huge Whoopup Canyon site in Wyoming depicts 14 men engaged in what appears to be a tug-of-war. Eight men are lined up on one side, and six others face them, each with his hands on the shoulders of the man in front of him—except for the central two, who grasp a stick or rod.

Many kinds of implements are shown in this Archaic rock art (fig. 5.14). Some of these are recognizable as spears, dart throwers (atlatls), and throwing sticks (a boomerang-like hunting weapon). One panel appears to show a rabbit snare. Other objects are not easily identified. They may depict wooden or fiber tools such as spring-snares that have not been preserved archaeologically.

A few Pecked Realistic designs apparently represent ideas rather than things. One panel shows a human figure apparently floating or flying above a hunting scene (fig. 5.15). He may express the flying sensation people sometimes experience while in a trance state. Several panels have depictions of mountain lions above the hunting scenes. Mountain lions may in some way express the idea of success in the hunt, because the big cats are unmatched in their ability to

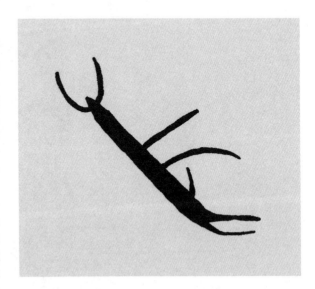

Figure 5.15. This horned human seems to float or fly above a deer-hunting scene. A feeling of floating or flying is common during trance states. Whoopup Canyon, Wyoming.

Figure 5.16. This faint panel from site 39FA688 shows a human, at right, partially transformed into a deer. The deer, at left, has humanlike feet, suggesting another transformation image. These deer-humans overlie an earlier and fainter deer image and perhaps were made in response to it. (Scale bar shows 30 cm.)

hunt deer.[9] They certainly would have been unlikely to approach a place where humans were staging a hunt, and they are not scavengers. These mountain lion images might symbolize the desired outcome of the hunt, or they might have been made to invoke a spirit helper represented by the mountain lion.

Pecked Realistic Rock Art and Transformation

Other Pecked Realistic rock art expresses the idea of transformation. Some human figures have antlerlike hands that seem to express the idea of a half-human, half-deer state. This idea is expressed even more clearly in a panel that shows two half-human, half-deer creatures in dancing posture (fig. 5.16). One can speculate that these indicate a deer cult, perhaps linked to cooperative deer hunting, or a ritual in which a person takes on the spiritual identity of the deer (fig. 5.17). This idea of transformation from a human state to an animal state—or, more accurately, of transforming one's essence from the ordinary to the extraordinary as represented by an animal—is common to hunter art throughout the world. Humans with animal attributes are found in Paleolithic cave art in Europe, in the ancient hunting art of South Africa,

Figure 5.17. The arms and heads of this line of men have deerlike features, suggesting either a dance imitating the animal or a trance state in which the person experiences a sensation of being transformed into an animal. The rock has broken away at left, removing the lower portions of at least two animal dancers. Whoopup Canyon, Wyoming. (Scale bar shows 20 cm.)

Figure 5.18. In this detailed hunt scene from Whoopup Canyon, women, children, and a man with a horned headdress help goad deer and antelope into an enclosure. A man is spearing an antelope between two nets or fences. The many-legged figure at left appears to be a human in costume or disguise. At the bottom of the panel, four men with elongated headdresses and staffs or wands form a line just outside the hunt scene. The images at the top of this panel appear much older than those lower down because they are extremely worn and indistinct. This suggests that the panel was created over a long period. (Scale bar shows 30 cm.)

and in the rock art of the Australian Aborigines. Hunters are uniquely attuned to the powers manifested in the animal world. For them, the animal becomes a metaphor for ideas such as agility, survival, and power over one's adversaries.

Overall, Pecked Realistic rock art reflects a culture with a high degree of social cooperation and a well-developed religion. It provides evidence that the entire group worked together to capture deer, pronghorn, and mountain sheep (fig. 5.18). Ceremonies and costumed humans scattered among the hunting scenes show that hunting and religion went hand-in-hand in this culture (fig. 5.19). A strong link to the animal world—including both its tangible and its spiritual aspects—is expressed throughout this remarkable art.

Figure 5.19. The actions of the three humans at the top of this scene are difficult to interpret but may represent one person helping two others achieve a state of "dreaming," or trance. Like the previous picture, this one may reflect a trance designed to invoke transformation into deer. This enigmatic scene is carved into and around a recessed area in the cliff face at Whoopup Canyon. (Scale bar shows 30 cm.)

Glimpses of an Ancient Art

One of the oldest rock art styles in the Black Hills country is also one of the most poorly represented. Only three examples from two sites are known so far. This style is termed Painted Geometric.

All three examples are geometric designs painted with a dark red pigment (fig. 6.1). One is a circle with a slanted line through it. Another is a line with smaller lines branching obliquely from it. The third looks something like a pitchfork. Both of the sites at which these occur are in the southern Black Hills near the Cheyenne River.

One of the paintings is superimposed by a pecked design belonging to the Pecked Abstract group (fig. 6.2). Pecked Abstract rock art was generally made later than Pecked Realistic art but may have overlapped it for a short time. The three Painted Geometric glyphs must be older than the Pecked Abstract art, but it is not yet clear whether they are older or younger than Painted Realistic hunting scenes. It may eventually be possible to radiocarbon-date tiny paint fragments from these paintings. Whatever their exact age, they certainly are the oldest *painted* art in the Black Hills country.

The other site containing Painted Geometric designs also displays both pecked and incised rock art, as well as several abraded grooves (figs. 6.3, 6.4). This combination indicates that the site was revisited by different groups over hundreds or thousands of years. It is possible that the early painted designs somehow prompted later people to create rock art there as well.

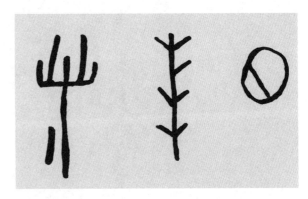

Figure 6.1. Sketches of the three Painted Geometric designs from the southern Black Hills: left, site 39FA1048; center and right, site 39FA767. All are finger-applied in dark red pigment.

Figure 6.2. Sketch of rock art panel at site 39FA1048, showing superimposition of pecked (dotted lines) and incised (solid lines) rock art over the pitchfork-like painted design (shaded lines). See figure 2.1 for a photograph of this panel. (Scale bar shows 30 cm.)

Figure 6.3. Drawing of rock art at site 39FA767, showing painted design (shaded lines at upper left) and pecked (dotted lines) and incised (solid lines) rock art. Thin lines designate natural breaks in the rock surface. (Scale bar shows 20 cm.)

One petroglyph at the site is a pecked human hand with a flowerlike extension at the end of the thumb (fig. 6.3).

The meaning and origin of these painted figures are not known. Neither site has been excavated, although one is known to contain artifacts. Similar geometric painted figures occur west of the Black Hills at the Medicine Lodge Creek site in the eastern Bighorn basin (fig. 6.5). The rock art at this impressive site—now a state park—has never been systematically studied, so it provides few clues to the Black Hills art.

Simple painted rock art is quite common in central and western Montana (fig. 6.6). Although it includes some geometric figures reminiscent of those in the Black Hills and at Medicine Lodge Creek, it is not strikingly similar. The single exception is a set of branched lines and a rayed circle at the Desrosier Rockshelter site.[1] Elsewhere, the Montana style is characterized by a mix of simple geometric designs, animals, humans, and impressed and stenciled handprints. A few complex, mazelike images also occur. Overall, these figures seem to be more closely related to rock art farther north and west on the Columbia Plateau than to rock art from elsewhere in the northwestern plains.[2]

With continued research, archaeologists may come to understand in more detail the distribution and significance of this elusive rock art style.

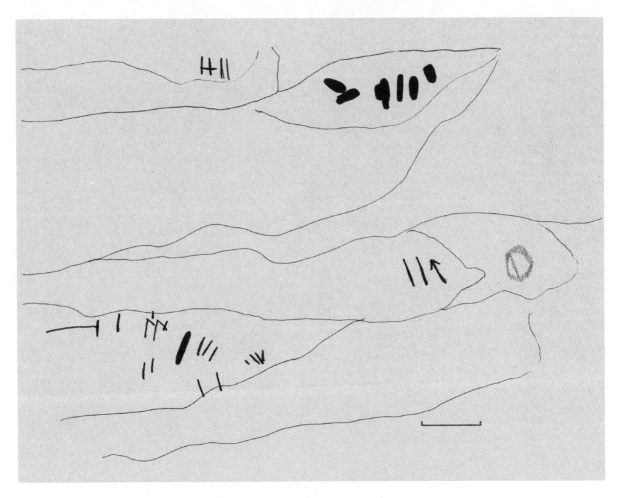

Figure 6.4. Sketch showing painted design (shaded lines at right) and incised and grooved rock art on adjacent rock surfaces at site 39FA767. (Scale bar shows 20 cm.)

Figure 6.5. Finger-painted geometric designs from Medicine Lodge Creek in the Bighorn Mountains of Wyoming.

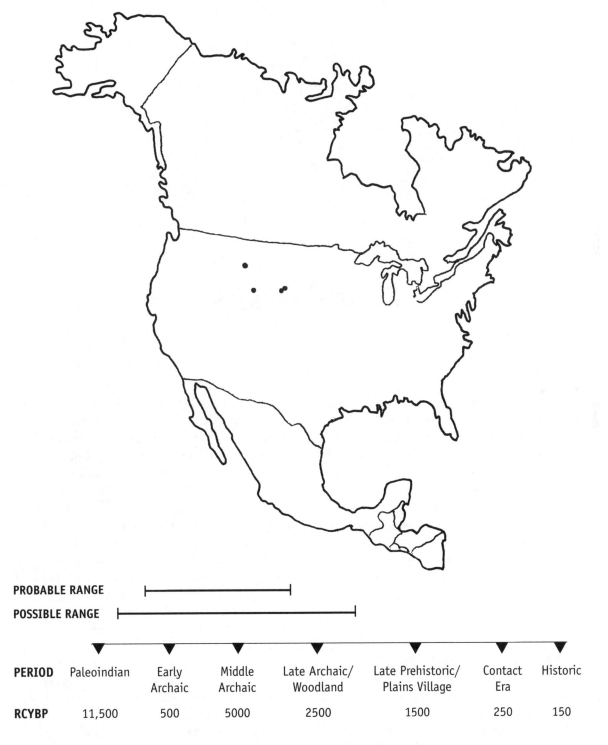

PERIOD	Paleoindian	Early Archaic	Middle Archaic	Late Archaic/ Woodland	Late Prehistoric/ Plains Village	Contact Era	Historic
RCYBP	11,500	500	5000	2500	1500	250	150

Figure 6.6. Locations of simple painted geometric designs: Desrosier Rockshelter, Montana; the Medicine Lodge Creek site, Wyoming; and two sites in the southern Black Hills. The time line shows the probable and possible ranges of dates for Painted Geometric–style rock art in the Black Hills.

Archaic Seekers

All human beings experience the sensation of "seeing" images that are not really perceived by the eye. These images are called *phosphenes* (light specks) or *entoptics* (things seen inside).[1] They are perceived by the brain as visual images but are not connected with visual stimuli. Examples of phosphenes are the "stars" one sees after receiving a blow to the head, the auras experienced by migraine sufferers, and the so-called prisoners' cinema—flashes of light people perceive after a few minutes in a totally dark place such as a deep cave. Children are reported to experience phosphenes in the moments before they fall asleep. Sensory deprivation, fasting, sleep deprivation, lack of oxygen, and hallucinogenic drugs also induce phosphenes.

Phosphene Images in Rock Art

Because phosphenes are essentially a consequence of eye and brain structure and chemistry, all people experience the same phosphene images. In translating these images to drawings or verbal descriptions, cultural training interferes, so that each artist produces a slightly different version of the same image. Thus, phosphenes may look somewhat different in the draw-

ings of different people, but the images they experience are the same. Scientists have identified a limited array of typical phosphene patterns. These include rayed circles, series of wavy lines, arrays of dots, concentric circles, asterisk-like figures, concentric arcs, spirals, checkerboards, lattices, and "fingers" (fig. 7.1).[2]

Images of phosphenes in art are strongly associated with altered states of consciousness. When shamans and religious supplicants enter a trance, they first experience a quasi-trance state in which they perceive vivid phosphene images.[3] Flashes of light, swirls of color and sound, and sensations of objects growing and shrinking to incredible dimensions are typical of this early stage of the trance. This is when the concentric circles, wavy lines, grids, checkerboards, starbursts, and other typical phosphenes are "seen." As the trance progresses, the person continues to experience intense images, but these begin to change into recognizable things. They often take the form of humanlike or animal beings. In this advanced trance state, the vision is experienced as part of the here and now. In such vivid visions, the spirit beings may approach the vision seeker and may transport him or her to other

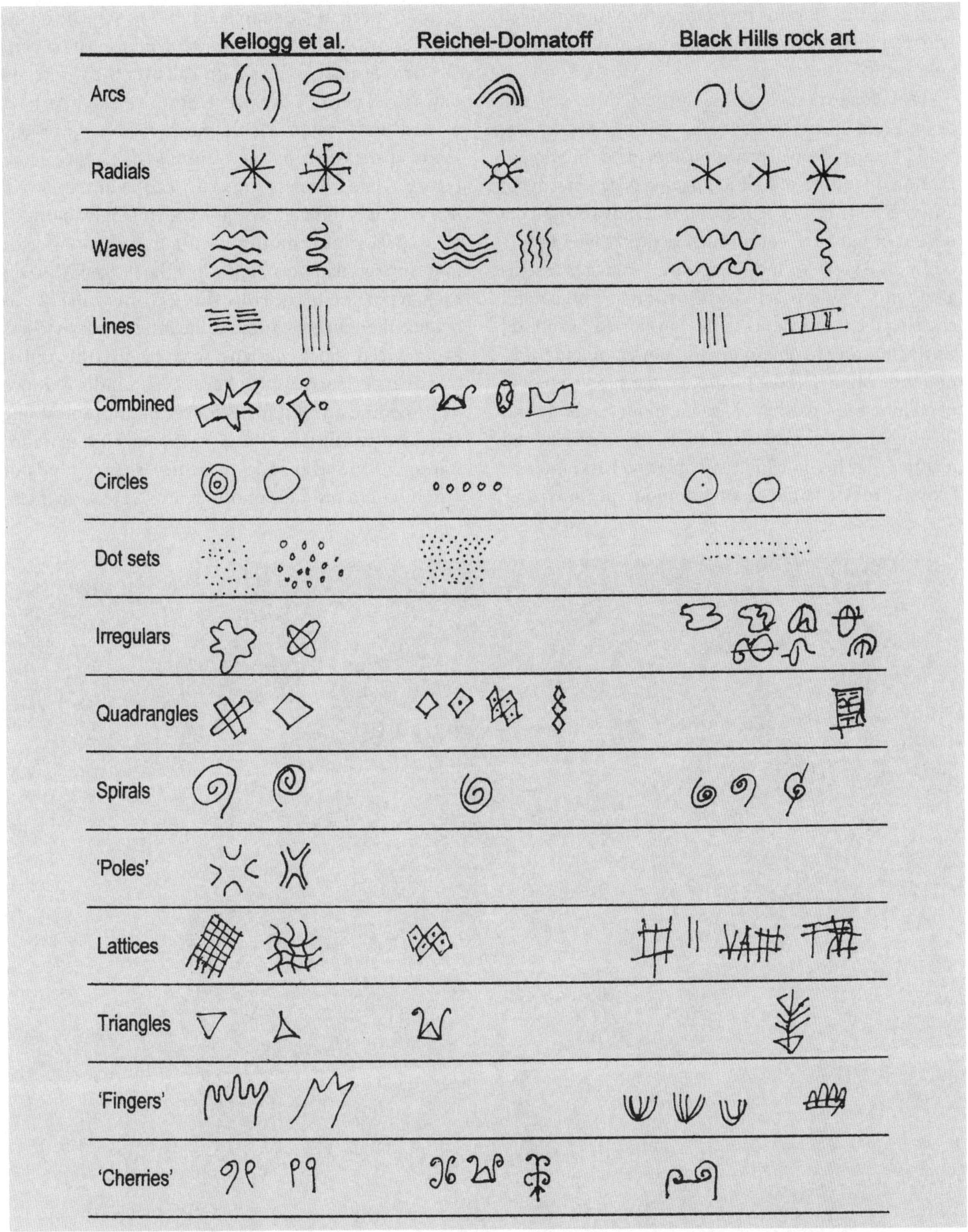

Figure 7.1. Typical phosphene or entoptic designs. Left column adapted from Kellogg, Knoll, and Kugler, "Form Similarity"; center column adapted from Reichel-Dolmatoff, "Drug-Induced Optical Sensations"; right column, examples of Pecked Abstract rock art from the southern Black Hills.

places. At this stage of the trance, the vision is filled with real things: rocks, plants, people, animals, clouds, and the like.

An altered state of consciousness, or trance, can be induced in many ways—by self-torture, loss of blood, fasting, sleep deprivation, repetitive chanting or motion, ingestion of hallucinogenic drugs, staring at an object for hours, isolation, or removal to places devoid of light and sound such as deep caves. In virtually all American Indian cultures, trance is associated with religious activity. Most often, the person entering the trance hopes to be transported to another world, in order to obtain insight, power, or supernatural protection. During the trance, the supplicant will often have the sensation of leaving his or her body and floating or flying in the air. Sounds, sights, smells, and textures may become indescribably vivid and intense. Clouds, rocks, animals, or luminous persons may

seem to speak to the supplicant. In this state he or she may receive the long-sought vision of a spirit helper.

Trance-related art is found all over the world and dates to all periods of history. Some researchers have argued that even art that appears to show everyday items such as people and animals is shamanic or trance-related. Unless the artist can be interviewed, however, it is difficult to argue convincingly that such art was religiously motivated. On the other hand, art that shows only phosphenes, like the Pecked Abstract rock art of the Black Hills (fig. 7.2), very likely was made either during a trance state or after a trance was experienced. Such designs may record the initial trance experience or may have helped induce trance by providing a visual focus for the supplicant. While religious specialists are the experts on achieving trance states, anyone who seeks or achieves these kinds of visions could produce phosphene art. Historic inter-

Figure 7.2. Pecked Abstract designs stand out clearly on this darkly patinated cliff at site 39FA788.

views with American Indians confirm that much of the rock art containing phosphene images in California and the Great Basin was made by people undergoing trances.[4] Other trance-related rock art has been identified in Texas, southern Ontario, and California.[5]

Phosphene Art in the Black Hills

Images of phosphenes make up a Black Hills rock art style. Known as the Pecked Abstract style, this rock art is widely scattered throughout the sandstones of the southern edge of the Black Hills. It consists of large or small panels with intricate designs made of circles, wavy lines, spirals, arcs, lattices, stars, and rows of dots (figs. 7.3–7.6). Practically no recognizable objects are depicted among the abstract designs. The rock art designs are formed with wide, shallowly pecked lines and have a general horizontal orientation. Unlike other rock art styles, the Pecked Abstract style reveals no attempt to frame the designs within a natural space. Instead, the designs spill over the rock edges, extending around corners, across fissures and ceilings, and over fallen boulders. Those who made the designs paid little attention to the natural boundaries of the

rock surfaces. Pecked Abstract designs occur in a variety of settings, including small rockshelters, large cliff exposures, low rock outcrops, and places with low visibility such as crevices and nooks.

Pecked Abstract rock art is strikingly different from the rock art styles that preceded and followed it (figs. 7.7–7.9). It is clearly the work of people operating outside of everyday experience. Like much of western American Indian rock art, this is art of the trance. The lack of attention to natural surface boundaries probably reflects the spontaneous and unbounded mental state of the artists,[6] just as the use of phosphene images reflects the trance experience. There is no evidence that the people who made Pecked Abstract rock art used hallucinogens. Instead, they probably induced trance states through fasting and isolation, as did later Plains Indians.

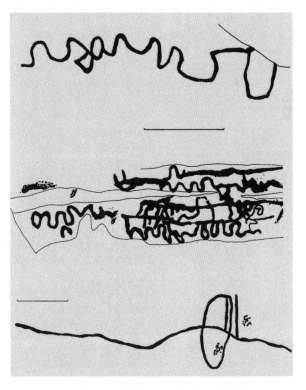

Figure 7.4. These Pecked Abstract panels display the typical horizontal orientation of the meandering designs. Top, site 39FA686; center, 39FA544; bottom, 39FA395. Pecked Realistic panels at the last site are about 20 feet higher on the cliff face than this Pecked Abstract panel. (Scale bars show 30 cm.)

Figure 7.3. Pecked Abstract panels from site 39FA684, southern Black Hills. A small incised man has been added to the first panel (top panel, right).

Figure 7.5. These panels from sites 39FA73 (top left and right) and 39FA79 (bottom) illustrate the complexity of some Pecked Abstract designs. At both sites the wide pecked lines making up the designs extend beyond the naturally defined rock surfaces, meandering around corners and across the ceiling of a rockshelter. (Scale bars show 30 cm.)

Figure 7.6. These Pecked Abstract panels occupy smaller rock surfaces than those in the preceding illustrations. Top left, site 39FA682; top right, 39FA389; center left and bottom right, 39FA89; center right, 39FA395; bottom left, 39FA695. (Scale bars show 30 cm.)

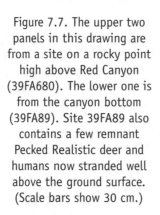

Figure 7.7. The upper two panels in this drawing are from a site on a rocky point high above Red Canyon (39FA680). The lower one is from the canyon bottom (39FA89). Site 39FA89 also contains a few remnant Pecked Realistic deer and humans now stranded well above the ground surface. (Scale bars show 30 cm.)

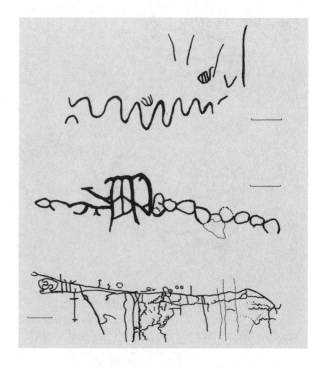

Pecked Abstract Art and Archaic Life-Ways

The Pecked Abstract style of the southern Black Hills is part of a much wider abstract petroglyph tradition that extends across much of the American West (fig. 7.10).[7] Found primarily in the western basins and nearby mountain ranges, this pecked art is nearly identical in some cases to the Black Hills examples. Some of this similarity can be attributed to the universality of phosphene imagery, but the similarities in technique, sizes of images, and orientation suggest actual cultural links between the Black Hills and areas to the west.

The exact age of Pecked Abstract art is unknown, but it perhaps dates to the latter half of the Archaic period, 5,000 to 2,000 years ago. Pecked Abstract panels in the Black Hills often superimpose Pecked Realistic panels. They also show less weathering and sediment displacement than the Pecked Realistic hunting-scene art (fig. 7.11). At one site, however, the two pecked styles occur nearly side by side and exhibit similar amounts of weathering. This suggests that the two styles may overlap somewhat in time. At another site, some Pecked Realistic designs occur at the same level above ground surface as Pecked

Figure 7.8. Pecked Abstract rock art sometimes takes the form of single or unconnected designs. Top row, from left: sites 39FA79, 39PN90, 39FA79, 39FA682; center group, panel from 39FA79; bottom left, 39FA687; bottom right, 39FA690. At first these isolated designs were thought to represent a separate style of abstract pecked art, but the discovery of intermediate examples showed that they were simply variations on the Pecked Abstract theme. (Scale bars show 30 cm.)

Abstract designs, whereas others occur higher up on the cliff face.

Pecked Abstract rock art tells a story of a people with an interest in matters outside of everyday concerns of food, shelter, and safety. These Archaic seekers created an art that would help them experience or remember trance states. While the exact form of their religious activity remains hidden, their art provides some of the earliest evidence of individualized vision or trance seeking in the northern plains. The long tradition of trance seeking indicated by Pecked Abstract rock art continued throughout the history of the Black Hills country (fig. 7.12). Even today, Indian men and women come to the lonely places of the Black Hills and butte country to seek the spiritual gift of the vision.

Figure 7.9. This complex Pecked Abstract panel at site 39FA86 has been damaged by the application of chalk and wax crayon to the pecked lines.

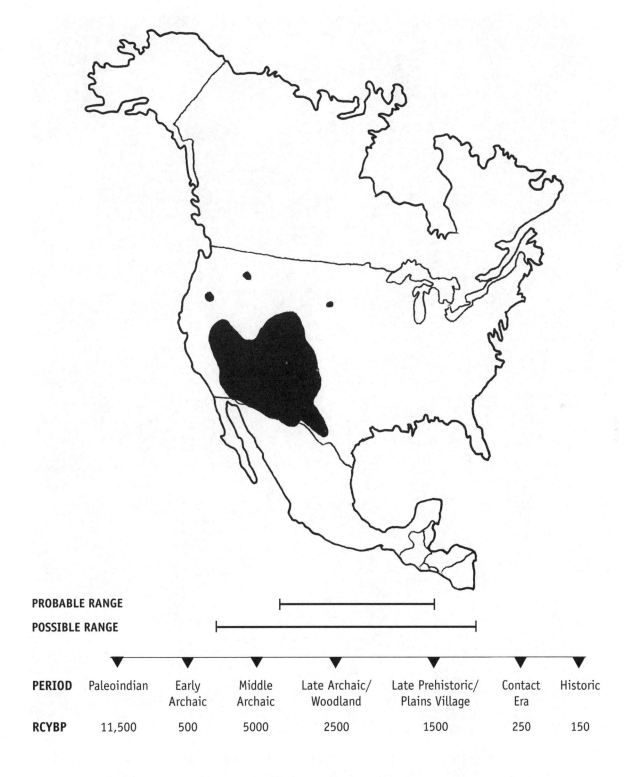

Figure 7.10. Approximate distribution of pecked abstract rock art and time line
for the Pecked Abstract style in the Black Hills.

Figure 7.11. This Pecked Abstract panel from site 39FA1032 is unusual in the angularity of the shapes making up its complex designs. Unlike many Pecked Realistic panels, it has not been completely repatinated by the mineral deposits that have blackened the surrounding rock surface.

Figure 7.12. The Lakota historian Battiste Good (or Brown Hat) drew this picture of a vision he received while fasting in the Black Hills in 1856. It reflects the vivid imagery experienced in the later stages of the trance. The hill represents the Black Hills, which were the Lakotas' home and responsibility, with the blue curve of the sky above it and flags representing the divisions of the earth. The drawing illustrates the use of the Black Hills for personal religious activities involving trances or visions—activities foreshadowed by the Pecked Abstract images of phosphenes or entoptics. It also illustrates the difficulty of recognizing some art as vision-based when phosphenes are not a main component of the image. (Reproduced from Mallery, *Picture-Writing*, 289.)

Themes of Life and Renewal

Sometime after the onset of the late prehistoric period, about 2,000 years ago, peoples of Siouan and Algonkian stock began to shift their territories from the eastern woodlands westward to the northern plains. Perhaps these people were the descendants of those who brought the distinctive Besant culture of the Late Archaic period, or perhaps they were newcomers to the plains.[1] By about 1000 C.E., more definite evidence places the ancestors of the Mandans, Hidatsas, and Crows as far west as the eastern Dakotas and the Missouri River.[2] The Algonkian-speaking Cheyennes and Arapahos may have reached the Missouri as early as 1500 C.E.[3] The ancestral Dakotas would follow later, reaching the Missouri River about 1650.[4] Another Siouan-speaking group, the Poncas, may have lived in the Black Hills vicinity for a few decades around 1700.[5]

With this influx of eastern and northern peoples came a radical shift in rock art. The older pecked rock art linked to Great Basin and western plains traditions gave way to rock art produced by incising, grinding, and abrading. This new art was more akin to traditions found in the eastern prairies and woodlands.

The familiar hunting scenes and the dizzying abstract designs were replaced by a combination of animal tracks, handprints, footprints, faces, bas-relief human figures, vulva and phallic designs (fig. 8.1), and scenes illustrating myths and personal accomplishments. In this art can be seen the beginnings of the pictographic notation system found in historic hide paintings and ledger drawings.

Although the details of this culture shift are unclear, it may be significant that some of the producers of incised rock art attempted to erase earlier glyphs. Some pecked petroglyphs have been deliberately rubbed out, with incised rock art placed over them (fig. 8.2). This incised petroglyph tradition includes several styles of rock art with differing geographic distributions and life spans. Its striking diversity probably represents movements of many different groups into the Black Hills country during the centuries preceding white contact. Its subject matter reflects the core ideas of peoples who were as concerned with spiritual matters as with success in warfare and hunting.

Figure 8.1. Panel of six vulva figures of various forms, made by incising and grinding the rock surface at site 39HN150. One petroglyph is superimposed by the 1925 graffiti.

Ludlow Cave, an Ancient Shrine

In 1874, as George A. Custer was preparing his famous expedition to the then-unmapped Black Hills, he befriended a northern Lakota-Arikara man named Goose. Goose told Custer of a wondrous cave, full of animal bones and with walls covered with magical pictures that changed before one's eyes (fig. 8.3). Custer detoured the expedition westward so he could see for himself this natural wonder, the Lakota name of which translated simply as "the cave."[6] After a long and difficult trek, the expedition arrived at the place now called Ludlow Cave.

William Ludlow, Custer's chief engineer, and the enlisted men were unanimous in their disappoint-ment at the cave. It was little more than a long crevice in the sandstone rimrock, covered with rudely scratched designs and littered with arrows and other offerings left there by the Indians. The men helped themselves to these offerings—an act for which Lakota and Cheyenne tradition promised severe con-sequences. According to one report, Goose looked on in regret as the soldiers, reporters, and young Santee scouts—who knew nothing of this western country—swarmed into the cave and rifled through the piles of offerings carefully placed there over the centuries.[7]

Indians and archaeologists alike seem to have for-gotten Ludlow Cave in the chaotic years following the Battle of the Little Bighorn, where Custer's Seventh

Figure 8.2. The light areas at upper center in this photograph show where the cliff face at site 39FA1190 was abraded with a rock or other hard object, apparently in an attempt to remove the pecked deer still visible under the abraded areas. At upper right, an incised line overlies the remains of a pecked figure.

Figure 8.3. View from Ludlow Cave, looking out. The large rock at center is part of a roof collapse. Although most of the rock art has been destroyed by graffiti, a few petroglyphs can still be seen on the walls of the cave and on the underside of the fallen rock. The large bison petroglyph shown in figure 8.4 is on the cliffs seen across the valley in this photo. (Photo by Paul Horsted; reproduced with permission.)

Cavalry met its fate. A few still remembered the place, however, when the anthropologist George Will began his fieldwork among the Mandans of central North Dakota early in the twentieth century. Mandan elders told him of a sacred cave north of the Black Hills. From this opening to the underworld, bison emerged periodically to replenish the herds, so the people might live. The people prayed and left offerings at Ludlow Cave and other "buffalo home" buttes to entreat the bison to continue to support human life.[8] The Mandans shared a belief in buffalo caverns with the Hidatsas, Cheyennes, Arapahos, Lakotas, and Crows.[9] Since these tribes once occupied this part of the northern plains, they, too, may have recognized Ludlow Cave as a sacred buffalo cave.

The biggest petroglyph at Ludlow Cave is a bas-relief carving of a buffalo cow and calf (fig. 8.4).[10] The bison cow, laboriously abraded into the rock to a depth of about an inch, is some seven feet long from nose to tail. She has strange, lyrelike horns, an extraordinarily long tail, and ears between her horns. These features indicate that this is a spirit bison, associated with the underground world, rather than an ordinary one (fig. 8.5).[11] Her lower back is humped in labor,[12] and a line apparently representing the afterbirth extends from her hindquarters. Her calf stands under her belly, ready to nurse. Across the deeply recessed abdomen of the buffalo are five deeply incised buffalo tracks. Around the bison is an array of other rock art designs of varying types and ages, including more bison tracks and deeply incised vulva designs. A loop is also deeply incised just behind the bison cow's throat. This probably represents a snare. The snare is a Mandan and Hidatsa symbol of the power to take animals in any kind of trap—a bison jump or pound, a catfish trap, or an eagle-catching pit.[13] In this case, it undoubtedly refers to bison trapping. This petroglyph is a visual prayer for regeneration of the buffalo herds and success in hunting.

A line extending from the buffalo's mouth may represent the idea of the visible breath of the animal. Bison were thought to give off a red breath when in labor or when transferring supernatural power to people.[14] In Lakota tradition, this visible breath also plays a part in accounts of the coming of the culture hero White Buffalo Woman. As White Buffalo Woman approached the Lakota camp on her sacred mission, she sang this song:

> With visible breath I am walking.
> A voice I am sending as I walk.
> In a sacred manner I am walking.
> With visible tracks I am walking.
> In a sacred manner I am walking.[15]

Figure 8.4. Main rock art panel on cliff facing the entrance to Ludlow Cave, site 39HN17. (Scale bar shows 20 cm.)

Figure 8.5. The long-tailed bison figure at Ludlow Cave is a Plains Indian variation on the theme of spirit creatures dwelling underground or underwater. Water-creature rock art from the eastern woodlands and Great Plains includes a variety of animals with long tails, scales, and horns or antlers: (A) Agawa Pictographs, Ontario; (B) Russell site, Kansas; (C) Quarry Ridge, Minnesota; (D) Painted Coulee, Montana; (E) Swift Creek Monolith, Saskatchewan; (F) LeMoille Cave, Kansas; (G) West Virginia; (H-L) 140T4, Kansas. (Figure E courtesy Jack Steinbring.)

To Lakotas, the phrase "visible breath" refers to the clouds of steam that showed the locations of bison herds during the coldest days of winter. It also denotes the smoke that rises from the Sacred Pipe, as well as the sacred red breath of the spirit bison.[16] This portion of the petroglyph, along with the eyes, still has a red stain adhering to it, showing that red pigment was applied to the image. The color red is strongly symbolic of new life, buffalo, and women's reproductive power in northern Plains Indian tradition.[17]

This impressive petroglyph—perhaps the largest one recorded anywhere in the northern plains—is not in Ludlow Cave but on the rimrock facing the cave entrance across a narrow valley. This location permitted the petroglyph to survive long after most other Ludlow Cave rock art was lost to roof collapse, vandalism, and collecting. A well-worn trail leads from the cave to the bison petroglyph.

Track-Vulva-Groove Rock Art and Its Symbolism

This buffalo petroglyph and Mandan beliefs about Ludlow Cave are the keys to understanding a style of rock art found throughout the Black Hills country and other portions of the northern plains. This rock art consists mostly of deeply ground and abraded animal tracks and human vulvas. Deeply incised intaglio and bas-relief human and animal figures are less typical of the style. Clearly, bison and women are its main focus. Apart from the bison cow at Ludlow Cave, one of the largest petroglyphs belonging to this style is a full-length, bas-relief figure of a woman in Medicine Creek Cave in the western foothills of the Black Hills (fig. 8.6; see also fig. 11.13).

The deeply incised images of the Track-Vulva-Groove style display considerable craftsmanship. First the outline of the figure was roughed out, then the interior was chipped and hacked away, and finally the carving was reshaped and smoothed through careful abrasion until a smooth texture was achieved. The animal tracks resemble actual hoofprints in soft sand or mud. The vulva representations are more varied in appearance, but most are also deeply carved into the rock.

A sacred connection between women, who give life, and bison, which sustain it, is expressed in many ways among the northern Plains Indians. For example, the story of the Lakotas' Sacred Calf Pipe illustrates the link between the two. One day two hunters were searching for game on the prairie. They saw someone approaching from far away. As the figure drew nearer, they saw that it was a lovely young woman, finely dressed and groomed. One of the men wished to overcome the maiden, but the other remained respectful toward her. The man with selfish desires was enveloped in a whirlwind when he tried to approach the young woman. When the wind died down, all that remained of him was a pile of bones covered with worms. The maiden spoke to the other man, telling him to gather the people together, for she had a message for them from the Great Spirit. The next day the people awaited her in a specially purified lodge. Soon the woman appeared, bearing a long bundle in one arm. The bundle contained the Sacred Pipe, which would become the principal religious symbol of the Lakota people. She showed the people how to care for and use the Sacred Pipe and instructed them in the first of seven ceremonies that would define and preserve them as a nation. She addressed the men, women, and children separately, explaining to each their duties and importance to the nation. After her visit was over, she walked out onto the prairie. There, as the people watched, she turned into a buffalo calf and disappeared in the distance.[18]

The woman-bison connection was also expressed in ritual. When a Lakota girl reached puberty, she retired to a small hut or tipi where an older woman instructed her in womanly matters. For four days she remained in the menstrual lodge, where she was expected to demonstrate her industry by constantly embroidering hides, moccasins, and other useful items with colorful porcupine and bird feather quills. Even though the girl already knew the art of quilling, she had to quill continuously during her four days of seclusion to ensure that she would always be "good with the awl"—the bone implement used in sewing and quillwork (fig. 8.7). Some girls actively sought a vision at this time by fasting in isolation for several days.[19]

The girl might then be honored in the "buffalo sing." This conferred the sacred protection of the buffalo spirit upon her.[20] The candidate spent the night

Figure 8.6. This deeply incised bas-relief woman from Medicine Creek Cave, Wyoming, is the second largest petroglyph in the Black Hills country, surpassed only by the bison shown in figure 8.4. A drawing of the woman appears in figure 11.13. (The ruler shows 10 cm intervals.)

Figure 8.7. Among the offerings found in excavations at Ludlow Cave were these dyed porcupine quills and bone sewing awls. (Courtesy South Dakota Archaeological Research Center, Rapid City.)

before the ceremony alone in a special lodge. At daybreak she emerged from the lodge bearing her menstrual bundle in her arms. She walked to the edge of the village and placed the bundle high in a plum tree where coyotes and wolves would not disturb it. This symbolized her desire to avoid bad influences, to seek an honorable marriage, and to be blessed with children. She was then escorted to a special ceremonial lodge. There a buffalo shaman instructed her in the highest ideals of womanhood and prayed for her protection and fruitfulness. At the end of the ceremony, the shaman acted the part of a buffalo bull in rut while the girl's mother placed sage in her lap and under her arms to empower her in resisting his advances. The girl was told that she was now holy, a buffalo woman, and the future of her nation. Enacting a bison cow, she drank from a bowl of chokecherry juice. The red color of the juice symbolized the sacredness of the buffalo spirit, the menstrual flow, and the renewal of life. Then she donned a new dress and had red paint applied to her forehead and hair-parting to show her new status as a buffalo woman.

Other Lakota ceremonies are equally direct in their expression of a sacred link between women and bison. This connection is manifested in the ceremony for releasing the soul of a beloved deceased relative, sometimes called the Making of Sacredness ceremony.[21] During one version of this ceremony, a white buffalo robe is carried by four young virgins, each

named for the sacred white buffalo cow who brought the people their religion. In one ceremony held on the Pine Ridge Reservation, the four girls were White Cow Woman, White Cow Comes Out, Scarlet White Cow, and Walking White Cow.[22] Later, chokecherry juice and sanctified meat from a buffalo cow were shared first with the four virgins, representing spiritual purity and the continuity of the nation, and then with the rest of the assembled people. The shaman reminded the assembled people that "all that we have done here today is *lela wakan* [very sacred], for it has all been done according to the instructions given to us by the holy woman, who was also a buffalo, and who brought to us our most holy pipe."[23]

Among the northern Lakotas, an elaborate set of rituals accompanied the killing of a rare white buffalo. During the central part of the ceremony, the fresh buffalo hide was dressed by a virgin of unquestioned repute. The young woman represented the reproductive potential of the people. The hide was then placed over a square of cleared ground symbolizing the life-giving powers of the earth. Lakota holy men explained the ceremony this way: "The old die, the new are born, and the race lives on forever. The white buffalo is the chief of the herd, and from the buffalo comes our animal food, and this gives life and strength. We put the dish with the cherries and water beside the head of the hide, because the buffalo likes these things; they make him to live. We eat the cherries and drink the water that there may be no end of fruit and water with us."[24]

The sacred connection between bison and women as givers and sustainers of life is also expressed in the Lakota Sun Dance, in which bison and young virgins play an important role, representing the promise of renewal of the nation. A respected women is chosen as the Sacred Pipe Woman. Representing the White Buffalo Woman, she dances and endures alongside those who have pledged the ordeal of four days of thirsting, fasting, and gazing at the sun.[25]

This idea is also expressed in the vision from which the Throwing of the Ball, a renewal ceremony, originated:

Then they brought forward a tiny girl, who sat down, and I saw that she was a little buffalo calf. She stood up and began to walk, but then she staggered and lay down. Her people, who I now saw were buffalo people, gathered around the little calf, and one buffalo cow snorted a red breath upon her, and when the calf lay down again I saw that she was now a white yearling buffalo. The mother continued to snort red and to nudge the yearling. When she got up again I saw that she had changed a second time, and was now a larger buffalo. The young buffalo then lay down, but when she got up again she was full grown; and then she ran away over the hill, and all the buffalo snorted, so that they shook the universe. I then saw buffalo at all the four quarters, but they were now people, and I saw the little girl standing at the center with a ball in her hand.[26]

The girl then tossed the ball, representing the universe, to each of the four directions and to the center. Then she gave the ball to the human people, saying, "This universe really belongs to the two-leggeds," for the ball represented the universe and the supreme being, Wakan Tanka. The Throwing of the Ball ceremony reenacted this vision, with a young girl playing the part of the buffalo girl. The girl wore a dress bearing an image of a sacred buffalo surrounded by stripes representing the rainbow (fig. 8.8).[27]

The Mandans, too, drew a close connection between women and the bison herds that sustained the people. The White Buffalo Cow Society, a women's group, fasted and prayed during winter to bring the bison herds close to the villages so that the people would not starve for lack of meat.[28] Women could help their husbands renew their *xo'pini,* personal power or medicine, by participating in a ceremony called "walking with the buffalo bulls." The young wives would symbolically have intercourse with the spirit buffalo by "walking with" (having real or feigned intercourse with) respected elders. This was achieved either by the woman's approaching the man and embracing a sacred bundle or by her retiring to a secluded area where she might briefly expose herself to either the man or the moon, in this context representing a buffalo bull.[29] Some of the buffalo's power would then be transferred back to the young men as they interacted with their wives.[30]

The connection between women and bison is not unique to the Lakotas and Mandans but is shared by many northern plains groups, including the Blackfeet, Arikaras, Hidatsas, Arapahos, Cheyennes, and Crows. Among the northern Cheyennes, the Sacred Buffalo Hat is the symbol and source of female renewing power.[31] The Hidatsas and Arapahos, like the Mandans, had special White Buffalo Cow societies for women. These societies sponsored a ceremony to bring the winter bison herds close to the camps. In it, a little girl played the part of a buffalo calf, beseeching her bison relatives to come back to visit her.[32] Crow midwives imitated the movements and sounds of bison when they assisted mothers giving birth.[33] The Arikaras, Arapahos, Mandans, Hidatsas, Blackfeet, and Cheyennes, like the Lakotas, have ceremonies and myths in which women and bison occupy interchangeable roles as sources of life.[34] The Omahas of the central plains echo these beliefs in their Sacred Buffalo Lodge rites. The buffalo lodge is associated with women because "the moon led the Omaha to the buffalo."[35] The hoop and javelin game of the Arikaras was said to have originated in a vision in which a cow turned into the hoop and two bulls turned into javelins. In enacting this vision, the dreamer was instructed to wrap the javelins with buffalo hide and to cover the hoop with the skin from a cow's vulva.[36] In this way, the game represents both success in hunting buffalo and success in procreation.

Whatever its ultimate origins or cultural affiliations, the recognition of women and bison as symbols of the powers that bring forth and maintain human life is deeply ingrained in northern plains thought. To many northern Plains Indians, the sky was a male world, whereas the female world was connected to earth's subterranean regions, entered through caverns, tunnels, and bubbling springs.[37] In these traditions the idea of buffalo and women as the bearers of life and the concept of the deep earth as the womb of all life intersect at special places such as Ludlow Cave (fig. 8.9).

Interpretation of Track-Vulva-Groove Rock Art

The abraded track and vulva petroglyphs can be understood in this context. On many panels, animal

Figure 8.8. Katie Roubideaux Blue Thunder, Rosebud Sioux (1890–1991), photographed at age eight. Note the buffalo and rainbow motif on the front of her dress, similar to that described for the dress used in the Throwing the Ball ceremony. (Photo by J. A. Anderson, 1898; Nebraska State Historical Society, John A. Anderson Collection; reproduced with permission.)

Figure 8.9. Vulva designs in Cave Hills rock art probably symbolize women's reproductive potential: (A) site 39HN690; (B) 39HN171; (C) 39HN208; (D–E) 39HN689; (F) 39HN800. (Scale bars show 20 cm.)

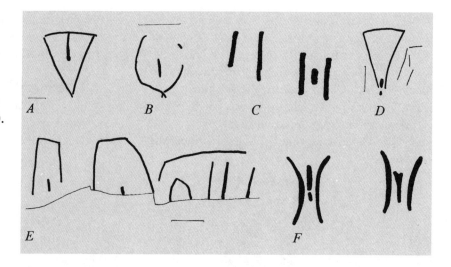

tracks and human vulvas appear together. Their forms are so similar it is sometimes hard to tell which was intended (figs. 8.10, 8.11). This ambiguity seems to be deliberate—a way of expressing the close link between female identity and the mainstay of life. Because bison and women are the providers and sustainers of life, the self-sacrifice of each is necessary for the survival of the nation. The rock art also expresses an old notion that can be traced to the cultures of Central America. The Quiché Mayan word for vulva is "deer," because the Quichés believed the first woman was thus formed by the kick of a deer.[38] Every woman since has born the mark of the deer's track that made human reproduction possible. This idea is also found on the northern plains and mountains. In a Shoshone sacred story, for example, the stars of Orion's belt came into being when a woman escaped from her husband by borrowing a wing from a spirit dragonfly and flying up into the sky. As the woman ran away, "she made tracks on the ground with her vulva; her husband saw these deer tracks made by the vulva."[39]

Tracks, hands, and vulvas can also be viewed as portals or receptacles—points of contact between beings or passage from one place or mental state to another. Deeply ground handprints and footprints are common in Track-Vulva-Groove style rock art in the Black Hills and Cave Hills. Farther east, handprints, footprints, bison or deer tracks, and small cupules are the most common elements in rock art. In the plains east of the Missouri River, these designs adorn isolated

boulders (fig. 8.12). Sometimes bison heads are found on these boulders as well.

This eastern plains rock art style appears to be related to both the Track-Vulva-Groove rock art of the Black Hills country and the "buffalo stones" of the plains north of the Missouri River. The latter are isolated boulders that either resemble reclining bison or were used by bison as rubbing stones. They contain deeply ground designs representing bison tracks or the ribs and head of the bison. These stones occur near buffalo kill sites used in during the Late Archaic and late prehistoric periods. Some are known to have been used by historic Blackfeet and Cree groups;[40] others are much older and may have been made by some earlier group, perhaps the Algonkian ancestors of today's Blackfeet tribes.

Track-Vulva-Groove style rock art clearly had its origins in the Algonkian and Siouan territories east and southeast of the plains (fig. 8.13).[41] It is more difficult to determine who made this rock art in the Black Hills country and why. Perhaps some was made by girls as part of a puberty ritual. In other parts of the West, girls sometimes made abraded grooves or other kinds of petroglyphs as part of their puberty rites.[42] This practice was recorded for the Thompson, Okanagon, Coeur d'Alene, Quinnault, Pomo, Cupeño, and Luiseño Indians.[43] There is no record of similar practices on the plains, but the rock art itself suggests this function. Track-Vulva-Groove rock art is produced by first deeply gouging the rough shape of the

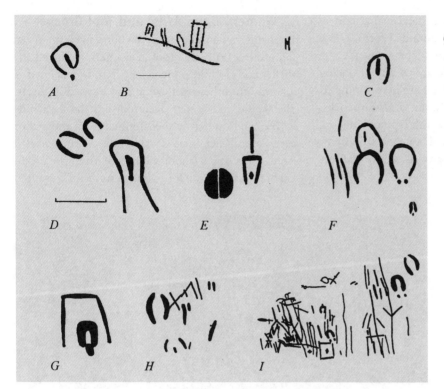

Figure 8.10. Incised and ground rock art from the Black Hills and Cave Hills showing track and vulva motifs, which closely resemble each other: (A) site 39FA79; (B) 39FA58; (C–D) 39FA7; (E) 39HN1; (F) 39HN227; (G) 39HN797; (H–I) 39FA7. (Scale bars show 30 cm.)

Figure 8.11. These panels from the north Cave Hills mix vulvas and track designs. Top, site 39HN779; center, 39HN150; bottom, 39HN234. (Scale bars show 20 cm.)

design into the rock. Then the design is painstakingly abraded to achieve a smooth, rounded form. Long, deeply abraded grooves often occur alongside the track and vulva designs. These are commonly called tool grooves and are assumed to have been produced as tools were sharpened against the sandstone rocks. Researchers have experimented with reproducing tool grooves. In sharpening elongated bone tools, they created abrasions identical to the grooves seen at rock art sites (fig. 8.14).[44]

Women, Bone Awls, and Tool Grooves

In northern plains cultures, the bone awl symbolized femininity. With this tool, a woman produced the shelter and clothing on which her family depended. A girl was given her own awl and awl case at puberty. She would record her accomplishments as a hide worker and quiller by incising marks on the awl or case. Several such incised awl handles were excavated from a historic Dakota village in Minnesota.[45] In Lakota tradition, the four young virgins who assisted

Figure 8.12. Three handprints were laboriously ground into this quartzite boulder near the Missouri River in South Dakota.

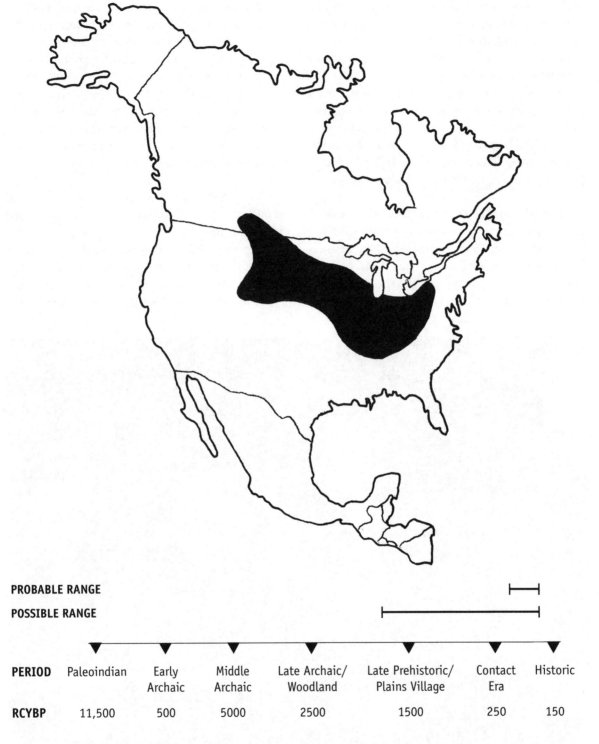

PROBABLE RANGE

POSSIBLE RANGE

PERIOD	Paleoindian	Early Archaic	Middle Archaic	Late Archaic/ Woodland	Late Prehistoric/ Plains Village	Contact Era	Historic
RCYBP	11,500	500	5000	2500	1500	250	150

Figure 8.13. Distribution of rock art sites with deeply incised tracks or tracks and vulvas. The time line shows the probable and possible ranges of dates for Track-Vulva-Groove rock art in the Black Hills vicinity.

in the Spirit Keeping or Making Sacredness ceremony were each given an awl.[46] At Ludlow Cave, with its bison tracks and bison birthing scene, bone awls and dyed porcupine quills were left as offerings, along with more typically "male" items.[47]

Just as a young man gained status through brave deeds, so a young woman gained status through creativity and industry. Fine work in dressing and decorating hides was the hallmark of an honorable woman. Waheenee, or Buffalo Bird Woman, recalled the honors she received from her Hidatsa people:

> For my industry in dressing skins, my clan aunt, Sage, gave me a woman's belt. It was as broad as my three fingers, and covered with blue beads. One end was made long, to hang down before me. Only a very industrious girl was given such a belt. She could not buy or make one. No relative could give her the belt; for a clan aunt, remember, was not a blood relative. To wear a woman's belt was an honor. I was as proud of mine as a war leader of his first scalp. I won other honors for my industry. For embroidering a robe for my father with porcupine quills I was given a brass ring, bought of the traders; and for embroidering a tent cover with gull quills dyed yellow and blue I was given a bracelet. There were few girls in the village who owned belt, ring, and bracelet.[48]

Were the tool grooves found at Ludlow Cave and at other Track-Vulva-Groove rock art sites produced as girls or their sponsors made the awls they would need as they entered womanhood? If so, it would explain the otherwise puzzling ethnographic references to these as "tool sharpening" grooves. Most of the tools used by northwestern Plains Indians were

Figure 8.14. The sandstone cliffs at site 39CU91 in the eastern Black Hills are covered with hundreds of abraded grooves.

Figure 8.15. Numerous deeply abraded bison and deer tracks and grooves are visible at site 39HN205, a north Cave Hills rockshelter. In setting, form, and technique of manufacture, they are strikingly similar to vulva petroglyphs.

made of chipped stone. They would have been dulled, not sharpened, by this kind of abrasion. A bone awl, however, would be both shaped and sharpened by abrasion on sandstone. I recently found a photograph from the 1920s or 1930s showing a set of abraded grooves at a Black Hills site. The inscription on the back—the source of which is not recorded—notes that these grooves were made by Indian women in sharpening their tools. The pioneer researcher W. H. Over also attributed the abraded grooves to the production and sharpening of bone awls and needles, but he did not give the source of this information.[49]

At one site in the eastern Black Hills, some of the abraded grooves contain a lengthwise stripe of red paint. This is difficult to account for in tool-sharpening terms, but not in symbolic terms. In traditional Lakota culture, for example, red is associated with life,

honor, the onset of womanhood, and bison. The red stripe on the forehead of the girl honored in the buffalo sing symbolized her status as a buffalo woman and her potential for motherhood. Again, the connection between bison tracks, vulvas, and grooves makes sense from this perspective (fig. 8.15). Other red-painted abraded grooves have been found in traditional Crow territory in the Pryor and Bighorn Mountains.[50] The Crows are an offshoot of the Hidatsa nation and might have carried Missouri River rock art traditions westward.

Repetitive, rhythmic motion is one means of attaining the altered state of awareness associated with the most intense forms of religious experience. Whether expressed in the chanting of Buddhist monks, the back-and-forth swaying of Orthodox Jews, or the dancing of Shakers, rhythm is one way of creating a receptive mental state during prayer. Rhythmic motion seems to help "erase" distractions and open the mind to new kinds of sensations. The long process of creating a deep groove in a sandstone rock face could have involved just such a repetitive, rhythmic action (fig. 8.16). Tool sharpening might not have been just tool sharpening—it might also have been an accompaniment to chanting, swaying, or other prayer activity.[51] The occurrence of such abraded grooves in locations that are hard to reach and uncomfortable to occupy lends support to this speculation. Why sharpen your tools lying flat on your back in a dark, cramped crevice overlooking a steep drop-off, when there are plenty of easily reached sandstone outcrops all around?

In many American Indian cultures, girls could actively seek a vision at the time of puberty (fig. 8.17).[52] Among the Kansa and some Great Lakes and Pacific coast tribes, a girl might undertake a formal, isolated vision quest like that undergone by boys of the same age. Among other groups, girls' visions were received more spontaneously. Perhaps the isolation of the Lakota candidate for the "buffalo sing" the night before the ceremony was such an opportunity. Sometimes the time alone in the menstrual lodge was when a dream or vision might come to a girl.[53]

Among the Lakotas, women were thought to be especially influenced by supernatural powers while menstruating. They were isolated not because they were thought to be unclean but because the powerful forces surrounding them during this time were likely to conflict with those of others in the community, men in particular. This isolation in many ways paralleled that of male vision seekers. In both cases, the individual removed him- or herself from the larger community for about four days. For both boys and

Figure 8.16. Abraded grooves cover the lower portion of the cliff (lower center) at site 39MD82, northeastern Black Hills.

Figure 8.17. This petroglyph from site 39HN165 in the north Cave Hills shows a woman with tears running from her eyes. Part of a second, smaller crying person is visible in the drawing at lower right. During a vision quest, the supplicant literally "cried for a vision," weeping that the spirits might take pity on him or her. (Scale bar shows 20 cm.)

girls, the first isolation usually took place at puberty. Both the menstruating woman and the male vision quester were thought to be especially open to the influences of sacred forces. Both were associated with the discharge of blood—women naturally, and men through voluntary self-wounding. Older members of the community watched over both the young man vision seeker "on the hill" and the young woman in the "moon-time" lodge, and both might seek the guidance of these elders in preparing for and understanding their experiences. Both boys' and girls' periods of isolation were followed by a sweat bath before the individual was allowed to return to the community and assume normal tasks and interactions. This pro-

vided a transition from the spiritually vulnerable states of menstruation and fasting back to everyday states of mind. The transition was thought to protect both the individual and the community from the supernatural forces to which the young person had been exposed.

Women's visions could take many forms, and from them women could obtain healing powers, use of herbal medicines, ceremonies, medicine bundles, war powers for their husbands or brothers, or instructions to follow an unconventional way of life such as becoming a warrior or remaining unmarried and childless. Significantly, many women's visions were related to skill with the awl—in quillwork, beadwork, or inventing new designs.[54] Such awl work was a sacred art: the application of beautiful or protective designs was thought to increase the usefulness and power of the item. Many designs were thought to have protective powers. Like the buffalo cow, the awl itself—whether seen in the vision or held in the hand—symbolized the woman's power to contribute to the well-being of her people as a giver and protector of life.

Among the Dakotas and Lakotas, such gifts were most often conferred during visions of Double Woman. This spirit was described as two women joined by a ropelike membrane from which dangled a lifeless baby.[55] Men who had visions of Double Woman thereafter lived as women. These men were renowned for their skill with the awl. Double Woman might also instruct a woman to shun the traditional ways of modest married life. Such Double Woman dreamers sought one another's company. They wandered about the camp laughing loudly and generally acting contrary to the normal reserve expected of women. They were feared for their unrestrained behavior but admired for their great skill in quillwork.[56] Double Woman dreamers formed secret societies to promote excellence in the women's arts.[57]

Old Dakota traditions specify that strange markings found on the rocky cliffs and boulders were made at night by mysterious female beings whose raucous laughter rang through the darkness.[58] Because loud laughter is associated with Double Woman, this suggests that the rock art was made by the spirit of Double Woman—perhaps acting through Double Woman dreamers. In speaking of sacred matters, Dakota and Lakota speakers often used metaphors in place of ordinary words;[59] thus, the description of cackling women refers to Double Woman without directly naming her. Dakota and Lakota oral traditions also say that the spirit of Double Woman dwelled in the rocky cliffs.[60] In explaining one of his own paintings showing Double Woman touching a rock with drawings on it, the Yanktonai Dakota artist Oscar Howe said, "Double Woman . . . carved drawings on rocks which foretold future events" (fig. 8.18).[61] A Mdewakantonwan Dakota story relates how Double Woman exacted revenge on two hunters who defaced petroglyphs of two deer she had inscribed into the rock near Pipestone, Minnesota.[62] The connection between Double Woman, the manufacture and use of bone tools in craftwork, and the creation of rock art again suggests that some rock

Figure 8.18. In this 1971 painting by Oscar Howe, Double Woman holds a piece of quillwork as adoringly as a mother would cradle an infant, while her other hand rests on a boulder covered with petroglyphs. (Copyright 1983, Adelheid Howe; reproduced with permission.)

art specifically reflects ideas about the essence of womanhood.

It appears that Double Woman traditions changed as trade in fur and hides became a dominant economic activity. Rather than making hides, robes, and clothing for their families, women turned their skills to mass-producing tanned and decorated hides that could be traded to non-Indians for metal tools, beads, commodities, and liquor.[63] Under the hide-trade system, a beaded or quilled robe was worth more in monetary terms than a plain one, but the designs no longer needed to impart special protective powers derived from sacred visions. Women had no reason to transfer these powers to hides that would be purchased and used by strangers, if not outright enemies.

Whatever powers were transferred from Double Woman's domain to the family by making bone awls at the fasting sites were best not imparted to hides and other items that would leave the community. No longer was it desirable to instill Double Woman's special powers into the awl, through which they might pass into items of clothing and shelter.

In practical terms, the high demand for hides probably meant that women had less time for spiritual pursuits. Women were increasingly valued for their ability to produce large numbers of tanned hides for trade, rather than fewer but more spiritually powerful items for use in the family and community. Providing women with iron awl bits was one means of increasing their efficiency in producing large numbers of

Figure 8.19. This panel from site 39HN160 shows a woman with her vulva exposed, a bison head, and other track and vulva designs. (Scale bar shows 20 cm.)

hides. These durable bits required much less resharp-ening than did the old bone awls. A woman could acquire them cheaply and with little effort. Lists of trade goods show that metal awls were in high demand throughout the hide-trade era.[64] This, too, led women away from making their own awls, to the point that the practice—and the association of Double Woman with rock art—was practically forgot-ten by the time ethnographers began recording Dakota and Lakota cultural traditions. The Lakota groups, in particular, retained few traditions about the connection between rocky places, petroglyphs, Double Woman, and the women's arts.

In Track-Vulva-Groove style rock art are expressed, side by side, ideas of female reproductive potential, renewal of life, and the metaphorical connection between women and bison as the source of life and the protective and nourishing spirits that sustain it (fig. 8.19). The style further expresses a connection between women's reproductive and nurturing poten-tial, on one hand, and, on the other, the rock and the awl, both symbols of endurance and longevity. We cannot know the exact context in which this rock art was produced, but we can recognize its unique sym-bolic message. Whether made by hunters praying for replenishment of the great bison herds, girls seeking visions on the threshold of young womanhood, craft-workers embodying the spirit of Double Woman, or shamans opening doors into another world, this rock art speaks powerfully of the crucial role played by women in the survival of the people.

Brave Deeds and Coup Counts

When a woman made marks on her awl handle to record the hides and lodge covers she had completed, she was participating in a tradition of keeping careful track of personal accomplishments and displaying the record for all to see. Boys and men were similarly celebrated for their accomplishments in war, horse raiding, and hunting.[1] No gathering or ceremony took place without a series of coup counts, or public listings of individuals' famous deeds.[2] These coup counts served to honor dedicated and industrious members of society, to inspire children to emulate the leaders, and to present a strong and unified appearance to enemies.[3] Deeds were recorded on robes (fig. 9.1), tipi liners, and war shirts, in personal names and nicknames, and in symbols such as eagle feather headdresses and moccasin decorations. Certain roles in ceremonies were reserved for men who had many brave deeds to their credit or women known for their industry, generosity, and devotion to family and community.

Much of historic plains Indian culture revolved around the warrior class.[4] Young men gained status by participating in raids on enemies. An elaborately graded system of "coups," or brave deeds, was used to confer war honors. The first to touch an enemy, alive or dead, had the honor of counting first coup; the second got second coup; and so on, up to four counts. Returning with horses or captive women and children also conveyed distinctive honors. Older warriors might "carry the pipe," that is, organize and lead a war party. To them fell either the credit for a successful raid or the blame for a failed one. Victorious war parties returned to their home camps in full daylight, their faces blackened in a symbol of victory and holding aloft long rods to which were attached the scalps or hands of their slain enemies. Then the entire village celebrated with dancing and coup recitations far into the night.[5]

Some rock art in the Black Hills country—like much historic Plains Indian art—records the accomplishments of individual warriors. This and similar rock art found throughout the plains shows that warriors were raiding their enemies and recording their successes in battle well before the horse and gun were introduced into the region. Because this tradition of recording events in pictures extended into the historic

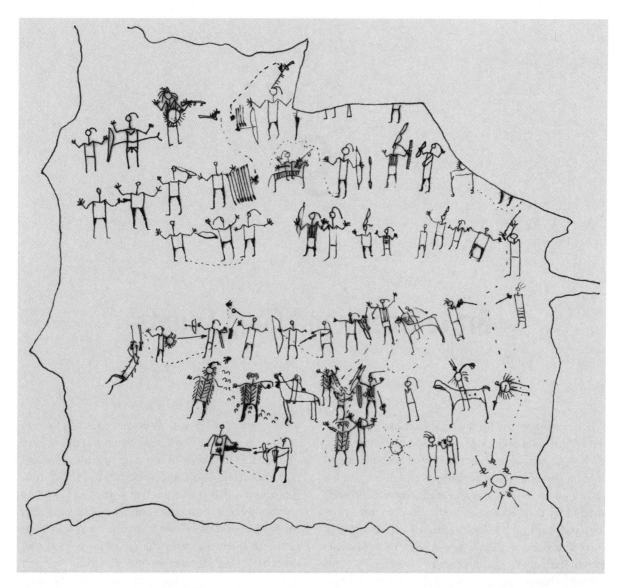

Figure 9.1. Drawing of a painted bison hide, Plains Indian, circa 1800–1850, from the Musée de l'Homme, Paris (specimen no. M.H.96.73.1). This early painted hide is strikingly similar to petroglyph panels showing simple rectangular or V-shouldered humans in scenes of warfare. Many of the pictographic conventions used in later Plains Indian ledger art—such as a weapon touching an enemy to represent the coup counted on that person and use of a line of tracks to show movement through time and space—appear on this and other early robes.

period, archaeologists and art historians can "read" the information contained in the rock drawings.[6] Using ledger art and hide paintings as a guide, they have developed a kind of pictographic dictionary for the symbolic conventions used in this art.[7]

In this biographical art tradition, as it has sometimes been termed,[8] every element included in a drawing conveys meaning. Hairstyle is often a clue to the subject's tribal identity. Personal attire may indicate his social status or warrior society membership. Shield designs or a distinctive article of clothing might indicate the personal identity of the individual pictured. A bow or gun indicates weapons captured or used to touch the enemy (fig. 9.2). Posture distinguishes the victorious subject from the less fortunate object of his attack. The victorious warrior is shown upright or leaning slightly toward the victim, as if to reach in and strike him or her. The victim is prone or leaning backward, as if dead, wounded, or recoiling from the coup strike. Some biographical art contains maplike elements to indicate the travels of the warrior. Often, direction of travel is shown by including a line of dots—representing tracks—in the drawing (fig. 9.3). Rivers, hills, and villages may be shown to complete the story of the war expedition.

Early Warrior Art: The Shield-Bearing Warrior Motif

Early examples of warrior rock art in the Black Hills country show men with large, decorated body shields (figs. 9.4, 9.5). The circle that forms the shield covers the entire torso, so that the figure is formed of a circle with just feet, hands, head, and sometimes weapons protruding from behind it. These shield-bearing warriors are often shown attacking enemies, whose bodies are represented as simple rectangles with appendages. The shield decorations probably were specific to individuals or members of elite warrior

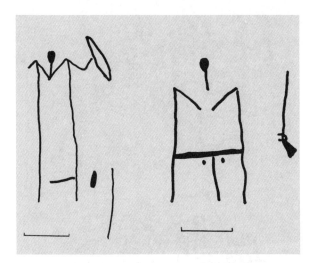

Figure 9.2. These V-shouldered human figures from site 39HN210 in the north Cave Hills bear an obvious resemblance to the figures shown on the painted hide illustrated in figure 9.1. The gun and bow probably indicate kills or coups accomplished with those weapons. (Scale bars indicate 20 cm.)

societies and thus identified the person to whom the scene referred. Often the shield-bearing warriors are shown in static postures, but on some panels they are engaged in combat. The shield-bearing warrior motif dates to the period before the northern Plains Indians acquired horses. It was probably largely abandoned around 1750, when warriors began to gain ready access to horses. With the advent of mounted warfare, the large body shields were of limited usefulness, for their bulkiness canceled out the natural advantage of height and maneuverability conferred by the horse.[9]

Because this art appears more concerned with warriors' prayers for supernatural help than with their actual deeds, this early shield-bearing warrior art has been termed ceremonial art.[10] The panels typically detail the shield designs and other symbols of a warrior's powers. Sometimes animals appear near the warrior figures, as if to indicate the men's spirit helpers. Ceremonial art typically shows individuals or groups of shield-bearing warriors. Not all scenes are free of action, however; some show combat scenes or record sexual exploits. In these scenes, shield-bearing warriors are shown with other humans depicted as rectangular figures with V-like shoulders and simple circular or oval heads. These V-shouldered humans often are cast in the role of enemy, but sometimes a one is visible "behind" a shield, as if the shield were transparent (fig. 9.6). Although the ceremonial art is distinct from later biographical art in its theme and artistic conventions, the two styles grade into each other. This seems to reflect a desire to record actual events as well as to commemorate the supernatural powers given to individual warriors. To the extent that success in war was attributed to help from the spirits, these are merely two variations on the same theme. While the term *ceremonial* is generally used for early warrior art, and *biographical* for later warrior art, both kinds of rock art have ceremonial and biographical aspects.

The beginning date for warrior art in the Black Hills country is unknown, but it probably began between 1100 and 1400 C.E. Four actual body shields found in a cave in Utah were radiocarbon dated to about 1500 C.E.[11] Similar art from Montana has been dated to around 1100 C.E. on the basis of archaeological deposits that partially covered the rock art.[12] At Medicine Creek Cave in the northern Black Hills, the single shield-bearing warrior petroglyph appears to postdate the other kinds of rock art, including Track-Vulva-Groove style rock art. This suggests a fairly late date for some shield-bearing warrior figures in the Black Hills and Cave Hills, but others are heavily eroded and appear quite old (fig. 9.7).

A petroglyph from the southeastern Black Hills may be one of the earliest examples of warrior art in the northern plains (fig. 9.8). It simply shows a round-bodied figure touching the head of a prone, rectangular-bodied figure. This petroglyph is pecked rather than incised, suggesting that it may be transitional between the early pecked styles and the later incised styles. In simplest pictographic terms, it tells the story of a shield-bearing warrior who counted coup on an unarmed enemy. This petroglyph is high on a cliff overlooking the valley of French Creek, one of the main passes into the Black Hills.

Two other early coup records from the north Cave Hills provide more detailed pictographic accounts of

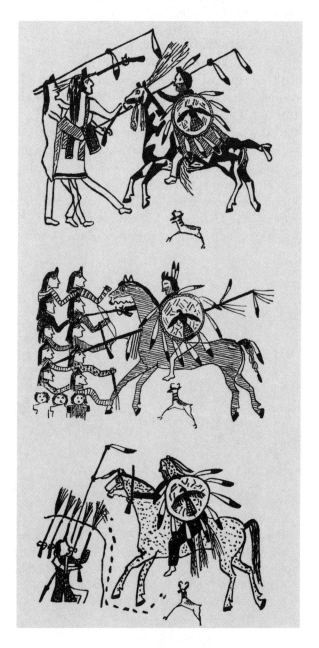

Figure 9.3. In 1873, the Lakota warrior Running Antelope drew these and other pictographs illustrating his coup count for W. J. Hoffman, an Indian agency physician. Running Antelope taught his friend how to interpret the pictures. The upper drawing records that Running Antelope killed two Arikara warriors in one day; one was lanced and the other shot with a gun and then struck with the lance to count the coup. The middle drawing records that Running Antelope killed ten Arikara men and three women, using lance and gun variously to kill and count coup on the victims. The horse quirt in one man's hand shows that he was a horse raider; the bow and gun in other men's hands indicate that they were armed with these weapons when killed. The lower drawing records the killing of five Arikaras in one day. The solid line represents an enclosure of brush in which the enemies hid. The dotted line shows that Running Antelope pursued them through the brush, killing them one by one. Maplike features (the enclosed hiding place and line of tracks to indicate a route or trail) shows up in rock art as well. (Reproduced from Mallery, *Picture-Writing*, 571–74.)

Figure 9.4. Large images of shield-bearing warriors flank this rock art panel from the Cave Hills (site 39HN162).

Figure 9.5. These shield-bearing warriors from the north Cave Hills probably date before about 1750, when horses became widely available on the northern plains. Upper left, site 39HN17; upper center, 39HN6; lower left, 39HN162; upper and lower right, 39HN199. (Scale bars indicate 20 cm.)

Figure 9.6. V-shouldered human and shield-bearing warrior motifs are combined in these Cave Hills petroglyphs. Left, site 39HN5; right, 39HN177. (Scale bar shows 20 cm).

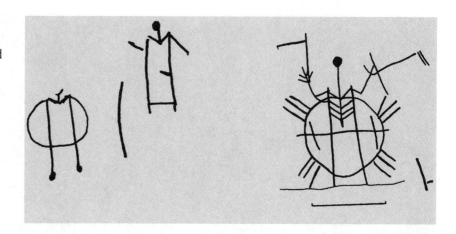

Figure 9.7. Shield-bearing warrior petroglyphs from the southern Black Hills are heavily eroded and may be older than examples from the Cave Hills. The lightly incised shield figure at left, from Crane Creek, Wyoming, has vertical stripes on its shield; it overlies a series of red painted figures. Most of the incised shield-bearing warrior at center, also from Crane Creek, was lost when the rock surface spalled away, but two horizontal stripes and fringe around the edge of the shield are still visible. Most of the shield-bearing warrior at right, from site 39FA316, was removed by erosion caused by water running down the rock surface; however, the design with dots at the four "corners" is typical of some historic shields. The rectangular figure to the left appears to be the remnant of a V-shouldered human lanced by the shield bearer. (Scale bars show 20 cm.)

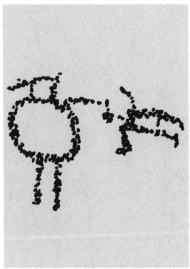

Figure 9.8. This simple coup scene from site 39CU91 in the southern Black Hills shows a shield-bearing warrior towering over a prone, V-shouldered human. The petroglyph is unusual in that it is pecked, rather than incised or painted, which suggests a relatively early date.

similar events. Both are near natural passes leading through the rocky buttes. The first was largely destroyed by vandalism. On the remaining fragments of the panel are a set of tracks (the dashed line in fig. 9.9) leading from the now indistinct lower right corner of the panel. The tracks lead past a simple M-shaped figure that is undoubtedly the remnant of a V-shouldered human. This may represent a slain enemy. One line of tracks then leads across a stream (whose side branches are represented at the top of the panel) to a V-shouldered human pierced by a lance point and an arrow. Another line of tracks continues across the bottom of the panel and along a second creek or river. Another human is shown along this path (center of panel). This figure is indistinct but clearly wields a spear or arrow. His or her lower torso is crossed by a forked line that may represent a spear or arrow. This panel thus seems to tell of a war expedition on which two or three enemies were killed in an area demarcated by two streams or rivers.

The other panel (fig. 9.10) shows a large shield-bearing warrior. His shield is depicted in great detail, probably to identify him. In one hand he holds a long rod from which two diamond-shaped objects are suspended. These probably represent either scalps or heads—a nearby rock art panel shows a human figure with an identical diamond-shaped head. Historic northern Plains Indian ledger art includes several pictures of returning warriors carrying long rods from which dangle enemy scalps or other trophies, just as this petroglyph shows. From the warrior's feet extends a line of tracks. These lead first to (and through) the remnants of a rectangular-bodied human figure, probably representing the warrior's first kill. (Interestingly, this panel appears to "read" right-to-left, like nearly all historic hide paintings and ledger drawings.) The tracks then cross a river and pass a village, indicated by a tipi. Beyond that point, a rectangular-bodied man is shown, evidently the second victim of the warrior's raid. The tracks return to their starting point via a different route. In other words, "Six-Dot Shield traveled across the river, far into enemy country, killing one enemy on the way. At the enemy village he killed another enemy, this one a man. He came back by a different route. He returned triumphantly with two scalps."

Superimposed over part of the scene is a large bear, the meaning of which is unclear. Perhaps it commemorates the powerful spirit helper or the warrior society membership of the shield bearer. Perhaps it

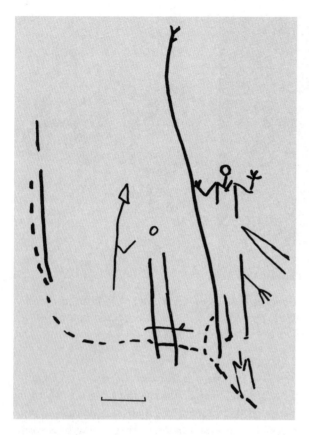

Figure 9.9. Coup scene from the north Cave Hills, site 39HN30, with streams and trails indicated by solid and dotted lines. (Scale bar indicates 20 cm.)

a branded horse and carries a carbine. His enemy appears to be wearing a breechcloth with horizontal stripes. He too carries a weapon, but it is not clear what type. Another scene showing mounted warriors (fig. 9.12) occurs at a different Cave Hills site (39HN210). It shows two men with horned head-dresses (perhaps the same warrior shown twice), each attempting to lance a much larger enemy figure. One of the enemies is completely impaled by a broken lance. The other is more eroded and is not clearly shown as wounded. Perhaps the most interesting aspect of this panel is the odd manner of depicting the horses. Both are shown with what appears to be horse armor or leather caparisons,[13] and both are rather poorly drawn. The warriors, their bodies covered by large circular shields, perch unnaturally atop the horses' humped backs. The persistence of the body-shield motif, the discrepancies of scale, and the awkwardness of the horses strongly suggest that this is a very early depiction of equestrian warfare.

Later Warrior Art: Biographical Themes

Another rock art site from horse days, but perhaps somewhat later, shows a rider with a horned head-dress and a small shield who has successfully run down at least one enemy, a figure at the bottom right of the panel who is doubled over and slashed by several lines (fig. 9.13). The rider holds a saber and gun as well as the horse's bridle. A bison head decorates his shield, which is shown in an enlarged version elsewhere on the panel. This shield and another at the same site are very similar to historic Cheyenne shields. They probably indicate that the artist and hero of the scene was Cheyenne.[14]

Toward the left in the panel, another mounted human—probably the same warrior—is escaping with a captured horse. The quirt in his hand indicates a horse raid. A second horse raid is recorded by a large but faint sketch of a horse and rider at the top right of the panel. A human handprint appears on the horse's flank. A warrior might paint a handprint on his horse to show that he had killed an enemy in hand-to-hand combat.[15] To capture the horse of such a powerful warrior was an impressive coup. A small drawing of a deer or mountain sheep in the center of the panel may indicate the name of the hero.[16]

was a tribal identifier that warned potential enemies away from the territory.

Other rock art panels in the Black Hills country combine the V-shouldered human and shield-bearing warrior motifs. A few show both conventions on the same figure. Whereas all shield bearers can be assumed to represent warriors, V-shouldered humans are shown in a variety of contexts (fig. 9.11). Some are the victims of the shield bearers; others appear to be warriors themselves because they carry weapons. Some V-shoulders represent women (see fig. 8.17). Both of these motifs are found throughout the northern plains, as well as on a few Blackfeet and Mandan painted robes and shirts collected around 1800.

At another Cave Hills site (39FA49), a mounted warrior is running down another warrior who faces him on foot (see fig. 15.1). The mounted warrior rides

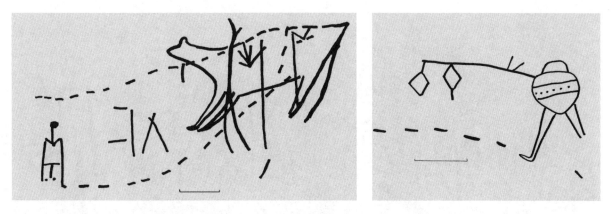

Figure 9.10. These drawings illustrate the left and right halves of a north Cave Hills rock art panel (site 39HN210) separated by a fissure in the cliff face. The shield-bearing warrior on the far right carries a pole from which hang shapes probably representing either scalps or heads. (Scale bars indicate 20 cm.)

Figure 9.11. V-shouldered humans occur in a variety of contexts, not all of which appear to be related to combat. Upper and center, north Cave Hills sites: 39HN5, 39HN22, 39HN219, 39HN217; lower, southern Black Hills sites: 39FA7, 39PN438; 39CU91. (Variable scales.)

Figure 9.12. This complex scene from site 39HN210 shows two warriors (or the same warrior twice) with shields, horned headdresses, and horses with leather armor lancing a woman (right) and bearing down on a less-detailed V-shouldered human (center). The meaning of the other designs on the panel is unclear. (Reproduced with permission from a tracing by James D. Keyser.) (Scale bar shows 20cm.)

Figure 9.13. Left and right portions of an incised petroglyph panel showing a series of warriors' exploits, site 39HN217, north Cave Hills. Horse at center is 40 cm long.

An unusual feature of this coup count is a drawing of the warrior touching a woman's genitals, at the far left of the panel. Her lack of hands may indicate that she was a captive.[17] Touching a woman's genitals —an act analogous to touching an enemy with one's hand or coup stick—was tantamount to despoiling her.[18] No girl was considered a virgin if she had suffered this indignity. Many families actually bound a daughter's legs together at night, lest a young man crawl under the tipi cover and claim her virginity in this way. In traditional Plains Indian warfare, men were rarely taken captive, but young women and small boys and girls were often taken and adopted as wives or children. Sometimes captives were little more than slaves, but they might instead be afforded status equal to that of regular members of the group. This scene thus seems to record that the warrior in question captured a woman and claimed her for his wife. Although the warrior is merely sketched in outline, his upraised arm shows a shirt with a quilled or beaded design

running along its length. Such decorated shirts were worn by high-ranking warriors.[19]

Another possible coup against a woman is shown on a cliff along the Cheyenne River in the Black Hills (fig. 9.14). An upside-down woman is shown next to a man. The woman wears a dress and has a spear-shaped figure on her torso. Her upside-down posture could indicate death, according to studies of Plains Indian pictography, or perhaps she is intended to be falling from the cliffs above. This petroglyph could have several meanings, not all of which are related to acts of counting coup.

Other petroglyphs are probably biographical but are less closely linked to coups. A partly pecked, partly incised human figure in the Black Hills shows a warrior with a small shield and a staff or lance. The lower portion of this petroglyph is now buried. A nearby incised petroglyph is a simple representation of a man holding a gun in his upraised arms. Both of these may refer to the capture of weapons. A horse-capture scene

Figure 9.14. This incised rock art panel from site 39FA7 in the southern Black Hills shows a man standing near a falling woman. The dark object below her head is an abraded groove. (Scale bar indicates 20 cm.)

in the north Cave Hills shows only the front portion of a running horse, with a lead rope dangling from its bridle (fig. 9.15). The rope shows that the horse was released from a picket pin. The most prized horses were picketed at night within the camp circle; to capture a horse under such dangerous circumstances was a highly admired accomplishment.[20] Because this petroglyph is lightly incised and in an out-of-the-way location, it may represent a prayer or vision of horse capture rather than an actual event. Other biographical petroglyphs show the warrior but not the action he accomplished (fig. 9.16).

A complex coup-count scene is found on the cliffs lining the Cheyenne River in the southern Black Hills (fig. 9.17). It shows a series of coup counts across the top of the panel. Toward the right side of this series of glyphs, the subject of the record is depicted with a large plume atop his head and a round-headed war club. Assuming the entire panel is one person's coup count, then four smaller drawings appear to illustrate events in his life. In two places he is shown next to a feathered staff. This indicates membership in a warrior society, perhaps the Stong Heart Society, as well as extraordinary success in battle.[21] Two other scenes represent his success in episodes of hand-to-hand combat. The largest and most detailed depiction of this warrior shows three severed enemy heads at his side, showing that he killed three in battle.

At the bottom of the panel are four long rows of sketchy human figures. Their positioning indicates that they were "taken," that is, killed. Because part of the panel is missing, it is impossible to make an exact count, but more than 200 must have been in the drawing before weathering erased some figures. A few rows of guns are intermingled with the rows of dead humans, probably indicating that many weapons were captured in this battle. Similar rows of guns occur at other biographical rock art sites (fig. 9.18). At the left end of the top row of corpses is an eagle like that seen on U.S. Army insignia. Because no single Indian ever killed that many U.S. soldiers, this count must represent a collective event of killing—probably the Battle of the Little Bighorn. In 1876, General George Armstrong Custer and 213 of his men were slain when they attacked a Lakota and Cheyenne summer encampment on the Little Bighorn River in Montana. No other battle in the region claimed so many U.S. casualties. A careful study of the coup scenes at the top of the panel might suggest which Lakota or Cheyenne warrior made the rock art. The coup count shown on the rock art panel tells the story of a real person with a unique record of coups.

Participants in the Warrior Art Tradition

Like the painted hides and ledger books, this rock art tradition probably was produced by many, if not all, of the groups inhabiting the Black Hills country. Archaeologists have proposed various origins for shield-bearing warrior petroglyphs in the northern plains, all of them to the west.[22] Among the shield designs themselves, Crow, Cheyenne, and Arapaho designs are specifically recognizable (fig. 9.19).[23]

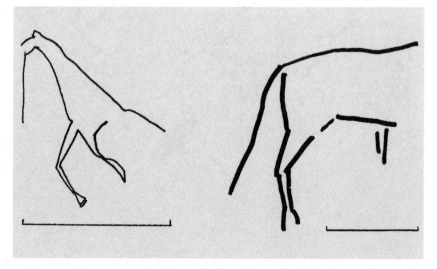

Figure 9.15. Stealing enemies' horses was considered a brave deed. These remnants of incised horses from the north Cave Hills may record successful horse raids. The lead rope dangling from the muzzle of the horse on the left may indicate that it was a favorite horse tethered within the camp circle. Cutting the tether and taking such a well-guarded horse was an especially daring exploit. Left, site 39HN486; right, 39HN17. (Scale bars show 20 cm.)

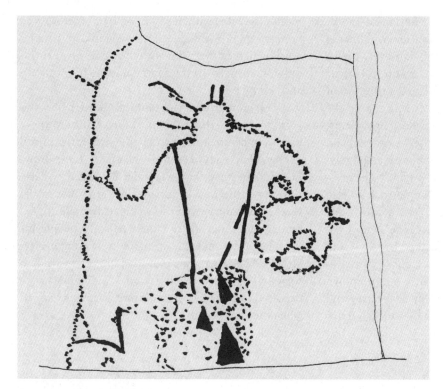

Figure 9.16. A warrior with lance and decorated shield is shown in this unusual petroglyph from site 39FA7. The dotted lines represent pecking; the solid lines are incised. The triangular objects were solidly ground into the rock surface. The legs of the figure are now buried. (Shield is 15 cm wide.)

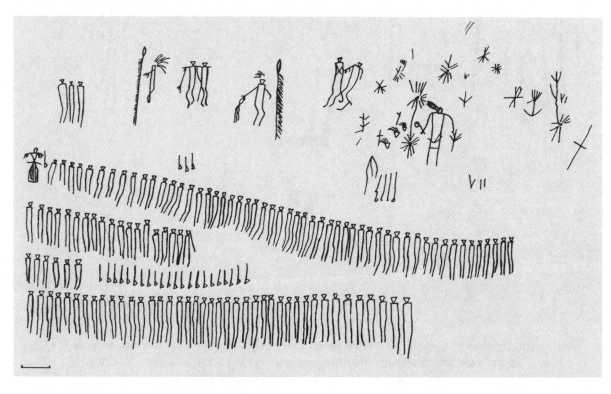

Figure 9.17. This complicated, lightly incised coup count from the Cheyenne River at site 39FA79 appears to show the brave deeds of a single warrior at top and the results of a large battle, perhaps the Battle of the Little Bighorn, on the lower half of the panel. (Scale bar shows 10 cm.)

In the Great Plains, the distribution of the V-shouldered human motif largely coincides with that of the shield-bearing warrior motif; however, unlike shield bearers, V-shouldered humans do not occur west of the Rockies (fig. 9.20).[24] The distribution of the V-shouldered humans coincides with that of the Algonkian-speaking tribes of the northern plains, specifically the various Cheyenne, Arapaho, and Blackfeet groups.[25] A V-shouldered human is still used today in Cheyenne religious iconography.[26] The presence of V-shouldered humans in Kansas rock art also suggests a Cheyenne origin for at least some of this rock art, because the southern Cheyenne bands lived in that area. The Mandans, Hidatsas, Dakotas, and Pawnees also made drawings on cliffs or trees to record victories in battle, although it is not known whether these included images of shield-bearing and V-shouldered humans.[27] If the shield-bearing warrior

motif originated with the Shoshones or other western groups, then the Siouan and Algonkian peoples quickly merged the motif with their narrative art tradition to form an art tradition unique to the northern and central plains.

Ceremonial and biographical petroglyphs and paintings are perhaps the most direct links to those who went before. In this art are the real stories of real people. Unlike more esoteric sacred art, these drawings were meant to be read by all who passed by. They show only the warlike aspects of Indian life in the Black Hills country, but this was an extremely important facet of life. These panels tell of a people for whom bravery and skill in battle were sought-after virtues. They also show that in earlier Plains Indian societies, as in contemporary ones, individuals were expected to do their best and were warmly rewarded when they succeeded.

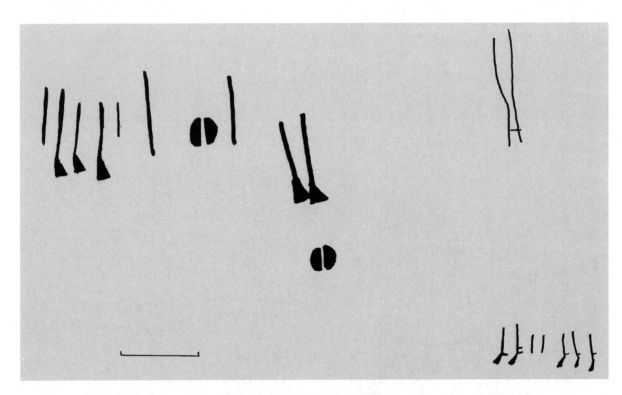

Figure 9.18. The rows of guns in this incised panel at site 39HN210 are similar to those in figure 9.17. In this case they represent either weapons captured in combat or coups counted with a particular weapon. (Scale bar shows 20 cm.)

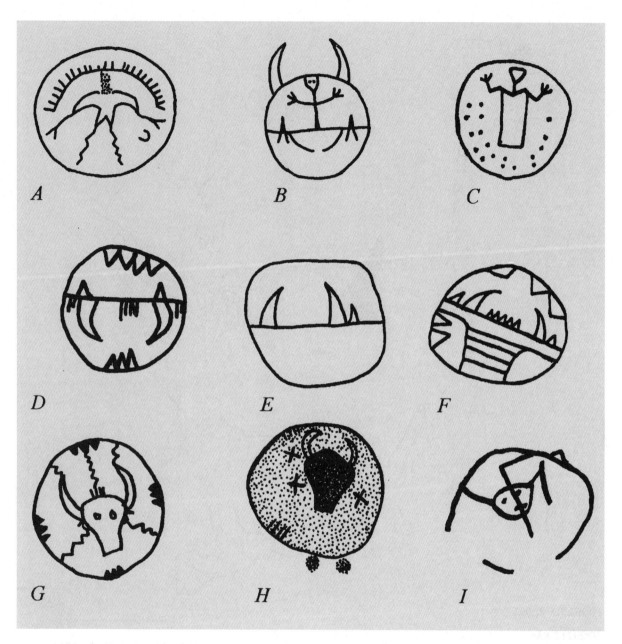

Figure 9.19. These shield petroglyphs can be identified as Cheyenne or Lakota on the basis of comparisons with historically recorded shield designs. The thunderbird shield at upper left is Lakota or Cheyenne; the remaining shields are Cheyenne. Shields A, B, D, E, G, and H are from the north Cave Hills; F and I are from the southern Black Hills; C is from the northwestern Black Hills. (A–B, site 39HN1; C, Culver site, Crook County, Wyoming; D, E, 39HN217; F, 48WE654; G, 39HN217; H, 39HN232; I, 48WE654.)

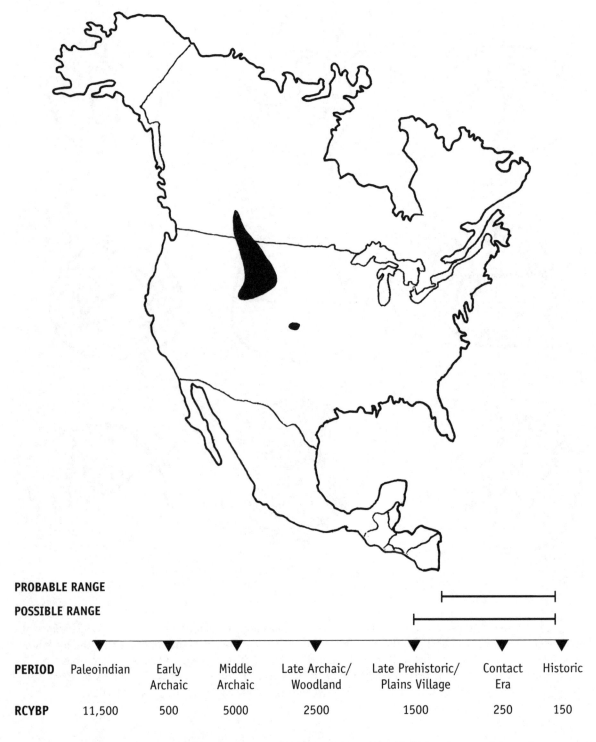

Figure 9.20. Distribution of rock art sites with plains-style shield-bearing warriors and V-shouldered humans. The time line shows the probable and possible ranges of dates for warrior rock art in the Black Hills country

Eagle Catchers

One of the greatest challenges Plains Indian warriors faced was eagle trapping. To obtain the highly desired eagle tail feathers, warriors captured the great birds alive. The basic technique was the same throughout the northern plains.[1] The would-be eagle catcher dug a pit on the southwestern slope of a butte or, more rarely, at its summit. The pit was large enough for the young man to lie down in on his back, with his knees partly drawn up, and still be completely hidden by a light cover made of grass and brush (fig. 10.1). The eagle catcher placed his bait, perhaps a freshly killed rabbit, atop the brush cover. Then began the long wait for one of the big raptors to take the bait. As the eagle alighted, the young man quickly reached through the brushy cover and seized it firmly by the leg. He then pulled the struggling bird down into the pit with him and either killed it outright or tied its wings and legs to render it immobile.

Eagle trapping demanded skill, bravery, patience, and luck. The eagle trapper could be severely and permanently wounded by the eagle's strong wings, piercing beak, and razor-sharp talons. The slightest error in timing would result in the bird's escape. The great birds were naturally wary of the traps. An eagle trapper might wait days or weeks without a single chance at a catch. A shift in wind direction or a sudden rainstorm might ruin his luck for a day or more. Still, eagle feathers were valuable and always in demand as symbols of personal achievement. Successful eagle trapping could be a poor man's ticket to greater social status, because the feathers could be traded for the equipment and horses that would improve his success in hunting and warfare. Among some groups, the valuable tail feathers were plucked out and the eagle was set free again; other groups allowed the birds to be killed.

Ritual enmeshed every aspect of eagle trapping. Eagle-trapping rites were especially complex among the Mandans and Hidatsas who made their homes along the Missouri River in what is now North Dakota (fig. 10.2). Hidatsa and Mandan men left their farming villages in the late summer and early fall, venturing west to hunt bison and trap eagles. The young men sought to increase their success in eagle trapping through careful adherence to a set of rituals, through the purchase and maintenance of sacred bundles associated with trapping, and through self-sacrifice

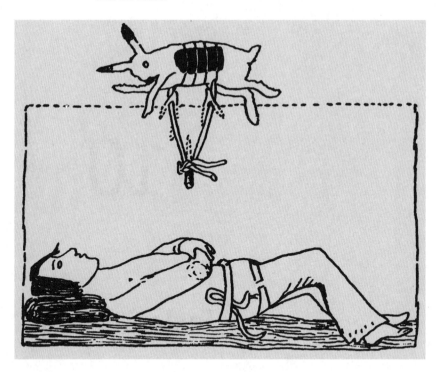

Figure 10.1. Cross-section drawing of a Hidatsa eagle pit by Edward Goodbird, circa 1915. The rabbit bait was placed atop a loose covering of branches that concealed the eagle trapper, who waited in the rectangular pit below. This hunter has slipped a thong into his belt for tying the eagle's wings. (Adapted from Wilson, *Hidatsa Eagle Trapping,* 130.)

(fig. 10.3). The Mandan elder Crow's Heart told the anthropologist Alfred Bowers of praying throughout a freezing night, naked and suspended by arrows thrust through the skin of his chest. He was rewarded by catching a handsome eagle the next day.[2]

The Cave Hills were part of the vast territory used by the Missouri River tribes for summer bison hunts and eagle-trapping expeditions. In 1908, the anthropologist George Will described several eagle pits and an eagle-trapping lodge in this area.[3] The lodge was a conical structure made of aspen poles with a grass and dirt covering. Inside was a central hearth and a painted buffalo skull. Although the buffalo skull is now gone, this and a second eagle-trapping lodge are still visible in the Slim Buttes, just east of the Cave Hills (fig. 10.4). Archaeologists find eagle catch pits in both the Slim Buttes and the Cave Hills.

The Sacred Stories of Eagle Trapping

A series of Mandan and Hidatsa stories tells of the exploits of Grandson.[4] Grandson was related to the sky people. His mother had gone to the sky to marry one of the sky beings. The young wife had a baby but eventually grew homesick for her earthly relatives. As she attempted to lower herself down through the sky, her angry husband cast a stone down after her. The stone struck and killed her, but her baby landed unhurt on the earth. He was discovered by Grandmother, or Old Woman Who Never Dies, patroness of gardening. The boy quickly grew up and began a series of adventures, magically subduing the supernatural creatures he encountered. His powers were unmatched until at last a snake overcame him and entered his skull. The boy's celestial father intervened and restored him to life again. When he returned to Grandmother's lodge, he noticed that she left a dish of food under her bed every day. It was always licked clean by the next day. Silently hiding in the lodge, he discovered a huge snake living under the bed. Without hesitation he attacked the snake and killed it, proudly announcing the coup to Grandmother. Fearing Grandson's great powers, she congratulated him, but secretly she mourned, for the great snake had been her husband.

Early in Grandson's sojourns, he visited the lodge of the snake people. There he saw two parallel ash logs that the snakes used as pillows. The snake people taught him about eagle trapping and how to arrange

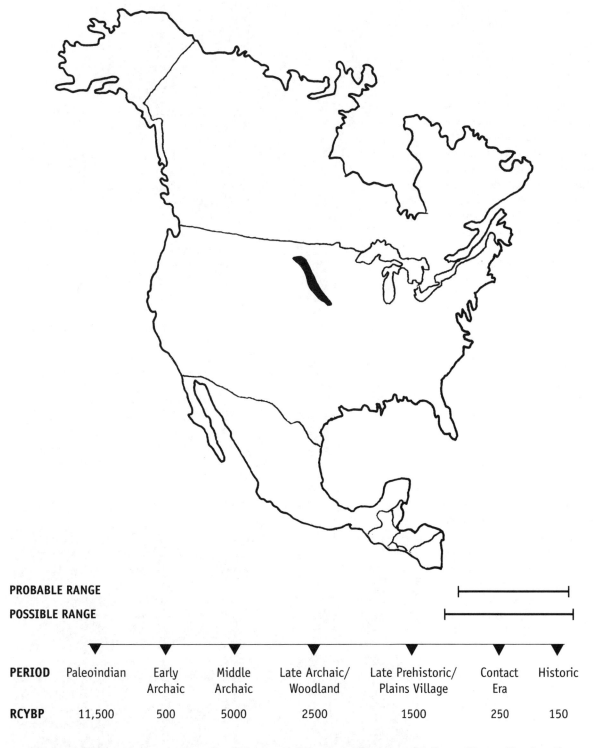

PROBABLE RANGE

POSSIBLE RANGE

PERIOD	Paleoindian	Early Archaic	Middle Archaic	Late Archaic/ Woodland	Late Prehistoric/ Plains Village	Contact Era	Historic
RCYBP	11,500	500	5000	2500	1500	250	150

Figure 10.2. Historical and archaeological extent of Mandan, Hidatsa, and Arikara villages. The time line shows the probable and possible ranges of dates for Middle Missouri rock art in the Cave Hills.

Figure 10.3. Bears Arm's drawing of a Mandan eagle-trapping camp. The tipis used by the women and others not engaged in trapping are shown at the bottom of the drawing. The ceremonial lodge is at center, with a sweat lodge in front of it. At the upper right, Bears Arm has drawn himself undergoing a torture he endured while on an eagle-trapping expedition at the age of 17. (Adapted from Bowers, *Mandan Social and Ceremonial Organization,* 209.)

Figure 10.4. Remains of a Hidatsa or Mandan ceremonial eagle-trapping lodge (site 39HN201) in the Slim Buttes, northwestern South Dakota, circa 1940. (Courtesy South Dakota Archaeological Research Center, Rapid City.)

an eagle-trapping lodge, with the two snake poles and other symbolic paraphernalia.[5]

Another account of the origin of eagle trapping occurs in the story of Black Wolf.[6] In this story, Black Wolf happens upon the den of the small black bears while trying to find his companions on the prairie. The bears' den is surrounded by cast-off eagle feathers, for the eagle is their preferred food. After Black Wolf proves himself worthy, Old Black Bear, chief of the small bears, teaches him how to catch eagles. The bears' chief gives Black Wolf nine songs to be used during ritual preparations for eagle trapping. He also teaches Black Wolf how to trap catfish. (Mandan-Hidatsa stories teach that all traps, including fish traps, eagle pits, and buffalo surrounds, were given to the people by the small black bears.)[7] Coyote, who is one incarnation of First Worker (one of two creator-heroes), teaches another song for the eagle-trapping rites. The snakes teach Black Wolf a song to be used while making the snake poles for the eagle-trapping lodge. These poles represent the huge mythological snakes visited by Grandson during his sojourns. Buffalo and Eagle also contribute songs for the ceremony.

Eagle Trapping in Cave Hills Rock Art

Eagle trapping is the theme of four rock art sites in the north Cave Hills. At one site, two lightly incised petroglyphs depict brush-and-pole structures identical to Mandan-Hidatsa eagle-trapping lodges. One of the lodges has a catfish supported above it on a pole, and the other has an arrow (fig. 10.5). The catfish and arrow glyphs almost certainly represent the sacred bundles owned by the eagle trappers whose lodges are depicted.[8] The exact age of this rock art is unknown.

Among the Mandans and Hidatsas, the same sacred bundle was used for both fish trapping and eagle trapping. Thus, the owner of eagle-trapping rites often also owned fish-trapping rites. Both the Hidatsas and the Mandans linked eagle trapping, fish trapping, and buffalo trapping, the small bears having conferred privileges for all three.[9] Among the Mandans, catfish- and eagle-trapping rites could be purchased at the same time, or the fish-trapping rites could be bought later.[10] The catfish atop the eagle-trapping lodge thus probably indicates that its owner possessed a sacred bundle associated with Black Bear rites that included both eagle-trapping and fish-trapping privileges.

 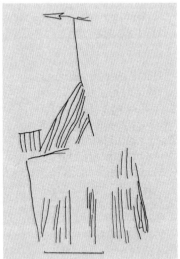

Figure 10.5. Drawings of lightly incised petroglyphs depicting eagle-trapping lodges from site 39HN486, north Cave Hills. A pole supporting a catfish extends from the top of the lodge at left; the partially obscured lodge at right has a pole with an arrow above it. Both pictures contain other, less distinct items. In the catfish lodge picture, the item at right probably represents the enclosure in which the eagles were kept. The object at left may be a catfish trap lying on its side. The arrow lodge drawing is even less distinct, but it, too, may show an eagle enclosure. (Scale bar shows 20 cm.)

Hidatsas and Mandans routinely placed emblems of their sacred bundles on the roofs of their houses or on votive poles erected in front of their lodges.[11] The Hidatsa Edward Goodbird recalled that even after his father built a modern log house, he still placed a bison skull on the roof, to show that he had been initiated into the Wolf Ceremony.[12] Drawings of eagle lodges, however, do not show votive poles (fig. 10.6). Thus, the catfish and the arrow in these petroglyphs may refer simply to sacred bundle ownership associated with that lodge. Catfish-trapping rites were closely associated with eagle- and buffalo-trapping rites; the catfish indicates that the owner of the lodge had the religious validation and practical training to conduct these rituals.

The arrow glyph probably also refers to sacred bundle rites. Although it could represent the Hidatsa Sacred Arrow bundle, this was associated with warfare rather than eagle trapping.[13] Alternatively, it could symbolize a sacred bundle associated with bears. Some bear bundles included sacred arrows as one of their components. These were indirectly associated with eagle trapping. A more direct connection is found in the Grizzly Bear bundle, which included a sacred bow and arrows.

The origin of this sacred bundle is found in Hidatsa mythology. The Hidatsa Grizzly Bear ceremony recalls a myth involving Spring Boy and Lodge Boy.[14] The hero boys, now grown, ask the Old Woman Who Never Dies to sponsor a ceremony at which all the sacred beings are to adopt as their sons prominent young men. Grizzly Bear agrees to participate and adopts a man named Brave While Young. After the ceremony, Brave While Young becomes a successful hunter and eagle trapper. He forgets to thank his benefactor, however, and must eventually make amends by sponsoring a ceremony to honor Grizzly Bear. During that ceremony, Spring Boy and Lodge Boy present the young man with their sacred bow and arrows. Besides the reference to Brave While Young's initial success in eagle trapping, the story tells that the creator-hero First Worker, also known as Coyote, gave the young man a sacred snare—an item associated with all kinds of trapping. The arrow petroglyph, then, could indicate that the leader of this eagle-trapping party had a sacred bundle—perhaps the Grizzly Bear bundle—that included a sacred arrow.

A small, bowl-shaped rockshelter less than half a mile from Ludlow Cave contains a very different set of petroglyphs that also seem to be related to Mandan or Hidatsa eagle trapping (fig. 10.7). They include three images of bears, one bison, what appears to be a fish trap, a large snake, and a creature that is part human and part dog or coyote. The fish trap is a set of slightly

Figure 10.6. Drawing of a ceremonial eagle lodge showing enclosure for captured eagles, by Edward Goodbird, Hidatsa, circa 1915. Note the absence of a votive pole. (Reproduced from Wilson, *Hidatsa Eagle Trapping*, 172.)

Figure 10.7. View of site 39HN696, north Cave Hills.

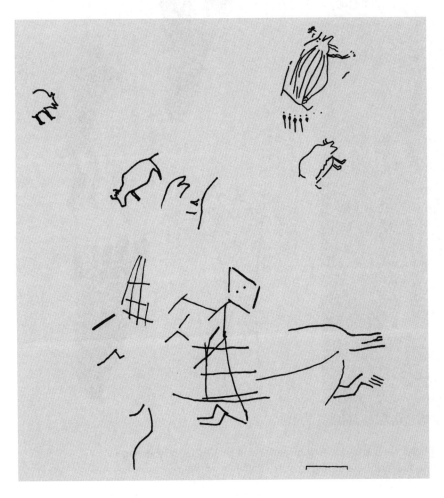

Figure 10.8. Incised panel at site 39HN696, showing bears, a bison, a stylized snake (head at center of picture, zigzag body extending to the left), and a possible catfish trap (center left, over snake's tail.) The long claws indicate that the badly eroded animal at lower right is a bear. (Scale shows 30 cm.)

curved lines, intersecting at the top, with perpendicular lines crossing them in several places, like bands around a barrel (fig. 10.8). In the Mandan story of the origin of eagle trapping, it is precisely these beings—Bear, Snake, Bison, and Coyote, but the small black bears in particular—who teach the young man Black Wolf how to trap eagles.[15]

This set of petroglyphs depicts various aspects of the story of Black Wolf. These particular spirits—small bears, snakes, coyote, bison, and eagle—are unique to this story and to the eagle-trapping ceremonies. The petroglyphs compare well with a drawing from the "Lion Boy" ledger book, a set of Hidatsa drawings of unknown authorship probably made about 1860.[16] Both show bears and fish traps, perhaps to show the bears conferring trapping powers.

The half-human, half-coyote figure also makes sense in the context of the eagle-trapping myth (fig. 10.9). The Coyote Chief in the eagle-trapping origin story is the same person known as First Worker. This unusual image perhaps represents his changeable nature. The bison referred to in the story is also present in the rock art.

The diamond-shaped image and the disconnected zigzag lines near the center of this panel (fig. 10.8) appear to go together to represent a huge snake.

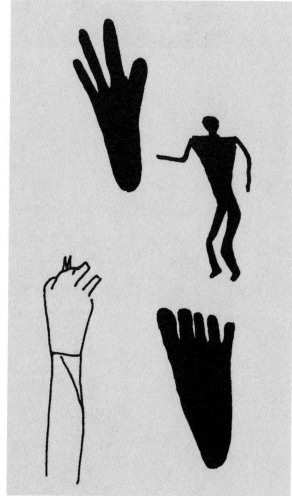

Figure 10.9. Photograph and drawing of panel at site 39HN696, showing human, footprints, and half-coyote, half-human figure.

Although badly eroded, it resembles snake glyphs elsewhere in the Cave Hills. On these panels, it is clear that mythic creatures and not ordinary snakes are depicted, because the snakes are enormous—longer than the people are tall—and sometimes have horns (figs. 10.10, 10.11).

These scenes may illustrate the story of Grandson slaying Grandmother's husband, the huge snake.[17]

This story is part of the same myth cycle as that of Black Wolf and the eagle-trapping rites. The snake at upper right in figure 10.11 may represent the Hidatsa-Crow being Snake-With-Legs, who sometimes appeared in visions to confer special powers on a supplicant.[18] At two sites, an eagle-trapping lodge is shown near the giant snakes (figs. 10.10, 10.12). Interestingly, the basic form of the eagle lodge is similar to that of the catfish

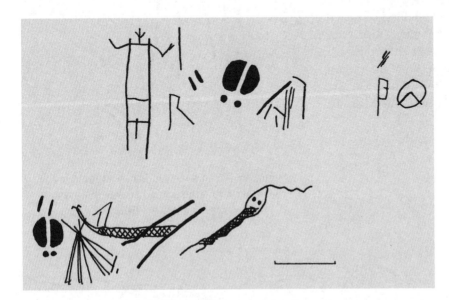

Figure 10.10. Rock art panel at site 39HN209 with two deeply abraded bison tracks and (at bottom) a more lightly incised scene depicting an eagle-trapping lodge with a snake (gridded pattern to right) next to it. Deep incised lines cut through the snake's body, which is longer than the human above it is tall. (Scale bar shows 20 cm.)

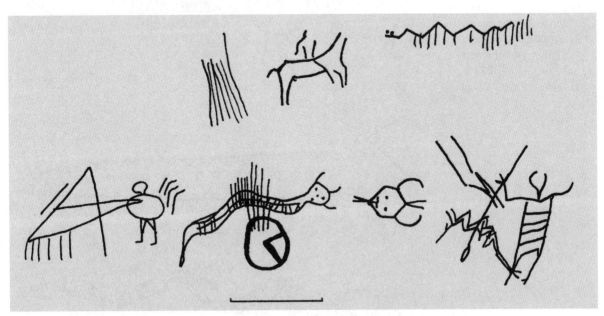

Figure 10.11. Another rock art panel at site 39HN209, again expressing the snake-killing theme. (Scale bar shows 20 cm.)

trap, so the two may express the same idea of drawing prey into an enclosure. Two sites show humans with large body shields spearing the huge snakes; this suggests that the petroglyphs date to the precontact era, before these weapons were abandoned. Other snake petroglyphs in the Cave Hills may also be related to eagle-trapping ritual (fig. 10.13).

There seems to be no memory or written record today of the use of rockshelters in eagle-trapping country for rites including the retelling of sacred stories. The rock art itself is the only evidence for this practice. Although we can never know the exact form these rites took, the discovery and interpretation of these sites adds a new dimension to Hidatsa and Mandan eagle trapping in the Little Missouri country.

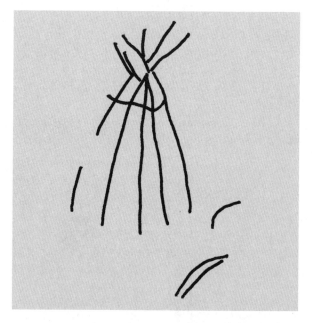

Figure 10.12. This incised eagle-trapping lodge overlooks two large horned snakes in a narrow crevice at site 39HN842.

Figure 10.13. Additional snake petroglyphs from the north Cave Hills. Top, site 39HN232; center, 39HN1, Ludlow Cave (from a drawing by W. H. Over); bottom, one of two similar pronghorned snakes at 39HN842. (Scale bars show 20 cm.)

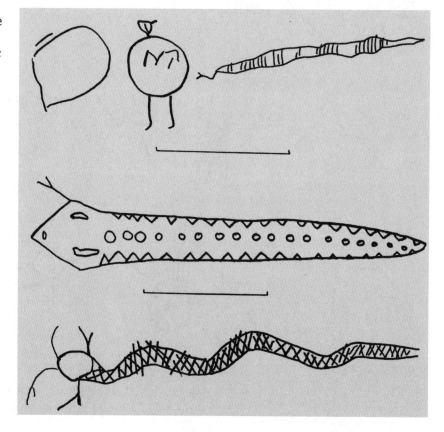

A Place Apart

Biographical rock art most frequently shows up near natural passes, on large, billboardlike cliffs, or along major trails. This pattern may reflect warriors' desire to warn away enemy intruders. In this case, the biographical art worked as a kind of "enter at your own risk" sign to keep outsiders out of a desired territory.[1] In the Black Hills proper, biographical rock art is found only along the Cheyenne River (fig. 11.1)—the main travel corridor around the mountains—and at frequently visited places such as stone quarries. In the Cave Hills, many biographical panels are found near passes and trails in highly visible locations. Other kinds of incised and painted rock art, by contrast, are limited to caves, rockshelters, and narrow canyons. These places are distinct from the rest of the landscape. They are natural portals to the underground world or isolated places where people can seek solitude.

Craven Canyon and Ponca Art Traditions

One such place is Craven Canyon. This narrow, twisting canyon contains numerous rockshelters and crannies as well as large, smooth cliff faces (fig. 11.2). It has long been "a place apart" for Black Hills dwellers. The earliest rock art there is a large, detailed hunting scene belonging to the Pecked Realistic style (see fig. 5.11). Unlike similar panels, this one does not occur in a major canyon leading from the interior Black Hills to the foothills and plains. Perhaps Archaic hunters pursued game into winding Craven Canyon, where it would have been easier to corral the animals. Perhaps they used the canyon as a shortcut between other important places. Or perhaps they, like later peoples, recognized something mysterious or sacred in the canyon's setting.

Pecked Abstract rock art, too, is found in Craven Canyon. One site has painted designs that echo Pecked Abstract forms and perhaps were created in response to them. One secluded rockshelter contains an incised bison with traces of red pigment. It also contains at least two sets of painted rock art that may record visions. A nearby cliff has many painted arrows or darts, a human figure, and a strange three-lobed object made with unusual care and skill (fig. 11.3).

This last figure is striking for its "three-ness." It has three lobes, each with a bell-shaped base to which

Figure 11.1. Overlapping drawings of left (above) and right (top of facing page) portions of a pecked, incised, and ground rock art panel at site 39FA7, adjacent to the Cheyenne River. The complex layering of rock art, representing all periods of the area's prehistory, includes biographical designs and reflects the location of the site on a major land and water route. (Scale bar shows 30 cm.)

three semicircles are attached. At the top of the figure are three "bumps," each with three semicircles attached. Use of the number three is unusual in historic Plains Indian religious symbolism, in which the principal numbers are four and seven and their multiples, such as 16 and 28.[2] The surface on which this image was painted was carefully prepared by being abraded completely smooth, and the red pigment was then applied with great precision. This suggests that the painting was important and that its form was carefully planned to symbolize some idea related to triple sets of three.

One style of rock art, which I call Painted Realistic, is unique to this canyon. It suggests that the area was indeed a place apart—that is, the only place where these kinds of images could be made. This set of rock art comprises a bison with large, round eyes, several

legless human and animal figures, and several odd, quasi-human figures with balloonlike heads (fig. 11.4). One of the animals is a large mountain sheep or pronghorn antelope with swept-back horns and distinctive rump patches (fig. 11.5). These figures appear to have been made by outlining the figure in black or dark blue pigment and then filling in the body with the same dark pigment. Interior features such as eyes and rump patches were left uncolored for contrast. The designs were made on four rock surfaces near a sharp bend of the canyon and within a half mile of each other. Interestingly, one set of panels faces south, one north, one east, and one west. It is unclear whether this arrangement was coincidental or deliberate. Although the various paintings included in this style are recognizably a group, they do not appear to have been made at the same time or by the same individ-

ual, because the pigments and drawing techniques vary from figure to figure.

An unusual painting in this style shows a half-human, half-animal figure (fig. 11.6). It has a curved horn or feather and a large, balloonlike extension at the top of its head. It has one thin, upraised arm, extremely short legs, humanlike feet, and three extensions that may be tails. A bison track is drawn as a body opening between the creature's legs. Above one of the "tails" extends a line or cord to which is attached a similar but smaller creature, similar to a baby still attached to its mother by its umbilical cord. Inside the larger figure is another "baby." This one, too, has upraised arms but lacks the balloonlike head extension. The exact meaning of this strange figure is unclear, but it seems to refer to themes of birth and reproduction.

A large painted bison at another site in Craven Canyon is easily linked to an art tradition much farther to the east (fig. 11.7).[3] Incised shells and stone tablets from the lower Missouri River in Iowa and Missouri contain essentially the same kind of figure. This art is part of an archaeological culture termed the Oneota complex. Oneota people lived along the central and upper Mississippi and the lower Missouri River. They farmed the river bottoms, built villages of earthlodges, and made distinctive pottery and art. These sites are linked to Cahokia, a large urban center whose immense earthen platforms are still seen outside St. Louis, Missouri. The smaller Oneota settlements may have been linked to Cahokia through trade, or they might have been formal colonies for the expanding Cahokia city-state. The earliest Oneota sites date to about 1000–1250 C.E. Oneota culture gave rise to the Ioway, Oto, Missouri, Omaha, Kansa, Quapaw, and Ponca nations of historic times. Of these groups, only the Poncas visited the Black Hills. A simpler bison figure found in another Craven Canyon rockshelter lacks the distinctive Oneota traits (fig. 11.8).

Did Poncas make the Craven Canyon rock art? History and archaeology place the Poncas and their immediate ancestors far to the east, near the Missouri River in what is now eastern Nebraska. The Black Hills lie several hundred miles west of the Oneota archaeological sites that are believed to represent the ancestors of the Ioway, Oto, and Ponca peoples of historic times. In their original homeland, the Poncas lived in earthlodge villages and supported themselves by farming and hunting with some plant gathering. In a study of ancestral Ponca archaeological sites and tribal histories, Ray Wood hypothesized that the Omahas and Poncas migrated from the vicinity of the mouth of the Missouri River sometime before 1670.[4] In 1700 they were living along the Big Sioux River near present-day Sioux City. About 1715, these tribes migrated to the mouth of the White River in what would become South Dakota. From there, the Poncas moved west into the Black Hills area. By about 1735 they returned to the mouth of White River, and the Omahas moved farther south into Nebraska. The Omahas continued to shift farther down the Missouri, leaving north-central Nebraska in the hands of their Ponca allies. A few pottery finds from the southern and northwestern edges of the Black Hills may mark the short-lived Ponca stay in the area.[5]

Although more definite Ponca sites have not yet been identified in the Black Hills, their oral history tells of visits to the area.[6] No Ponca name for Craven Canyon was preserved, but the tribe did have a name for nearby Wind Cave. Interestingly, Ponca oral tradition tells of the priests making rock art images at various places across the northern plains, to mark the Poncas' migrations. These were pictures of "medicine men." The part-animal forms suggest shamanic practices in which holy men or women are transformed into the animals representing their spirit helpers. Perhaps the Craven Canyon designs, like those spoken of in the oral history of the Ponca people, represent the medicine men who demarcated migration routes.

Much more research in needed before these ideas can be considered valid. They do, however, point out

Figure 11.2. Craven Canyon in the southern Black Hills is recognized as a sacred site by Lakota people.

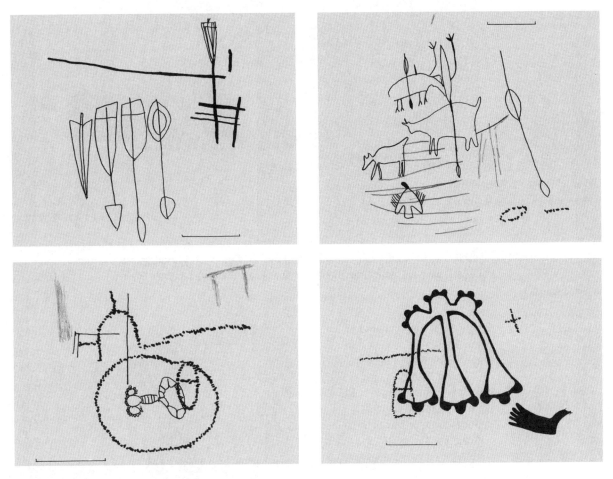

Figure 11.3. Four portions of a rock art panel at site 39FA88. Stippled lines represent pecking; remaining figures are painted red (trilobed figure, light lines over animals, and marks near pecked designs) or black (arrows, animals, foot, complex figure inside pecked oval). (Scale bars show 30 cm.)

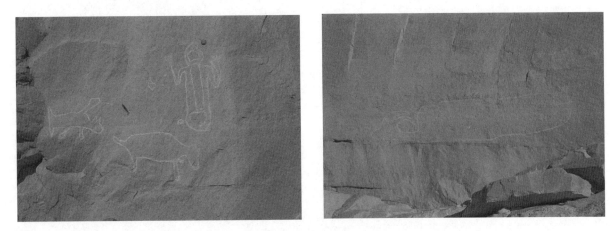

Figure 11.4. Painted Realistic panels at site 39FA321 in Craven Canyon. Visitors to the site have outlined the figures in chalk, obscuring their original appearance.

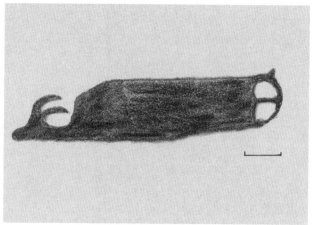

Figure 11.5. Sketches of Painted Realistic rock art shown in figure 11.4. Figures are painted in blue or black pigment with unpainted interior areas. (Scale bars show 30 cm.)

Figure 11.6. Line drawing of black or blue painted design at site 39FA88 in Craven Canyon. The eyes, ear opening, interior figure, and oval shape inside the "balloon" were left unpainted. (Scale bar shows 30 cm.)

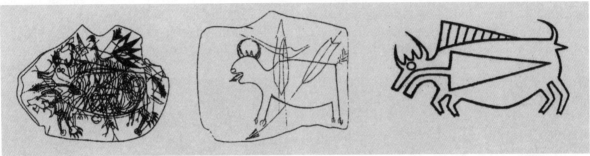

Figure 11.7. The bison at site 39FA316 in Craven Canyon (top) shows clear stylistic similarities to designs on engraved stone tablets from Oneota sites in Iowa (bottom left and center) and to a stone pipe from an Oneota site in Illinois (bottom right), probably made by the ancestors of the historic Ioways, Omahas, or Poncas. Note especially the pointed ears between the bison's horns. Because this is contrary to actual bison anatomy, it is clear that some other, possibly mythical creature is intended.
(For sources, see note 3, chapter 11.) (Scale bar shows 30 cm.)

Figure 11.8. This bison figure occurs alongside rock art of various types and ages in a rockshelter (site 39FA819) near the Painted Realistic panels. The bison is incised and retains traces of red pigment in its eyes and on its mouth. Other red and black designs (shaded lines) were added to the panel later.

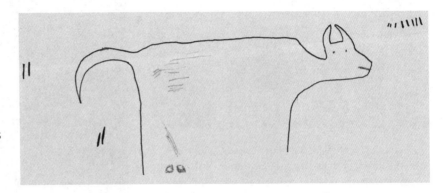

an interesting possibility. Perhaps Craven Canyon was a special place that Ponca bands visited over the generations, renewing the rock drawings that made it their own. Perhaps the unique configuration of the canyon or the existence of earlier rock art designated this a sacred spot for the Poncas. Or perhaps Ponca bands used the nearby rockshelters as base camps when they visited the Black Hills. Does the rock art give us a glimpse of an otherwise unseen culture in the Black Hills? Or is there an alternative explanation for this apparent link to Oneota art? Only further searches for Oneota traces in the Black Hills will tell.

Ludlow Cave

Ludlow Cave (see chapter 8) is another place apart. Its walls were covered with rock art and its floor blanketed with offerings when non-Indians first described it in 1874. Excavated in 1920, the cave contained many articles identifiable as offerings, including unused tools, feathers, arrows, and jewelry. Artifacts and radiocarbon dates from the cave suggest it was used for at least 2,000 years. It contained artifacts from the Mandans, Hidatsas, Cheyennes, Lakotas, and probably Crows. These diverse and often adversarial groups found common ground in their shared knowledge of and reverence for the cave. The Mandans and Hidatsas viewed the narrow crevice extending back from the main cave some 400 feet as a passageway to the underworld. It probably had similar meaning for the other groups as well. A story collected from the Arikaras suggests that Lakota people associated Ludlow Cave with Double Woman (see chapter 8).[7] Those who brave the dark and confinement of the crevice report hearing strange sounds. Indians believe these are the voices of the spirits who dwell in the rock or in the underground world. Like many other American Indian sacred sites, Ludlow Cave appears to have special acoustic properties.

Medicine Creek Cave

Another place apart, with rock art similar to that found in Ludlow Cave, is Medicine Creek Cave. It lies in the northwestern foothills of the Black Hills in a secluded canyon. This cave is really a narrow crack

Figure 11.9. Most of Medicine Creek Cave is less than three feet wide; petroglyphs cover both sides of its narrow passageway. Views from outside (left) and inside (right).

extending back into the rock about 50 feet (fig. 11.9). Like the walls of Ludlow Cave before its destruction, those of Medicine Creek Cave are covered with a confusing array of petroglyphs. Artifacts taken from the cave in the 1930s indicate that it, like Ludlow Cave, was used for at least 2,000 years.[8] The artifacts included numerous unused arrow points and other tools. The pristine condition of these items suggests that they were left as offerings, not as discards. Medicine Creek Cave did not contain the numerous wooden arrow shafts and bone and shell beads found in Ludlow Cave, probably because these items were not preserved in its damp environment. A bed made of pine boughs was found within the cave deposits. This probably was a fasting bed used by a vision seeker,[9] because the cave is generally unsuitable for shelter. It receives rain and very little sunlight. It is a cramped, damp, and forbidding space. Its rock art probably spans the entire period when the archaeological deposits were formed. In other words, for nearly 2,000 years, people visited the cave, left offerings there, and created rock art to reflect their experience (fig. 11.10).

Figure 11.10. A series of deeply pecked bison heads is unique to Medicine Creek Cave. (Ruler shows 10 cm intervals.)

As at Ludlow Cave, female reproductive powers are a major theme of the rock art. A large bas-relief woman with a prominent vulva is carved near the entrance to the cave (see figs. 8.6, 11.13). Elaborate ground vulva designs are scattered throughout the cave (fig. 11.11), as are the animal tracks so often associated with vulva designs.

The reuse of Medicine Creek Cave over at least 20 centuries is even more remarkable than that of Ludlow Cave. The opening to the crevice is practically invisible from the valley below, so it is unlikely that the cave's location was often rediscovered by chance. People's repeated visits to the cave must have been deliberate and made for special activities. The repetition of certain designs raises the possibility that some of these activities were related to warrior or dream societies—associations made up of people who had experienced similar visions. Repeated designs include pecked bison heads (14), birds (10), human heads with pointed noses and interior "swirls" (about 26), bear paws (6), and mountain sheep (about 6). Another possibility is that the cave was used for vision questing. Like other sites with Track-Vulva-Groove style rock art, it may have been used as a part of girls' puberty rites. But while the art's outward form may have symbolized female reproduction and the renewal of the bison herds, use of the cave seems to have gone beyond fertility-related themes (fig. 11.12). Unlike Ludlow Cave, no historical accounts are available to help us understand what it meant to native people.

More than any other site in the Black Hills country, Medicine Creek Cave raises a basic but seldom explored question about Plains Indian rock art. Why is so much of the rock art carved rather than painted? Certainly it is easier to create an image by applying pigment to a surface than by cutting away part of the surface. Depending on the kind of rock, painted images may also be easier to see than carved ones. Paint, moreover, allows the artist to use color to produce a more elaborate or symbolically charged image. In the context of traditional Plains Indian culture, various pigments had complex symbolic associations, thus adding another layer of meaning to the painted image.

No painted designs are discernible at Medicine Creek Cave today. This probably was not always the case, however. A small paint container was found in the sediments below the rock art panels, suggesting that at least some of the rock art was painted at one time. Because the walls are so densely covered with petroglyphs, it seems likely that paint was being applied to the incised designs rather than used to create entirely new images. This painting of carved designs may have been a means of renewing both the appearance and the power of the images.

Yet this does not explain why the figures were carved rather than painted in the first place. Although some paint may eventually wear off, a properly formulated pigment can penetrate the sandstone and endure even longer than the outer surface of the rock. A more plausible explanation lies in the unique way in which carved rock art interacts with light. As light passes over a rock surface, the incised designs seem to emerge and disappear. Some petroglyphs are visible only in full light, whereas others can be seen only in shadow. The play of light over the rock thus produces an illusion of movement. It brings to life the otherwise static images incised into the rock.

This effect would have been especially pronounced at Medicine Creek Cave. The entrance to the cave faces south, and the sun's path runs perpendicular to the axis of the narrow passageway. A supplicant lying in the crevice of Medicine Creek Cave and looking up would receive direct sunlight for only a short time at midday. At the sun climbed slowly toward, then over, and finally past the crevice, the petroglyphs would seem to pop into view and then as suddenly to recede into the rock. Similarly, the moon would be visible for only a short time and might produce similar "movement" of the carvings. In choosing carved over painted images, those who made the rock art might have been deliberately producing this effect of movement, which meshes so perfectly with the vision seeker's vigil. Movement itself is an expression of the sacred in Lakota tradition and in many other American Indian religions.[10]

The human figures in Medicine Creek Cave are unlike others in the region. The large bas-relief woman has one hand raised (fig. 11.13; see also fig. 8.6). She has three bands at her neck, perhaps representing the strands of a collarlike necklace, and a thick line across her waist like a belt. Between her legs is a very large and deeply carved vulva. Her face has two pits for eyes and an incised, crossed circle for the

Figure 11.11. Close-up view of elaborate vulva design at Medicine Creek Cave.

Figure 11.12. The abraded grooves, ground tracks, and vulvas symbolizing women's potential to produce and nurture the next generation occur alongside a large bear paw and various lightly incised designs in this photograph of the interior of Medicine Creek Cave.

mouth. The nose is formed by two parallel lines running from the top of the head nearly to the mouth. The form of the face is vaguely like that seen on shell maskettes from the northern plains and central Mississippi Valley (see chapter 13). The woman's upper torso is covered with a tangle of lightly incised swirls and lines. The elaborate swirled design links this figure to the other humans at Medicine Creek Cave, although it is the only one shown in full frontal view and as a complete person.

The other human figures are profiled heads or busts with long, upturned noses and a wide variety of headdresses (fig. 11.14). They typically have circles or swirled lines covering most or all of the face. One figure has mountain sheep horns like those on other glyphs in the cave depicting actual mountain sheep. A single mountain sheep horn also extends from the mouth to the shoulder of the female figure described in the preceding paragraph. Other headdresses shown

on the heads include two that appear to have birds attached, one with an attachment that looks like a tiny deer, one with two thin, forked "horns," and one with a small arrow.

Hairstyles on the human heads are shown in detail and vary widely. One figure has long, backswept hair. Another head appears to have been shaved except for a tuft of hair at the crown, with a lock of longer hair hanging down from this. Three others each have a similar tuft of hair on top, with a lock of hair or a feather hanging down the back of the head. One of these has a mountain sheep horn design extending down the side of the head. An elaborate head appears to show a thick tuft of hair extending back from the forehead, with a ducktail-like lock at the nape of the neck. A handprint or bear claw appears at the upper side of the face, and several lines run vertically between mouth and chin. Other heads are less elaborate but include the characteristic long, upturned nose, minimized eye, and swirls or circles across the face. Six of the faces each have a small knob on the center of the forehead.

These varied hairstyles and headdresses bring to mind the elaborate personal ornamentation of members of some Plains Indian warrior societies.[11] For example, among the Mandans and Hidatsas, members of the Kit Fox Society wore headdresses of painted fox jaws. Warriors of the Black Mouth Society painted the lower halves of their faces black. Members of the Coarse Hair Society wore headdresses of buffalo hair hanging down in long strands in front of their faces. Young Dog Society members cut their hair short on one side of the head, wore a black headband with a single feather upright in it, and hung long strings of beads at the sides of their faces. A boy being initiated into the Stone Hammer Society of the Hidatsas daubed clay on his back or chest. His hair was tied in a bunch on one side of the forehead, and feathers or bags of medicine were tied to the hair. None of the recorded insignia, however, exactly matches those shown on the sharp-nosed figures in Medicine Creek Cave.

Long-Nose Images

Other northern plains rock art offers few clues to the meaning of these strange long-nosed images. The most noticeable features of the Medicine Creek Cave faces are their elaborate hair and headdress styles and face paints or tattoos. These images may ultimately be related to tiny masks found in archaeological sites in the U.S. Southeast belonging to the early Mississippian tradition (700–1300 C.E.). These spoon-shaped maskettes typically have very long, pointed, and sometimes upturned noses. Without exception, the maskettes are made of copper or marine shell. Both shell and copper are strongly associated symbolically with underwater spirits. At least some of the maskettes were worn as earrings. Known as Long-Nose (or Long-Nosed God) earrings, these maskettes occur in archaeological sites from Florida to Wisconsin (fig. 11.15). The maskettes seem to have spread onto the northern Great Plains in the form of shell pendants, lacking the elongated nose but otherwise essentially similar to their eastern counterparts.

One of the many groups who shared in the Mississippian tradition emerged historically as the

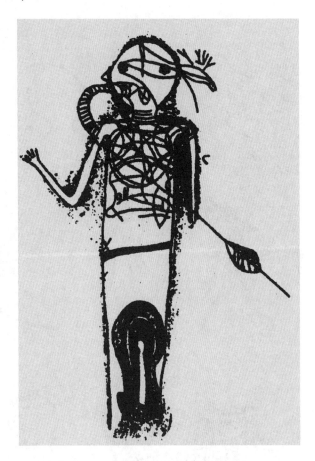

Figure 11.13. Drawing of large bas-relief woman with keyhole-shaped vulva, Medicine Creek Cave. A photograph of the image appears in figure 8.6. (Reproduced with permission from Buckles, "Analysis of Primitive Rock Art," 120.)

Winnebago and Ioway Indians. Winnebago and Ioway myths tell of a hero who overcomes various monsters to ensure the survival of the people. This hero is known at various points of his life as He-who-is-hit-with-deer-lungs, Red Horn, and He-who-wears-human-heads-as-earrings. We know from rock art at Gotschall Rockshelter in south-central Wisconsin and at Liehrmann Cave in east-central Missouri that the earrings the hero wore were Long-Nose maskettes identical to those found in archaeological sites. These two caves both have detailed paintings of this Mississippian culture hero.[12] He is easily recognized by his physical form and by the events shown in the rock art that closely match those included in the Red Horn myth cycle recorded historically. Besides illustrating

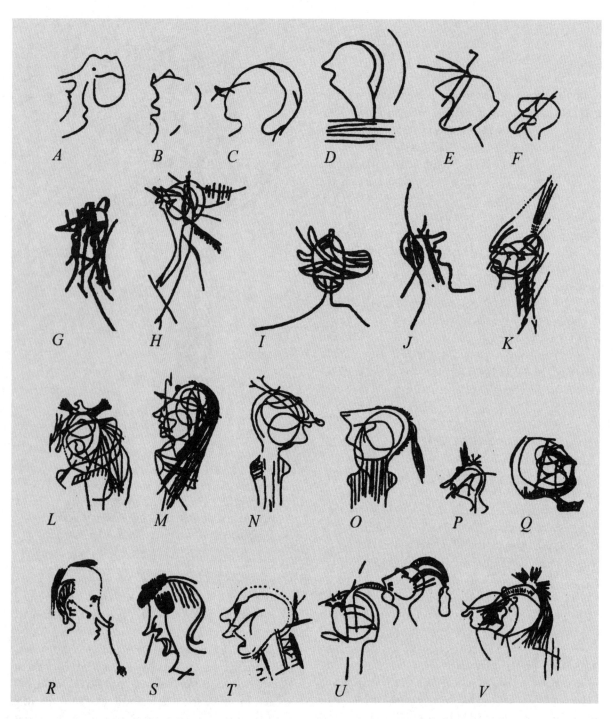

Figure 11.14. Human heads from Medicine Creek Cave. Although varied in appearance, most have long, pointed noses, and many have knobs or protrusions at the forehead. The more detailed figures (L–V) have bird (L), antelope (N), and mountain sheep (R, U) headdresses. Hairstyles include a "Mohawk" (O), long, loose hair (M), and shaved heads with tufts at top and back (R and V). Figure S appears to wear face paint or tattoos in the form of a handprint and vertical lines at the chin and sides of the head. (Reproduced with permission from Buckles, "Analysis of Primitive Rock Art," 106.)

the astonishing longevity of this religious tradition, these sites demonstrate that rock art with mythological themes was made in caves near—but not very near—Mississippian population centers.

The human figures at Medicine Creek Cave have strange, pointed noses. The profile heads bring to mind the Long-Nose maskettes, except that they include more detailed headdresses and hairstyles than are seen on the maskettes, and the noses are not as extended. They clearly represent entire heads and torsos, not just masks (fig. 11.16). The lone front-facing figure (figs. 8.6, 11.13) brings to mind the shell maskettes of the northern plains. Such maskettes seem to be a rather late variation on the Long-Nose theme. They lack the very long noses, perhaps because the shape of the shell was not conducive to them. On the shell maskettes and on the front-facing figure at Medicine Creek Cave, two parallel lines extending from the forehead to the mouth take the place of the protruding nose. At this site, we have neither Red Horn nor his earrings but something that may conflate the idea of the Long-Nose maskette with actual beings, whether human or supernatural.

Who might have brought such an idea to the northern Black Hills? Two of three divisions of the Hidatsa people trace their origins to the wild rice district of central Wisconsin and eastern Minnesota. Artifacts found in ancestral Hidatsa sites along the Missouri River provide some support for these migration stories.[13] In particular, a style of pottery with castellated and braced rims and a doughnut-shaped stone used in playing a game called chunkee have distinctive counterparts in southern Wisconsin sites. The long Hidatsa migration from southern and central Wisconsin to the Knife River in North Dakota probably took place just before 1600, the time when these kinds of artifacts first show up on the Missouri. Although none of the artifacts found in Medicine Creek Cave can be directly linked to the Hidatsas or their Mandan allies, much of the rock art is similar to that found at Ludlow Cave. Ethnographic accounts and pottery finds clearly link the Hidatsas and Mandans to Ludlow Cave.

The strands that form these connections are thin indeed. Neither archaeology nor history provides any conclusive proof that the Medicine Creek Cave "long noses" are derived from the Mississippian Long-Nose tradition. We know only that the faces at the cave look vaguely like the eastern Long-Nose maskettes and the northern plains incised shell pendants that probably developed from them. Nor can the present data prove this was a Hidatsa site. Yet the possible connections are worth considering. Hidatsa myths refer to "sharp noses"—dreaded supernatural creatures that the culture hero had to overcome—but the storytellers provided no descriptions of them. Hidatsa myths also refer to the use of "shells that have noses" to placate the underwater monsters, but again they provide no specific descriptions of these shells. It is interesting to note, however, that both of these ideas occurred only among the Hidatsa divisions that traced their origins to the wild rice country of eastern Wisconsin. That area was well within the Mississippian sphere, as the Gotschall and Aztalan sites of southern and eastern Wisconsin demonstrate.

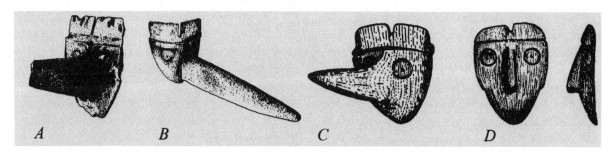

Figure 11.15. Long-Nose maskettes: (A) copper mask, Big Mound, St. Louis, Missouri; (B) copper mask, Gahagan Mound, Louisiana; (C) shell mask, Rogana, Tennessee; (D) shell mask, Diamond Bluff, Wisconsin. (Reproduced with permission from Williams and Goggin, "Long Nosed God Mask," 120; copyright 1956, Missouri Archaeological Society.)

Figure 11.16. These incised petroglyphs from the interior of Medicine Creek Cave have been damaged by the application of colored chalk to the incised lines. Left, incised "sharp-nose" with three interior circles and a "knob" (unchalked) in the forehead area. Right, mountain sheep carved in the same technique as the human heads and with the same kinds of horns as those shown on several of the heads.

If Medicine Creek Cave was a Hidatsa sacred site, how was it used? The lack of any specific ethnographic or historic reference to the cave makes this a matter of speculation. The anthropologist Robert Hall connects the Long-Nose imagery with historic ceremonies involving ritual adoption.[14] Such adoptions were a means of recognizing young persons of exceptional promise, ensuring their leadership training, and solidifying positive relations between families, tribes, and generations. Among the various plains tribes, the person so adopted was first ritually "killed." He or she was then ritually revived in the new role of adopted son or daughter. This mortuary theme may be echoed at the Gotschall Site, which the archaeologist Robert Saltzer believes was a place where ancestral leaders were venerated and "reborn" as young persons.[15]

As discussed earlier, human figures at Gotschall in Wisconsin and at Liehrmann Cave in Missouri depict the culture hero Red Horn. In each case, the face of the orphan-hero, who was adopted by powerful helper spirits, is covered with vertical red stripes. The same pattern of face painting was used throughout the plains to designate those honored in the ritual adoption ceremony.[16] One of the faces at Medicine Creek Cave (fig. 11.14S) has a series of vertical lines extending down the side of the head, a longer vertical line at the side of the face, and several vertical lines on the chin. This raises the possibility that the rock art was associated in some way with ritual adoption ceremonies, but no tangible evidence has been found to support this speculation.

Clearly, the rock art at Medicine Creek Cave has specific religious meanings, but its exact interpretation is impossible. The themes of bear spirit power and female reproductive potential, the strange, sharp-nosed beings, and the possible pine-bough fasting bed all suggest that this was long recognized as a place of special powers.

Below Sacred Mountains

People everywhere attach meaning to place. Distinctive features such as mountains, rivers, lakes, and unusual rock formations can evoke powerful memories of tribal history, origin stories, and personal experiences. Traveling through a landscape over the course of a season, a year, or a lifetime, one is reminded again and again of the stories that define and shape a people. Mountains are universally recognized as places of power. Perhaps nowhere is this more true than in the northern plains, where isolated buttes and mountains punctuate the prairie landscape like exclamation points.

Sacred Mountains in the Black Hills

Several sacred mountains grace the Black Hills country. Bear Butte, at the northeast corner of the Black Hills (fig. 12.1, and see fig. 1.3), is the sanctuary of the Cheyenne people.[1] Here their hero Sweet Medicine received the religious and cultural instruction that would allow his people to prosper in the northern plains. The Naishan Dene (Kiowa-Apaches), who left the Black Hills about 200 years ago, still honor their cultural hero Half Boy, who disappeared into the waters of Bear Butte Lake. His twin brother turned himself into the ten Sacred Bundles that would sustain the nation in years to come.[2] Bear Butte is also holy to Lakotas, who traditionally believed that the spirits of their dead congregated there.[3] Lakotas passing the volcanic eminence would place stones in the crooks of trees to commemorate those who had gone before. Both Lakotas and Cheyennes believe to this day that Bear Butte is a special place of power. Like their ancestors, young people still go there to fast and pray in hope of a vision. Others gather for ceremonies at the base of the mountain.

Bears' Lodge Butte, better known as Devils Tower (fig. 12.2), is considered sacred by all the northern plains nations and by the Kiowas and Naishan Dene now living in the southern plains.[4] Their stories tell how the gigantic rock tower was formed to save a group of brothers and sisters from a monster bear that had destroyed their camp. The children climbed from the tower into the sky, where they became the stars of the Pleiades. The towering rock is a reminder of the gods' mercy and the power of faith.

Inyan Kara (fig. 12.3) was another gathering place of the spirits.[5] Its name translates as Stone Creator or Stone Enactor, probably referring to the creation of

Earth by Inyan, the stone. Inyan literally bled himself dry to accomplish this creative task. For the Lakotas, the tower of rock symbolizes their most sacred ceremony, the Sun Dance, and the idea of self-sacrifice for the good of the people. Nearby Sundance Mountain marked the location of traditional Kiowa, Cheyenne, and Lakota summer ceremonies. Young men preparing for the ordeals of the Sun Dance retired to its slopes to fast and pray.[6]

Harney Peak, at the center of the Black Hills, was considered by the renowned Oglala Lakota holy man Black Elk to represent the center of the universe. It was there that Black Elk dream-traveled to receive the great vision recorded in *Black Elk Speaks*.[7] Some Lakotas fasted at Harney Peak and other places in the Black Hills.[8] The Lakota historian Brown Hat was told in his vision that the Black Hills were the home of the Above Spirits and the center of the Lakota universe.[9]

Perhaps, like Black Elk, he viewed Harney Peak as the heart of the Lakota world.

Rock Art at Bears' Lodge Butte

Like the bison birthing scene at Ludlow Cave (see chapter 8), petroglyphs located on a ridge within distant view of Devils Tower reflect a link between landscape and rock art. Although they are part of the incised rock art tradition, these petroglyphs are unlike others in the area. Some of the rock art represents thunder beings—eagle- or hawklike creatures with outspread wings (fig. 12.4). One petroglyph shows a creature with some human and some thunderbird characteristics. Perhaps these record the trance of some vision seeker. Throughout the world, the trance experience is symbolized by winged or birdlike humans, probably because during a trance one often experiences a sensation of flying high above the ground.

Figure 12.1. Bear Butte, or Medicine Pipe Mountain, is sacred to many northern Plains Indian tribes. This volcanic peak lies just outside the northeastern Black Hills.

Near these thunderbird images are two figures representing upside-down heads (fig. 12.4). Each is a simple design formed by a circle with a gridlike mouth. One has simple half-circle ears and almond-shaped eyes. The other lacks ears and has eyes like asterisks. At first these heads were thought to represent slain enemies, because upside-down posture and decapitated heads sometimes carry this meaning in Plains Indian picture writing. The gridlike mouths of the figures, however, suggest a different meaning.

Figure 12.2. Devils Tower was called Bears' Lodge Butte by most of the tribes who knew of the great rock tower. It is the setting of an ancient story, and a Lakota constellation is named for it.

The Kiowas traditionally conducted a unique ceremony in conjunction with the annual Sun Dance.[10] During this ceremony, sacred shields were displayed in a special lodge. Among them was a set of four identical shields called the *taime* shields (fig. 12.5). The *taime,* the principal holy object of the Kiowas, was a stone shaped like the head and torso of a man. This figurine was lavishly dressed in feathers and ornaments so that the stone itself was barely visible. A feather or a stalk of tobacco stood like a plume above its head. The *taime* was an essential part of the Kiowa Sun Dance.[11] A drawing of the *taime* shield suspended in the Sun Dance lodge, published in a 1911 article by Hugh Lenox Scott, shows two bulblike shapes hanging down from the top of the shield. A photograph of the same kind of shield, published by Ron McCoy in 1995, shows more clearly that the hanging objects are upside-down heads.[12] Like the petroglyphs, these have almond-shaped eyes and gridlike mouths.

Several petroglyphs from near Medicine Creek Cave were apparently drawn by the same person who made the upside-down faces near Bears' Lodge Butte. The incising technique is virtually identical in the two sets of petroglyphs. A face and a design vaguely resembling a buffalo show a remarkable similarity to the petroglyphs from the site near Bears' Lodge Butte (fig. 12.6). This is the only instance in the Black Hills country where rock art from two different sites can be attributed to the same artist. Even more significant is a third petroglyph at Medicine Creek Cave, also by the same artist, that shows paired upside-down heads like those on the Kiowa *taime* shields (fig. 12.7). These twin heads have circular eyes, gridlike mouths, and sprigs or feathers on their heads. They are carved just below yet a third bisonlike design—this one with moon and sun symbols incised within the main figure and rays extending outward from one edge.

Figure 12.3. Inyan Kara rises abruptly on the western edge of the Black Hills.

The symbolic meaning of the *taime* figurine is not clearly expressed in descriptions of the Kiowa Sun Dance. At one time, the *taime* was accompanied by two smaller stone images, referred to as man and woman. No exact descriptions of these exist, but they were said to have resembled the main *taime*. These smaller images seem to have represented the man who lives in the sun and the woman who lives in the moon. The paired heads on some *taime* shields represent these, rather than the *taime* itself. A Kiowa elder told the anthropologist James Mooney that these faces were actually seen in the patterns of dark spots on the sun and the moon.[13]

Figurines similar to the Kiowa *taime* used in the Crow Sun Dance (fig. 12.5) probably represent the culture heroes Lodge Boy and Spring Boy. These, too, are simple figures with gridlike mouths and almond-shaped eyes with tear streaks. In the Crow and Hidatsa myth accounting for the origin of the Sun Dance, Lodge Boy is taken captive by the sky people and is suspended from the rafters of the Sun Dance lodge, where is he to be killed. His brother manages to save him by climbing up the lodge and untying him. In the Hidatsa and Crow versions of the story of Lodge Boy and Spring Boy, the cannibalistic Long Arm tortures the twins by hanging them upside-down from the poles. In letting the boys escape, Long Arm demands that they thereafter perform a torture ceremony as part of the Sun Dance.[14]

Like the Kiowa shield designs, Crow images of Spring Boy and Lodge Boy, including petroglyphs, shield designs, and the Sun Dance effigy, may have been derived from patterns seen in the sun or moon.[15] These Crow designs are similar to the paired heads at Medicine Creek Cave in having circular eyes with dots in the center, as well as the characteristic gridded mouth. Like the Kiowa sun-man and moon-woman images, Crow images of Spring Boy and Lodge Boy were associated with the Sun Dance.

There seems little doubt that Plains Indians sought and received powerful visions through prolonged gazing at the sun and moon.[16] The term Sun Dance has become a generic term for various complex tribal festivals held during the summer and involving construction of a large dance lodge and several days of ceremony. It originated, however, as a short form of the Lakotas' term for one portion of their great annual ceremony: "gazing at the sun, they dance." This is the most demanding portion of the Sun Dance, attempted by only a few, but it is during the sun gazing that a candidate might receive a communication from the spirits that will aid him throughout his lifetime.[17] In one such vision, the candidate saw the face of a man in the sun; in another, a man appeared beneath the sun.[18] A Lakota healer received his power to treat disease in a spontaneous vision in which a face appeared in the rising sun and gave him instruction.[19] The Crows reported that they saw their shield designs and other images in the sky during visions.[20] A Pawnee man received a vision from a bear that came out of the sun after he prayed and gazed at the sun for seven days.[21] Thus, the identification of the images on the *taime* shield as the man in the sun and the woman in the moon can be linked to vision seeking that involved sky gazing. The similar structure of several of the petroglyphs at Devils Tower and Medicine Creek Cave suggests that they may have been based on patterns seen in the sun or moon (fig. 12.8).

The rock art images do not exactly match the Kiowa *taime* or the Crow Sun Dance effigies. One important feature of the Kiowa *taime* is a set of disks and crescents painted on the figurine's torso and across its forehead. These represent the sun and moon. These symbols do not appear in the petroglyphs near Bears' Lodge Butte, but they show up on one of the buffalo-shaped petroglyphs at Medicine Creek Cave (fig. 12.7). The *taime* figurine, when displayed, always has a single upright feather on its head, but earlier *taime* images made of buckskin had tobacco sprigs rather than feathers for plumes.[22] A feather or tobacco sprig plume seems to be shown on only one of the petroglyphs at Bears' Lodge Butte, but the twin heads at Medicine Creek Cave have two and three "plumes," respectively. The characteristic tear streaks are also missing from the petroglyphs. Without these important symbols, particularly the crescent at the forehead, it is not certain that these petroglyphs depict the sun and moon faces seen on the *taime* shields. Nevertheless, the almond eyes, the gridded mouth, the

Figure 12.4. Left (above) and right (top of facing page) portions of the main rock art panel at site 48CK1544, within view of Devils Tower. Larger human head is about 40 cm wide.

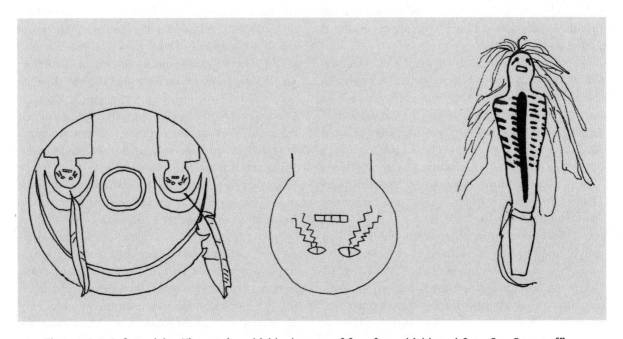

Figure 12.5. Left to right: Kiowa *taime* shield, close-up of face from shield, and Crow Sun Dance effigy.

Figure 12.6. Incised face and other designs from site 48CK1544, near Bears' Lodge Butte.

Figure 12.7. Twin inverted heads and animal outline with sun and moon symbols, site 48CK64, Medicine Creek Cave.

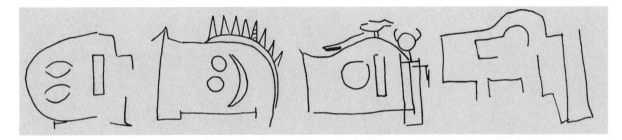

Figure 12.8. Incised petroglyphs from Medicine Creek Cave (first three from left) and site 48CK1544 (right) are similar in form, perhaps indicating a common origin in patterns seen in the sun or moon. Some images have been reversed or rotated for comparison.

plume on one figure's head, and the inverted posture of the petroglyph heads are strikingly reminiscent of the Kiowa figurine. The Crow Sun Dance effigies typically have inverted triangles painted on their torsos and often have star or moon symbols. Again, these are not evident in the petroglyphs, except on one of the Medicine Creek Cave figures.

The Kiowas say their original *taime* came from the Crows, who in turn acquired it from the Arapahos.[23] The Kiowas and Crows were close allies during the time the Kiowas lived in the eastern Powder River basin and the Black Hills. Although the Kiowas do not specifically refer to Bears' Lodge Butte as the preferred site of their summer Sun Dance, it was (and still is) one of their most important holy places.[24] With abundant water and grass, the area near Bears' Lodge Butte was a favorite Sun Dance ground for later peoples (fig. 12.9). These latecomers may have borrowed this ceremonial ground, and even the Sun Dance itself, from the Kiowas, much as they adopted the legends surrounding Bears' Lodge Butte, Bear Butte, and other sacred landmarks.[25] Perhaps this rock art was made by a young man preparing for the Sun Dance or by a relative who prayed for his success in the ceremony to come. Perhaps the rock art records actual visions of the man in the sun and the woman in the moon—images seen after hours of gazing at the sky. The information that might confirm or refute this idea is beyond reach now, but it is plain to see that whatever its specific meaning, this collection of rock art records a journey outside the everyday world.

In View of Bear Butte

A narrow, wooded canyon at the eastern edge of the Black Hills is lined with low outcrops and fallen boulders. These contain a collection of rock art different from any other in the Black Hills country. Pecked into the cliffs and rocks is a confusing jumble of abstract designs and images of humans and animals (fig. 12.10). These designs all appear to be of the same age and manufacture.

Although the canyon itself is narrow, dark, and deep, the plateau it dissects lies in full view of Bear Butte on one side and the high mountains of the central Black Hills on the other. The view was probably even less obstructed before white settlement led to increased forestation throughout the Black Hills. Was the rock art placed deliberately to allow a view of these peaks? This seems a reasonable guess, given that Bear Butte has long been considered a sacred place.

At the head of the small canyon, where it narrows to a crevice, water running off the plateau has carved deep niches in the sandstone rock, forming alcoves just large enough for one or two people to sit in. One of these is now blocked by fallen rock, but rock art is visible behind the fallen boulders, showing that it once was open. Another alcove is at the side of the canyon. A sandstone ledge forms a natural chair inside the alcove, and a deep groove has been cut around the back edge of the seat. This groove may be a natural feature that was enlarged by grinding away the rock, or it may be completely man-made. The walls and ceiling of this tiny alcove are covered with petroglyphs. Whatever its specific use, this clearly was a place apart—a tiny dark world distinct from the sunny plateau above (figs. 12.11–12.15).

Closer to Bear Butte was a single large boulder carved with fantastic animal designs. The boulder was found in a wide meadow traditionally used as a Sun Dance and council ground. The boulder is now at the

Old Fort Meade Cavalry Museum, east of Sturgis, South Dakota (fig. 12.16). The age and meaning of this rock art are unknown. Presumably it was made by one of the many groups—including the Cheyennes, Lakotas, Kiowas, and Naishan Apaches—who regularly camped near the base of their sacred mountain.

The Cave Hills Dance Circle

A line of high, isolated buttes skirts the southern Cave Hills like a broken string of beads. The Indian names for these are forgotten, replaced by English and Finnish family names. No record exists of their place in the native landscape. The buttes still guard the old trail running north to the Cave Hills and Ludlow Cave, now a U.S. highway. The largest, McKenzie Butte, lies 80 miles due north of Bear Butte and looks vaguely like a smaller version of it. The east side of the sandstone rimrock capping McKenzie Butte has a

small series of petroglyphs. They include two bison tracks, two bear paws, a mountain lion paw print, and a bison with antlers (figs. 12.17, 12.18). These overlook a flat prairie forming a low divide between two creeks. On this prairie is a huge ring, not of stone but of unusually dark green grass. Local people call this the Indian dance ring. The ring of dark grass, as wide as a footpath, is estimated to measure about 230 feet across. According to local residents, it once had a small pile of stones at each of the four cardinal directions and a single stone exactly in its center. No one today knows when, by whom, or for what purpose the ring was made. It is marked only by the change in vegetation, but it is clearly visible from the east side of McKenzie Butte (fig. 12.19).

One clue to McKenzie Butte and the great ring comes from a Mandan and Hidatsa sacred site in Grant County, North Dakota. Known as the Medicine

Figure 12.9. View from site 48CK1544, which contains rock art with inverted human head petroglyphs. Devils Tower, or Bears' Lodge Butte, was a Sun Dance site for several tribes.

Figure 12.10. View of the Tilford site, 39MD1, in the small canyon in view of Bear Butte. Rock art is inside the deep crevice in the foreground of the photograph.

Figure 12.11. Drawings of two panels of pecked rock art from the Tilford site, 39MD1, show a variety of complex, abstract designs. (Scale bars show 20 cm.)

Figure 12.12. Two pecked panels from site 39MD1 depict a variety of abstract designs. (Scale bars show 20 cm.)

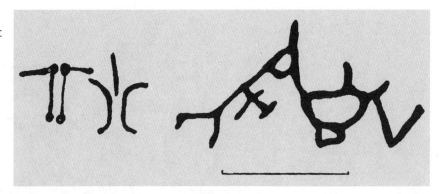

Rock, this place was long a landmark for Indians and white explorers alike. Lewis and Clark heard of the Medicine Rock while camped near the Mandan villages near present-day Bismarck, North Dakota. Their journal entry for February 21, 1805, recorded Mandan traditions about the sacred stone:

Visited by the big White & Big Man[.] they informed me that Several men of their nation was gone to Consult their Medison Stone about 3 day march to the South West to know what was to be the result of the ensuing year. They have great confidence in this stone, and say that it informs them of every thing which is to happen, & visit it everry Spring & Sometimes in the Summer. They haveing arrived at the Stone give it smoke and proceed to the Wood at Some distance to Sleep the next morning return to the Stone, and find marks white & raised on the stone representing

the peece or War which they are to meet with, and other changes, which they are to meet[.] This Stone has a leavel Surface of about 20 feet in Surcumfrance, thick and porus, and no doubt has Some mineral quallities effected by the Sun.[26]

Other early explorers provided similar descriptions of the Medicine Rock and its significance.[27] They recorded that both Mandans and Hidatsas left valuable offerings there. Individuals and war parties would fast and pray overnight or for several days, pleading for success in warfare and hunting. After the prescribed period of prayer, the outcome of their expedition would be revealed to them in the markings on the rock. Sometimes these signs were carefully copied onto a piece of hide and brought back to the village so that the wisest elders could assist in their interpretation. Sacred stories also told of a hill near the Medicine Rock as the place where the Mandans' ancestors were saved after a flood covered the earth. A wooden enclosure stood there, symbolizing the canoe in which these ancient ones floated to safety. Smaller versions of this wooden ark were constructed in the centers of Mandan villages as constant reminders of the sacred legends.

The devastating smallpox epidemic of 1837 forced the surviving Mandans and Hidatsas to abandon their old villages and to band together in a single new village farther north on the Missouri. After this, they seldom visited the Medicine Rock, which had played such an important role in their religion. The place was never forgotten, however, and continues to receive offerings to this day.

The Medicine Rock looks down upon a large circular area with little vegetation, estimated at 240 feet in diameter. Like the nearly identical circle at McKenzie Butte, this one has long been identified by

local residents as an old ceremonial ground. Although no one knows the specific purpose of these rings, their placement near prominent buttes with rock art cannot be mere coincidence. The rock art on the Medicine Rock is similar to that at McKenzie Butte. Both contain deeply ground bison tracks as well as tracks and outlines of other animals (fig. 12.20). Mandan traditions about Ludlow Cave, as well as discoveries there of pottery identical to that found in ancestral Mandan and Hidatsa sites along the Missouri, confirm that the Cave Hills were part of the Mandan and Hidatsa sphere. The Medicine Rock lies on a straight line between McKenzie Butte and the old Mandan-Hidatsa villages near Bismarck, at about its midpoint. This line roughly approximates the old Indian trail between the Missouri and the Black Hills country used by war parties, bison hunters, and eagle seekers. This route was later used by Custer's 1874 Black Hills expedition and

Figure 12.13. The main panel near the end of the crevice at site 39MD1 includes rakelike figures, a spiral, and other designs (see figure 12.14, top). (Photo by Phil Henry; reproduced with permission.)

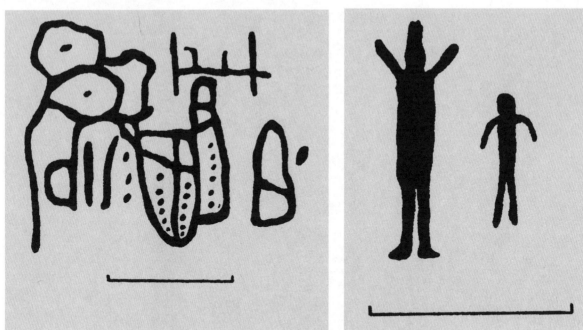

Figure 12.14. The human and animal figures on these three panels at site 39MD1 are interspersed with abstract images. (Scale bars show 20 cm.)

Figure 12.15. Deeply incised panel at site 39MD1 includes a horned human figure. (Scale intervals are 10 cm.)

Figure 12.16. Boulder found near Bear Butte, currently on display in the Old Fort Meade Cavalry Museum. The boulder is adorned with finely pecked animal figures, including a deer, bighorn sheep, possible pronghorn, and three birds. The placement of a "ground line" beneath some of the animals' feet is unique to this site.

later still as the main stagecoach and freight road to the gold rush towns of the Black Hills.

Even less is known about a third such ring that lies below Killdeer Mountain in western North Dakota. Killdeer Mountain was the Hidatsas' Singer Butte—the principal home of the animal spirits. A cave or crevice at the top of the mountain was considered the doorway of the animals' lodge. It was there that the animal spirits revealed the names of the different parts of the land in the Earthnaming or Earth mystery. It was also the first of the buffalo home buttes. The Hidatsas performed an Earthnaming ritual there and left offerings at the top of the butte for the buffalo spirits.[28]

The rock art and ceremonial circles thus seem to stand both as milestones along an ancient trail and

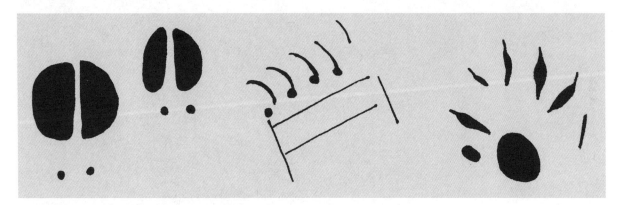

Figure 12.17. Bison tracks, bear paw, and mountain lion paw print from separate panels at McKenzie Butte, site 39HN433.

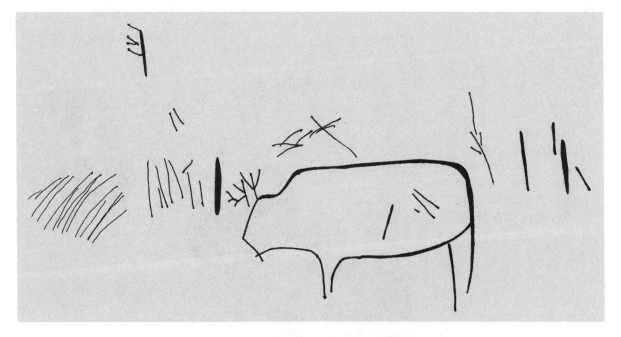

Figure 12.18. The antlers on this bison may indicate that it represents a spirit creature. McKenzie Butte, site 39HN433.

Figure 12.19. "Indian dance ring" (site 39HN533) as viewed from McKenzie Butte.
(Photo by Phil Henry; reproduced with permission.)

Figure 12.20. Sketch of rock
art at the Medicine Rock site
(32GT129), Grant County,
North Dakota. Other
petroglyphs on the rock
include human footprints,
turtles, deer, and a
vulva design. (Scale
bar shows 10 cm.)

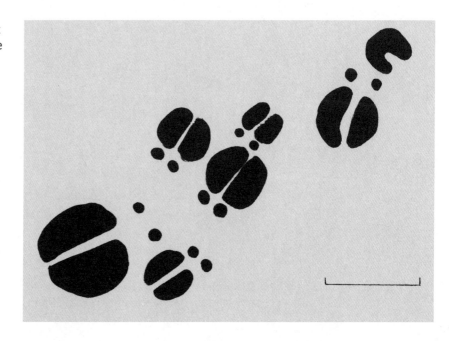

as the faint echoes of an ancient religion. Perhaps when Mandan and Hidatsa hunters and warriors ventured far from the safety of their villages into hostile territory, they discovered sacred places to which they could resort for supernatural protection and guidance.

The link between rock art and sacred places has long been recognized in the American Southwest.[29] It has been less universally recognized in the northern plains. There are many examples, however, in addition to those I have mentioned. Rock art is found at the Pipestone Quarries in Minnesota, an area held sacred by all northern Plains Indian groups.[30] Petroglyph boulders dot the areas of the eastern Dakotas believed to be the dwelling places of the thunder beings, especially the Coteau des Prairies and the north-south continental divide at Big Stone Lake and Lake Traverse.[31] Caves in the Bighorn Mountains contain rock art referring to the sacred Tobacco Ceremonies.[32] Petroglyphs of mythical beings in the Wind River Mountains both mark and create sacred sites used for prayer and fasting.[33]

Rock art below and on sacred mountains testifies to the special significance of these places. Its own sacred aspects echo those of the mountains, where wondrous events took place in mythic time.

The Face in the Rock

The human face is one of the most striking images in art. Babies display an inborn ability to recognize faces. Even a tiny infant will respond to a picture of a face placed within its range of vision. A simple face is often the first representational art young children attempt. They draw faces over and over throughout the early years of childhood. Faces thus are perhaps the most familiar of images. This may explain in part why faces in rock art are so striking. To find a familiar image in an unexpected place is startling. It also puts the viewer into a new role: you are looking at the rock, and the rock is looking back at you.

Because Plains Indian religion assigns everything a spirit, placing a face on a cliff or boulder was essentially a religious act. By giving the rock a face, the petroglyph made its spirit both visible and tangible. Perhaps this explains why face petroglyphs occur quite rarely and are often carved with extreme care and precision.

Pecked Heads in Black Hills Rock Art

Images of faces (apart from the faces on human figures) are uncommon in the rock art of the Black Hills

country. About five simple human heads are deeply pecked into a cliff overlooking the Cheyenne River, along with hundreds of other petroglyphs (figs. 13.1, 13.2). These are circles with lines added for eyes, ears, mouths, and sometimes a lock or two of hair. The age and meaning of these face petroglyphs are unknown. Superimposition and weathering show that they are older than—and perhaps in some way inspired—a later set of elaborate human figures, including some with snakelike designs extending down their torsos. One of the pecked face petroglyphs was later changed into a shield-bearing warrior. This means the faces could date before about 1100 C.E., when it is estimated that the first shield-bearing warrior petroglyphs were made in this area, although it is possible that the modifications were made as late as 1750, when horses came in and the body shield was abandoned.

The later "snake dancers," as they are sometimes nicknamed (see fig. 11.1), show a clear link to art from the Mississippi Valley and probably are a simplification of a common eastern motif, a combined snake and human.[1] Since no comparable images occur in historic Plains Indian art, it is impossible to propose a

Figure 13.1. An outline-pecked head with upright tufts or horns stands alone in this panel at site 39FA7, along the Cheyenne River. (Photo board is 30 cm wide.)

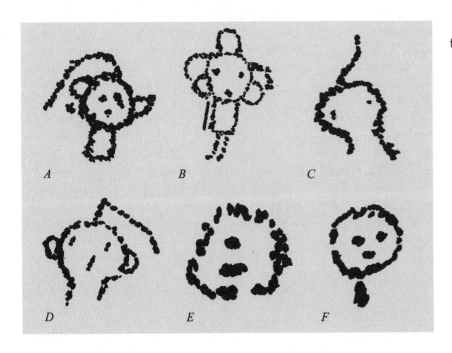

A   B   C

D   E   F

Figure 13.2. Pecked heads from site 39FA7. One head (B) was changed into a shield-bearing warrior by the addition of legs, arms, and head to the basic figure.

meaning for these puzzling images. The small pecked heads may have been part of the same culture that produced the larger "snake dancers," but the connections between the two are unclear. Without more clues, the story of these pecked heads remains a mystery.

A Southeastern Face Motif

Farther west along the Cheyenne is a very different face petroglyph. With a circular outline, eyes formed by concentric rings, and a series of curved bands across the neck, the petroglyph looks like a play on circles (fig. 13.3). It is unlike any other rock art in or even near the Black Hills country. It is not alone on the northern plains, however. Similar faces with eyes formed of concentric rings and with parallel lines between the eyes, banded foreheads, and multiple necklace strands are deeply carved into six boulders from widely scattered locations on the plains of southern Saskatchewan (fig. 13.4).[2] Each was found on a high hill overlooking a major river valley. These faces have been linked to prehistoric art from the lower Mississippi Valley. Their age, meaning, and creators are unknown. The single Black Hills example probably also has some connection to art traditions from the Southeast. When and by whom it was made are matters of guesswork. The southeastern motif suggests a Siouan origin, but none that can be confidently linked to any historic tribe. It probably was made sometime after 1250, when similar faces begin to appear in other kinds of prehistoric art. It may date to a much later era, because southeastern influences continued in the plains into the historic period.[3]

The meaning of this petroglyph is even more elusive than that of the small pecked heads. It is located in a small, secluded side canyon. Perhaps it was made in response to a series of much earlier pecked rock art adorning the higher reaches of the cliffs. Whether a territory marker or a religious icon or both, this petroglyph seems to represent a temporary venture into the Black Hills. Long before white settlers entered the area, someone smashed away the central portion of the face, as if to render it powerless.

Spirit Faces

Before the rock art of Ludlow Cave was destroyed by rock collapse and vandalism, a series of faces carved in relief looked down from the high rocks at the cave entrance. One was later found, face down, in the cave deposits and was collected for the South Dakota state museum. This bas-relief face was made in the same way as the Track-Vulva-Groove rock art discussed in chapter 8 and probably had the same origin. The features of the single remaining example are simple but strikingly human (fig. 13.5). Whether the others were more elaborate is unknown, because no photographs or sketches of them exist.

A petroglyph placed lower on the walls of Ludlow Cave is a simple circle with two lines for the neck and two dots for eyes (fig. 13.6). Curved horns extending from the sides of the head show that the face is that of a spirit being rather than an ordinary human. In Cheyenne and Lakota tradition, spirits are often shown with horns like this.[4] Because Ludlow Cave was a sacred site, this image may have been made to invoke the aid of a particular spirit. A similar horned face is carved in a small rockshelter not far from Ludlow Cave (fig. 13.7, right).

A Cheyenne religious tradition may be represented in these and a third horned face (fig. 13.7, left).[5] On a west-facing point at the southwest edge of the north Cave Hills is a deeply incised face with bisonlike horns. In traditional Cheyenne religion, the thunder spirit is Nonoma, depicted as a speckled face (representing hailstones) with bison horns (fig. 13.8).[6] Nonoma is strongly associated with the southwest, the direction from which the thunderstorms come. Nonoma is one of two keepers of the spirits of animals and is thus associated with hunting and life renewal. The other spirit animal keeper is the female spirit, sometimes described as a bison cow, associated with the below world and the animal caves. The Cave Hills petroglyph is heavily pitted, but it is not clear now whether it was deliberately pitted or simply affected by natural weathering.

The unusual placement of this petroglyph on an open, west-facing cliff, its form, and its location in known historic Cheyenne territory are important clues to its possible meaning. Although Cheyennes today do not retain specific memories of the Cave Hills, uniquely Cheyenne shield designs are found at Ludlow Cave and elsewhere in Cave Hills rock art. This indicates that the Cave Hills, like the adjacent Little Missouri country, were once part of Cheyenne territory. The anthropologist E. Adamson Hoebel

Figure 13.3. Concentric circles give the eyes of this face petroglyph an almost hypnotic effect. The mouth and nose of the incised face were battered away by later precontact visitors to the site, who may also have made the deep abraded groove that cuts through the right edge of the petroglyph. Site 39FA1336, southern Black Hills. (Abraded groove is about 15 cm long.)

Figure 13.4. Face petroglyphs from southern Saskatchewan.

Figure 13.5. Bas-relief face petroglyph collected from rock rubble in Ludlow Cave, 1920. (Courtesy South Dakota Archaeological Research Center, Rapid City; reproduced with permission.)

Figure 13.6. A deeply incised and ground horned head is still visible near the entrance to Ludlow Cave among the graffiti covering the cave walls (lower right of photo). (Photo by Phil Henry; reproduced with permission.)

recorded that the Cheyennes believed that spirit bison dwelled under the ground and sometimes emerged through caves to repopulate the earthly herds. According to Hoebel, this belief was borrowed from the Mandans, with whom the Cheyennes had lived for a time before migrating west to the Black Hills country.[7] It is likely that Ludlow Cave was a sacred buffalo home to both of these otherwise very different peoples. If the horned heads represent Nonoma, then they reflect the Cheyennes' redefinition of the sacred landscape of the Cave Hills as they established their new homeland west of the Missouri.

Shell Masks and Plains Indians

The key to understanding a very different incised face petroglyph in the southern Black Hills lies far away in the southeastern United States. Except for being carved

Figure 13.7. Horned head petroglyphs from the north Cave Hills may represent the Cheyenne thunder spirit. Left, site 39HN174; right, 39HN18. (Scale bars indicate 20 cm.)

on sandstone instead of fashioned from a shell disk, the Black Hills petroglyph would be right at home among some shell masks found in archaeological sites in the Southeast.

Among the most intriguing finds in Great Plains archaeological sites are shell maskettes (fig. 13.9). These are small, pear-shaped miniature masks made of marine shell. Because these shell faces may have been worn at the neck, they are sometimes referred to as shell gorgets. Shell mask gorgets have been found in northwestern Montana, eastern North Dakota, western, central, and eastern South Dakota, southern Manitoba, and northeastern Iowa.[8] They are clearly related to similar specimens from the middle Mississippi and the Southeast. James Howard recognized this in his classic monograph *The Southern Cult on the*

Figure 13.8. The tipi in which the Cheyennes' sacred Medicine Hat bundle was kept was decorated with images of Nomoma, the thunder spirit. (Courtesy W. H. Over Museum, Morrow Collection; reproduced with permission.)

Northern Plains, but few plains archaeologists have followed Howard's lead in recognizing a link between the cultures of the northern plains and those of the Southeast.[9] Recent discoveries have prompted some archaeologists to reexamine the cultural connections indicated by such artifacts.

Shell masks or gorgets are typically associated with the later years of the Southeastern Ceremonial Complex art tradition.[10] This was a widespread religious and artistic tradition adopted by many groups in the Southeast beginning about 1250 C.E. and lasting several centuries. Shell masks are typically manufactured on ovoid pieces of whelk or other marine shell. They usually have a long, narrow nose, often carved in low relief, eyes formed by perforation of the shell, and small round or oval engraved mouths (fig. 13.10). The eyes are usually surrounded by sets of jagged points extending down and away from the eyes. This "forked eye" or "weeping eye" motif is the hallmark of the late prehistoric shell masks discussed here. Shell masks were perhaps first manufactured in the Southeast between 1450 and 1550 or later.[11] At least one specimen from South Dakota dates from the Initial Coalescent period (1400–1550) of the Middle Missouri archaeological sequence.[12] Thus, shell masks do not appear earlier in the Southeast than in the plains, despite their greater abundance in the Southeast. They are assigned to the late prehistoric period in both areas. In the plains, use of shell masks continued into the early contact and historic periods.

Shell masks or gorgets have been found in several archaeological contexts. In the Southeastern and cen-tral Mississippi River sites, they are invariably associated with burials. With one questionable exception, these are the remains of men, infants, and children. The shell masks occur in various positions in these burials, suggesting use as gorgets, masks, and headrests. Shell masks are found in village graves as well as in burial mounds. This means they were used by both ordinary and powerful people.[13]

In the Great Plains, contexts are more varied. A shell mask formed part of a Kansa war bundle still used in the 1880s.[14] Another was found in northeastern Iowa with a child burial. It appears to have been worn as a necklace strung with copper or brass and glass beads.[15] Several shell masks have been found in North Dakota.[16] Two came from a mound in eastern North Dakota along with other shell artifacts, a straight stone pipe, a fossil, a few pottery sherds, bison bone, and the fragmentary remains of two individuals: an adult male and an elderly male. Three shell masks and two copper liners for shell masks were found eroding from a creek bank in central North Dakota. One of the three masks has a horse scratched into its reverse side. Another shell gorget, representing a rattlesnake rather than a face, was found on Shell Butte in south-central North Dakota. The motif is typical of Southeastern Ceremonial Complex materials from Tennessee. Two shell masks have been reported from Manitoba, one from a burial mound at Calf Mountain.[17]

Other shell masks have been found in South Dakota and Montana.[18] A shell mask was found in a cave in northwestern Montana among what appear to

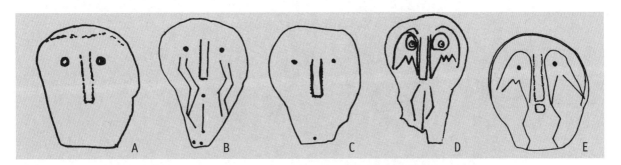

Figure 13.9. Shell maskettes from sites in the northern and central plains: (A) Alamakee County, Iowa; (B–C) Burleigh County, North Dakota; (D) Heimdal Mound, Wells County, North Dakota; (E) Calf Mountain Mound, Manitoba. Variable scale.

be religious offerings. Another was found on the lower slopes of Bear Butte, one of the sacred sites of the Black Hills. Another shell mask was plowed up from a field in eastern South Dakota. Although the last two masks lack the characteristic forked eye incisions, they are otherwise typical of late prehistoric shell masks from the northern plains. Two tiny maskettes of shell were found in village sites on the Missouri River in

South Dakota, in trash pits or in the remains of houses dated between 1250 and 1550 (fig. 13.11).

Uses and Meaning of Shell Maskettes

Researchers have proposed several uses and symbolic associations for these masks. Their ideas are based on the occurrence of the masks in burials, their association with males, and their similarity to other late pre-

Figure 13.10. Shell maskettes from the Southeast: (A–B) McMahan Mound, Tennessee; (C) Brakebill Mound, Tennessee; (D) Lick Creek Mound, Tennessee; (E) Acquia Creek, Virginia; (F) Ely County, Virginia. (Adapted from Holmes, *Art in Shell*, pl. 69; variable scale.)

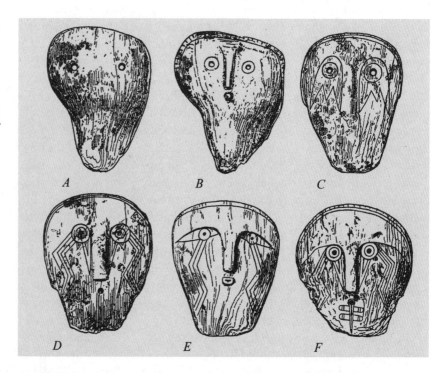

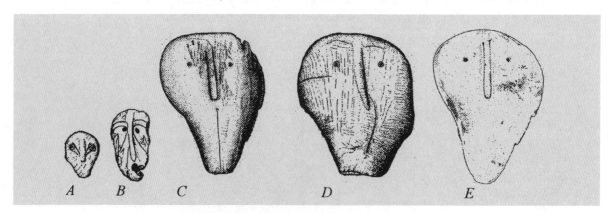

Figure 13.11. Shell maskettes from South Dakota: (A–B) miniature masks from the Demory site (39CO1) and Black Partizan site (39LM218); (C) Kingsbury County; (D) Bear Butte, Meade County, (E) Missouri River, site unknown. (Variable scales.)

historic art from the Southeast. Some may have served as death masks, with the eye decorations perhaps representing tears.[19] Several researchers have noted a connection between the forked eye motif and peregrine falcons and, in turn, between the falcons and warfare.[20] Others have proposed that shell masks were symbolic trophy heads.[21] The addition of forked extensions to the basic falcon eye-marking suggests a reference to thunder beings, again leading to an association with warfare in many eastern and plains cultures.[22] Hunting prowess is similarly associated with thunder gods in Creek and Cherokee belief systems. This suggests that the shell masks might have played a part in hunting as well as in warfare in the Southeast.[23]

Among the Kansa, shell masks apparently served as icons for the thunder god, who controlled success in warfare. Warriors might remove the shell mask from a sacred bundle and wear it as a pledge to kill an enemy or die in the attempt.[24]

The thunder symbolism indicated by these beliefs is balanced by the shell itself, which represents the "below" powers that both oppose and complement the "above" (thunder) powers. In Algonkian and Siouan tradition, shell is associated with the powers dwelling below water or below ground. The copper that lined many shell masks is also strongly associated with the underwater beings, probably because large copper deposits occur near the Great Lakes. This balance between the underwater symbolism of the shell and the sky symbolism of the forks of thunder might have been designed to appeal to both sets of powers.

Among some groups associated with the late prehistoric Oneota culture, shell masks may have been presented to persons honored in ritual adoption ceremonies.[25] This hypothesis draws a connection between shell masks and the Long Nose or Short Nose God maskettes found in the Southeast. These maskettes are, in turn, related to ritual adoption ceremonies practiced by various Siouan groups. Variations of the calumet, or adoption, ceremony were practiced by Siouan-speaking groups from the Southeast and the central Mississippi Valley and into the northwestern plains.[26]

Ritual adoption played an important part in traditional Lakota religion. Although the calumet, a cylindrical pipe typical of the southeastern traditions, is echoed in the form of the sacred wand and sacred corn ear used in the Lakota adoption ceremony, shell masks appear not to have been retained in any form in this tradition.[27] Candidates for ritual adoption were given a talisman or fetish, but it is not recorded whether such items included shell masks. The use of a polished conch shell disc in the wrappings of the Sacred Calf Pipe bundle of the Lakota hints at a possible connection between the calumet and shell masks, but it is no more than suggestive. In general terms, shell is a symbol of long life among the Lakotas, because of its durability.[28]

Shell masks appear to have taken on a different significance in Lakota tradition. Rather than being tokens of ritual adoption, they served in healing ceremonies. According to information supplied by the anthropologist Ben Rhodd, based on conversations with Lakota elders, shell masks were owned, maintained, and used by healers. Each mask was unique in its healing properties and in its ceremonial treatment. Each had its own song and could be used only by its owner. The owner of a shell mask could pass it down to his or her child or could have it have it "put away" by having it buried with him or placed where it would not be found again.[29]

A Shell Mask Petroglyph

A single panel of rock art from the southern Black Hills contains a face identical to those on the shell masks (fig. 13.12). It shows that plains dwellers were making their own forked-eyed images, not just obtaining them through trade. This panel was discovered at site 39FA91 by Smithsonian archaeologists working on the Angostura Reservoir project in 1946. It consists of a human face and arms lightly scratched into the back of a small sandstone rockshelter. The rockshelter is about 8 feet wide, 6 feet deep, and 4.5 feet at its maximum height—just large enough for a few people to sit in. It is located on a high bluff overlooking the narrows of the Cheyenne River.

In 1948 the Smithsonian archaeologists returned to excavate the rockshelter. The surface contained stone chips, a chipped stone implement, a gypsum fragment, and two unworked stone fragments. Archaeologists found an oblong, saucer-shaped hearth with a stone lining near the center of the outer edge of

Figure 13.12. The very lightly incised "shell mask" petoglyph from site 39FA91 on the Cheyenne River, southern Black Hills. (Scale bar shows 15 cm.)

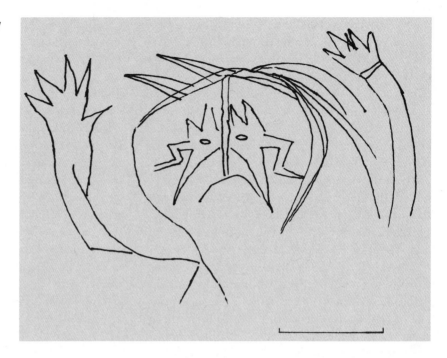

the rockshelter, just above bedrock. The rockshelter sediments contained a broken triangular arrow point, a stone scraper, 2 stone knives, a stone tool with edges used for drilling, cutting, and scraping, a core, a "stone formation" (apparently meaning a fossil or other odd-shaped stone), 64 stone fragments, 3 gypsum fragments, 3 unidentifiable animal bone fragments, and 3 unidentifiable shell fragments. A stone knife and a quartz crystal fragment were found in front of the rockshelter.[30]

Despite the rockshelter's small size, the Smithsonian archaeologists concluded that it had been used by a family. The presence of gypsum or selenite crystals was thought to indicate arrow making or some other activity involving gluing, because northern Plains Indians used selenite powder to absorb excess glue and impart a smooth finish to arrows and other glued objects. The "stone formation" listed in the field notes is not mentioned in the project report. Like the petroglyphs, the arrow point suggested a late prehistoric age. No explanation was offered for the rock art. The Smithsonian archaeologists apparently suspected that the incised face or mask, like the initials *S* and *N* they observed on the roof of the shelter, was of recent, Euro-American origin.

If the face petroglyph is a fake, it was made by someone with a secure knowledge of incised shell masks. My opinion, based on degree of repatination and comparison with other Black Hills rock art, is that the petroglyph was made during the late prehistoric or early contact period by a Lakota or Crow person. The incised face is typical of shell masks or gorgets from the Southeast, the Ohio Valley, and the northern plains dating between 1600 and 1880 (fig. 13.13). The petroglyph face is intermediate between the circular and pear-shaped forms typical of actual shell masks and gorgets.[31] It has a double line extending from the forehead to the mouth to represent the nose, two small round eyes set close to the nose, and weeping or forked eye designs. The eye decoration is nearly identical to that found on maskettes both east and west of the Mississippi. It is generally considered a late form. The form of the nose is very similar to forms appearing on shell gorgets, although lacking the slight relief. The downturned mouth is unusual. The figure is shown with long, unbound hair and what appear to be two feathers projecting from the top of the head.

The petroglyph has an incised line across the very top of the head. Many shell masks have a simple border line engraved around the top of the head, and the

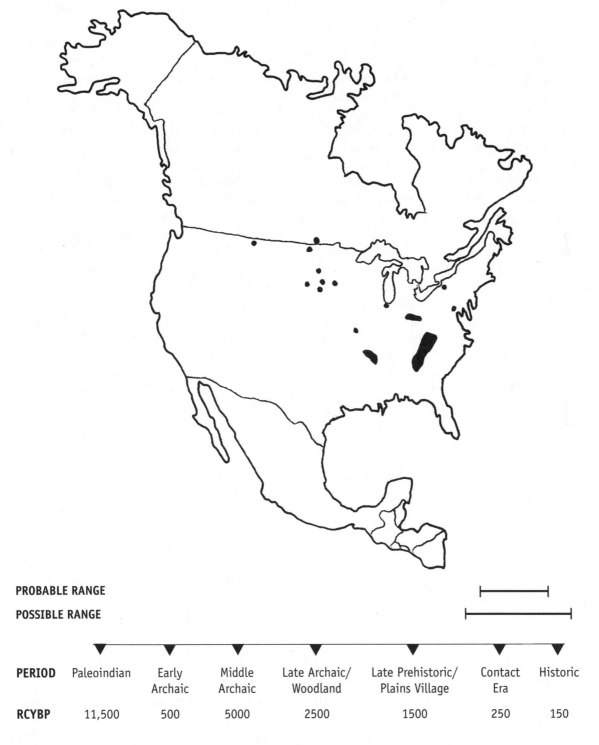

PROBABLE RANGE

POSSIBLE RANGE

PERIOD	Paleoindian	Early Archaic	Middle Archaic	Late Archaic/ Woodland	Late Prehistoric/ Plains Village	Contact Era	Historic
RCYBP	11,500	500	5000	2500	1500	250	150

Figure 13.13. Distribution of shell maskettes and gorgets with forked-eye designs, and associated time line.

line on the petroglyph apparently corresponds to it. On the northern plains, persons who had undergone ritual adoption were entitled to wear an arc of red paint across their forehead.[32] This raises the possibility that the line might have a special meaning related to the honoring ceremony. The hair and feathers correspond to hair designs on masks from east of the Mississippi. This design element does not occur on masks from western sites. The larger "palette" available to the petroglyph artist allowed a more realistic and elaborate depiction of hairstyle than can be achieved on a shell mask. Nothing on the petroglyph corresponds to the chin decorations found on many shell masks.

The artifacts found at the site reveal little about the meaning of the shell mask petroglyph. With the possible exception of the single arrow point, the gypsum and quartz crystals, and the undescribed "stone formation," the artifact assemblage is no different from what might be expected from short-term occupation by one or two people seeking shelter from inclement weather. It is possible that the arrow point and crystals represent offerings, but the number of items is too small to indicate a shrine. The site does not appear to have been revisited, as would be expected for a known sacred site.

The presence of gypsum crystals in the rockshelter is unusual but ambiguous. Several uses for gypsum have been recorded ethnographically. The Cheyennes, like the Arikaras, used gypsum as a finish over glue. They also used it to attach down or horsehair tips to eagle feathers on warbonnets and as a coating on the hands of hide workers to prevent them from soiling the robes they made. The Cheyennes also used gypsum powder to mark out a cross, representing thunder and lightning, on the altar for the Massaum ceremony. The name of the Cheyenne culture hero Lime refers to the baked gypsum powder used for white ceremonial paint.[33] During the 1874 Black Hills expedition, chief engineer William Ludlow observed a huge gypsum deposit where generations of Indians had split off pieces for ornaments, eventually leaving a shoulder several feet deep.[34] Gypsum is common in the Black Hills. The gypsum in the rockshelter might have been found nearby and brought to the site to be ground into powder. Whether it was being processed for use

as a paint or varnish, used for ornamentation, or prepared for ceremonial use is unknown. It is tempting to draw a connection between lightning symbolism, arrows, and the lightninglike face-paint design on the petroglyph, but definite evidence of such a link is lacking.

Because it depicts the head, hair, neck, shoulder, and arms—not just a mask—this petroglyph suggests that northern Plains Indians may have used face-paint designs identical to those seen on artifacts from the Southeast. The petroglyph hints that at least some religious beliefs were shared across large portions of the continent. Unlike the portable shell masks, the petroglyph implies that ideas—not just objects—were being exchanged between the Southeast and the northern plains during the late prehistoric or protohistoric period.

The petroglyph also provides an additional context for shell mask symbolism. Shell masks have been found in at least six contexts in the Great Plains: on or near prominent buttes; in a cave containing religious offerings or paraphernalia; in graves; as part of Kansa war bundles; among the paraphernalia of Lakota healers; and in the houses of middle Missouri River villagers. Ethnographic and archaeological evidence suggests the masks might also have been used in the ritual adoption ceremony practiced by various Siouan groups. The rock art at site 39FA91 provides an eighth context. There is no evidence that the petroglyph was associated with a burial. Clearly, it does not represent a trophy head, because the arms and upper torso are depicted intact. Because few artifacts were found there, it is unlikely that the rockshelter containing the petroglyph served as a shrine. The shelter is too small to have been a comfortable habitation site. The isolated and relatively inaccessible setting of the petroglyph precludes a connection with ritual adoption. Candidates for ritual adoption did not undergo isolation, and the adoption itself was a public gathering.

A more plausible explanation is that the petroglyph accompanied prayers for success in warfare, hunting, or healing. In the plains area, men traditionally retired to high buttes or caves for a period of isolation, prayer, and fasting in the hope of attaining help in warfare, eagle trapping, and hunting. Both men and women might engage in such devotions to seek aid for a relative whose life was threatened by sickness or the dangers of war. The size, inaccessibility, and setting of the rockshelter, overlooking the Cheyenne River, fit with use as an individual's prayer or vision-quest site. The hearth and artifacts suggested that the rockshelter was used as a temporary shelter. These items could have been left behind by a vision seeker or by an individual or group using the same rockshelter on a different occasion.

The age of the petroglyph is unknown. It probably dates to the late prehistoric or early contact period, judging from dates for shell masks from other sites in the northern plains. Other lightly incised rock art in the Black Hills dates to this period as well. Its cultural affiliation is unknown, although it looks similar to historic Lakota, Cheyenne, and Crow drawings. Shell masks and other Southeastern Ceremonial Complex–related artifacts are strongly associated with Siouan groups throughout the plains. This suggests a Lakota, Crow, Mandan, or Hidatsa affiliation for the petroglyph, as well as for other forms of shell masks in the northern plains.

The Smithsonian archaeologists excavated this rockshelter in 1948 because, "although the site would not be in danger of flooding by reservoir water, its close proximity to the future pool would make it subject inevitably to vandalism." That prediction eventually came true. The petroglyph is now ruined by deep cuts in the rock spelling out RYAN BATLEY 1994 FISHING TRIP. Ego and ignorance thus destroyed one of the most informative and striking artworks in the northern plains.

Visions and Oracles

Widely scattered across the northern plains is a style of rock art made up of arrays of symbols. These include crescents, crosses, figures that resemble the letter *H*, a three-rayed figure like a capital *E* turned on its side with a dot below it, and many others. Some of these symbols are found in historic Plains Indian art, but others are known only from this rock art style. Because the symbols are often arranged in columns, it is named the Vertical Series style. It was first defined in Montana, where several sites are found.[1]

Vertical Series Rock Art

The largest Vertical Series panel in the Black Hills is strikingly similar to a rock art panel from a site in central Montana (fig. 14.1). Like the Montana site, the Black Hills site is a large, smooth cliff face with a variety of painted geometric designs. A vertical series of crescent moons forms one edge of the panel, balanced by a column of crosses, probably representing stars, along the opposite edge. In between are several different symbols—some single examples and some repeated (figs. 14.2, 14.3). The central Montana site also has a set of symbols enclosed on two sides by ver-

tical series of repeated designs. In this case, one is a set of *H*s and the other a set of crosses (fig. 14.2). Other Vertical Series sites are scattered from northern Wyoming to southern Alberta, Canada. Sites occur in southern Alberta, central and western Montana, the Bighorn Mountains of northern Wyoming, and the southern and central Black Hills.

Only three Vertical Series sites are known from the Black Hills. The panel just described is one of two Vertical Series panels located in a southern Black Hills canyon. The other Vertical Series panel at the site is a smaller group of similar designs painted inside a narrow crevice (fig. 14.4). Another Vertical Series panel was in a rockshelter along the Cheyenne River described in the 1940s.[2] Researchers have failed to relocate this site in recent years, and it may no longer exist. Along the back wall of the rock overhang was a single panel of painted designs. Most of these were downward-pointing triangles with lines trailing from one side or the point (fig. 14.5). The third site is hidden high in the central Black Hills, where a complex panel of triangles and other designs covers the lower portion of a towering granite outcrop near a spring-fed pool (fig. 14.6).

Figure 14.1. Painted Vertical Series rock art at Atherton Canyon, Montana. See figure 14.2 for a drawing of the panel. (Photo by Stu Conner; reproduced with permission.)

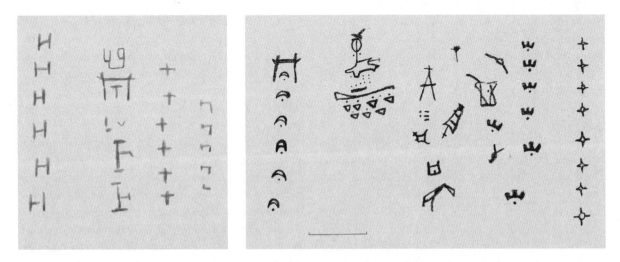

Figure 14.2. Drawing of red painted Vertical Series rock art at Atherton Canyon, Montana (left), and site 39FA321 in the southern Black Hills (right). (Scale shows 10 cm.)

Figure 14.3. Red painted Vertical Series rock art at site 39FA321, southern Black Hills. Designs are indistinct due to chalking and subsequent scrubbing of the rock face. See figure 14.2 for a drawing of the panel.

The meaning of Vertical Series rock art is enigmatic. Some of the symbols can be recognized from Plains Indian picture writing. The crescent represents a moon and probably, by extension, a month. The equilateral cross represents a star, or night, and thus perhaps another unit of time. An open rectangle represents a meat-drying rack. This design was used in picture writing to convey the concepts of plenty (if the rack is full) or famine (if the rack is empty).[3]

Other symbols must have had specific meanings, because they appear in identical forms at widely scattered Vertical Series sites (fig. 14.7). These include the "lazy *E*" with a dot under it, an *H*-like design, a downward-pointing triangle (sometimes with a dot over it), a design like a table crossed by a *T,* and open or closed rectangles with paired dots or short lines inside. The meaning of these cannot be extrapolated from existing examples of Plains Indian picture writing. They may have been special symbols used only by religious specialists, indecipherable to the average person. Perhaps this was the kind of rock art the Lakota holy man Black Elk said could be read only by religious specialists (see chapter 4). If so, the meaning of the designs would have been revealed to them after an intense period of fasting and prayer. The specific interpretation of a Vertical Series panel would change each time the holy man or woman visited it.

Another possibility is that the symbols had specific meanings within a particular religious tradition. Clearly, many of these designs were used in religious symbolism. For example, crescent moons and the four-pointed star are found in the symbolism of many Plains Indian ceremonies. Even the meat-drying rack is an important religious symbol among the Lakotas. The Sun Dance altar contains a miniature meat rack, painted blue, against which the sacred pipe was rested during the ceremony. In this context, the meat rack represents heaven and the people's prayer that their racks will always be as full as heaven.[4] The Poncas and Omahas had a tradition of tattooing honored young women with special symbols. These included a dot to represent the sun, a four-rayed star to represent night, a figure like a triangle topped by a cross to represent a person, a crescent moon, and a turtle to represent water and wind. Although rattlesnake tattoos are not reported, the rattlesnake was represented in the tattooing ceremony by a set of rattles or bells. Only women so honored could participate in certain ceremonies, including renewal of the Sacred White Buffalo

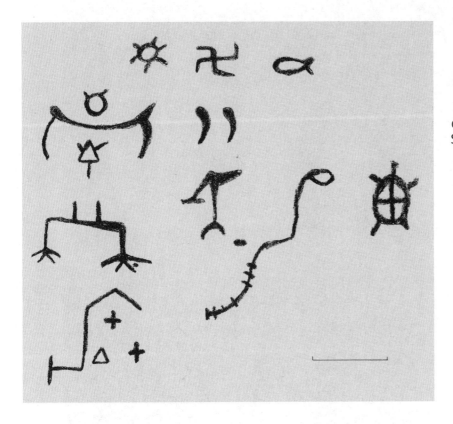

Figure 14.4. The authenticity of this panel of red painted designs from the southern Black Hills (the second panel at site 39FA321) has been questioned, but most of the designs occur at other Vertical Series sites either in the Black Hills or elsewhere on the northern plains. Perhaps this represents a later variant of the Vertical Series tradition. (Scale bar shows 30 cm.)

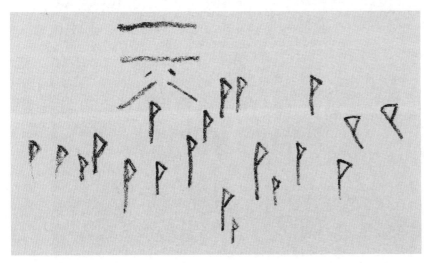

Figure 14.5. This rock art panel was recorded in the southern Black Hills in the 1940s. Its exact location is unknown. (Adapted from a Smithsonian Institution River Basin Surveys field sketch on file at the South Dakota Archaeological Research Center, Rapid City.)

Figure 14.6. This red painted rock art from the central Black Hills includes many inverted triangles and a variety of other symbols. Inverted triangles occur at all three Vertical Series sites in the Black Hills.

Hide. Interestingly, versions of all of these symbols occur in Vertical Series rock art.

The distribution of Vertical Series rock art does not exactly match that of any Indian nation (fig. 14.8). Within the Black Hills, some occurs near other rock art that may be of Ponca origin, but other examples are far from any other rock art sites. In the Bighorns, such rock art is also within the hunting territory of the western Ponca division, but similar rock art is not found in the heart of Ponca country along the Missouri and Niobrara Rivers. The style extends too far north for the Lakotas, Cheyennes, Poncas, and Crows and too far south and east for the Blackfeet nations. The specific symbolism has similarities to traditional Ponca women's tattoos, and similarities to historic picture writing suggest a Siouan or Algonkian

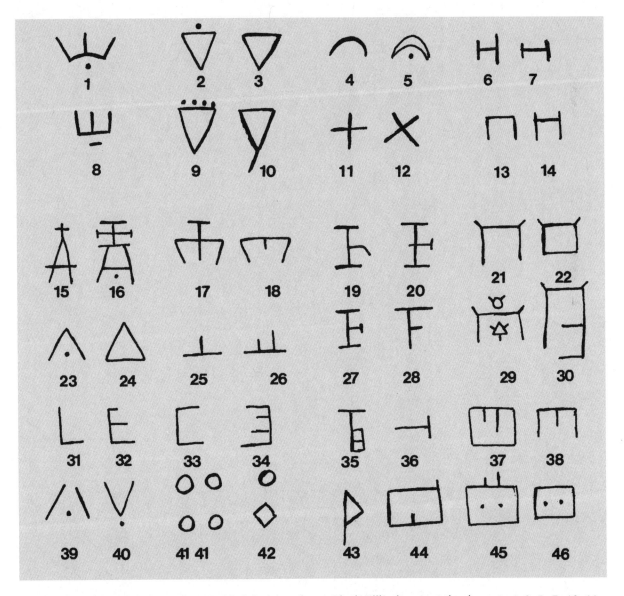

Figure 14.7. Design elements from Vertical Series rock art. Black Hills sites contain elements 1–3, 5, 7, 10–11, 15, 21, 24, 29, and 43–44; Bighorn sites contain 3, 6–7, 9, 11–12, 16, 21–22, 26, 28, 32–34, 36–37, 40, and 45–46; central and western Montana sites contain 6–8, 11, 13, 17–19, 21, 23, 27, 30–31, 35–36, and 38; and southern Alberta sites contain 1, 8, 11–12, 39, and 41–43.

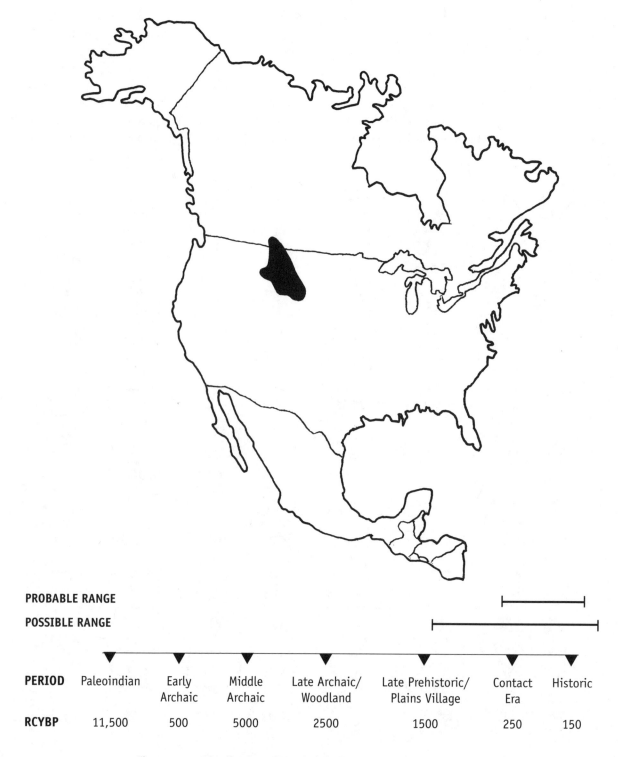

Figure 14.8. Distribution of Vertical Series rock art, and its time line.

origin. This would include all the groups mentioned, as well as the Assiniboins, Arapahos, and most of the Missouri River groups. It is not known whether many or few or only one of these groups made the Vertical Series rock art so widely scattered across the northern plains.

The Art of the Vision

A different kind of vision-related rock art was recently found in the north Cave Hills. The main image that can still be discerned at this site is a zigzag line forming an arc (fig. 14.9). In historic and contemporary Plains Indian art, lightning symbolizes spiritual power. At one end of the lightning arc is a bison, and at the other end an animal that most closely resembles a mountain sheep. Under the arc is a bull elk and a seated human figure. The combination of the power symbol and the animal figures suggests that this petroglyph was made as a part of vision-quest rituals, either to record a vision received or to evoke the help of the spirit animals.[5] Although it has long been believed that some animal images in northern plains rock art represent spirit helpers, few are as unambiguous as this example.

Another possible vision-quest site in the Cave Hills has images of bears, humans, elk, and bear paws

scratched into the ceiling of a tiny cave perched high up in the rimrock (fig. 14.10). Bear and elk were often seen in visions. Such visions conferred special powers of healing and seduction. A heavily eroded shield design at this site is typical of Cheyenne and Arapaho shields, but the rock art seems to have been made over several episodes. A deeply ground bison track and a vulva suggest that the site perhaps was used by the Lakotas or Missouri River village groups as well.

Elk Dreamers Society Rock Art from the North Cave Hills

Another kind of vision-related rock art is found in the north Cave Hills. A small, bowl-shaped rockshelter retains a few remnants of finely incised rock art. One panel consists of four human figures; another contains an archlike figure filled with parallel vertical lines, as well as a few other incised lines; and the remaining panel contains a few vertical incised lines, a set of converging vertical lines, and a human figure. All of these petroglyphs are very lightly incised and heavily eroded, making them quite difficult to see.

Four costumed humans make up the main panel. The most distinct of these wears a long, almost trailing breechcloth and a mask or headdress with branched antlers on each side (fig. 14.11, second from left). At

Figure 14.9. In this drawing of a very lightly incised rock art panel from the north Cave Hills (site 39HN694), three game animals and a lightning or power design dominate. From left to right are a bison, a seated human, an elk, and a mountain sheep.

his left side is a branched staff or wand. A less distinct adjacent figure also has an antlered mask, a long breechcloth, and a branched wand. On the other side of the first figure is a man with a triangular mask or headdress bearing long but indistinct antlers. Except for this, he is nude. The remaining human figure is very difficult to see but appears to have a mask or headdress with long horizontal extensions on each side. This human holds an object composed of a circular item with a long "tail" and a cross-piece. It appears to be some sort of wand, coup stick, club, or similar object. The "tail" or streamer has three small lines extending obliquely from near its end, suggesting feathers (fig. 14.11, right).

Figure 14.10. Human and bear figures from the ceiling of a perched rockshelter (site 39HN121) in the north Cave Hills. For historic Lakota and Cheyenne people, bears were powerful spirit helpers who might convey special powers of herbal medicine and healing. (Figures rearranged for illustration; bear at right is about 45 cm wide.)

Figure 14.11. This very lightly incised rock art from site 39HN745 in the north Cave Hills shows men in the costume of the Elk Dreamers ceremony. The three figures at left were traced from slides; the figure at right was drawn freehand from photographs and a field sketch. The figures are about 20 cm from head to foot.

The first three petroglyphs probably depict Lakota Elk Dreamers. The Elk Dreamers were a society of men who had experienced sacred visions of elk.[6] Such elk visions were thought to convey special sexual powers over women or special success in battle or healing. To fulfill an elk vision, the vision seeker had to perform one or more ceremonies, commonly referred to as the Elk Dance.[7] The performers wore masks constructed of the skin of an elk head with the antlers still attached, or ones made of willow branches and cloth or of rawhide and sticks. The more commonly used trapezoidal masks covered the dancer's entire head (fig. 14.12).

Each elk dancer carried a long wand with leafy branches at the top in one hand and a large fur-covered hoop in the other. Sometimes the Elk Dreamers carried leafy wands in both hands during part of the ceremony. The leafy wand was the special emblem of the elk, as opposed to other antlered animals. The hoop was the embodiment of the circle, emblematic of all antlered animals. It also symbolized a snare or trap, expressing the dancer's ability to overcome enemies or women (fig. 14.13). A mirror might be fastened in the middle of the hoop by four thongs, illustrating the "capture" of the desired "prey," although this was more typical of Deer Dreamer costumes than those of Elk Dreamers.[8] Except for the mask, Elk Dreamers wore only a breechcloth. Body painting made up the rest of the costume (fig. 14.14).

During their dance, the Elk Dreamers moved in a procession around the camp, preceded by two holy women walking side by side and holding prayer pipes. As a demonstration of their power, each man would endeavor to leave elk tracks in a patch of soft dirt.[9] As they moved singing through the camp, the Elk Dreamers were pursued, but never overcome, by other

Figure 14.12. In this Lakota drawing of the mysterious power of the elk, the elk dancer at center wears a trapezoidal mask with antlers and carries a branched bough and a hoop with a mirror at its center. The elk is uttering its mysterious whistle; its power to captivate is symbolized by the woman at right, connected to the elk by wavy "power" lines flowing from a sacred pipe. (Courtesy American Museum of Natural History.)

visionaries, including the Heyoka (Thunder Dreamers or Contraries) and Bear Dreamers.[10] The indistinct human figure in the Cave Hills rock art panel (fig. 14.11, right) may represent a Heyoka. During one part of the ceremony (or during one variation of it), the Elk Dreamers ran about with a long, leafy sapling in each hand. With these saplings, they knocked down a bark image of a thunder being that had been suspended from the top of a pole.[11] Both of these actions represented the Elk Dreamers' ability to overcome the power of thunder.

An alternative possibility is that the petroglyphs illustrate one part of the Cheyenne Massaum ceremony, also known as the Animal Dance or Contrary Dance.[12] This ceremony enacts world creation and the origins of animal hunting. According to oral tradition, it was brought to the Tsistsistas division of the Cheyennes by their culture hero Sweet Medicine soon after they took up residence on the Great Plains. On the final day of this five-day ceremony, a sacred hunt was enacted. Costumed humans imitated bison and elk, among many other species. These elk dancers wore sage wreaths on their heads, into which branches were thrust to represent antlers. They went naked except for body paint and breechcloth. Like the Lakota Elk Dreamers, each of them carried a long cane with leafy branches at the top.

George Bird Grinnell described the elk imitators of the 1911 Massaum ceremony as follows: "Their lower legs, arms, and shoulders were painted black,

Figure 14.13. Lakota drawing showing the Elk Dreamers' ceremony and its connection to the elk vision. The dancers with branched antlers and the woman pipe carrier have been directly empowered by the elk vision, as symbolized by the wavy lines extending from the elk's mouth. The other dancers represent a bison and an antelope, showing other dreamer status. Each Elk Dreamer carries a hoop and a small square mirror to symbolize his ability to capture women and enemies. The woman pipe bearer also carries a branched bough. (Courtesy American Museum of Natural History.)

and the rest of the body yellow. On the head they wore wreaths of white sage and carried in the right hand long willows with leaves on the upper end. Stuck in the wreaths of sage were bare twigs 18 inches or two feet long, which represented antlers.[13] One photograph from the 1911 Massaum ceremony appears to show a dancer with a wreath-and-twig headdress standing next to a similarly costumed dancer carrying a leafy bough.[14] Another person present at the 1911 ceremony recalled that the "the deer are painted yellow and have sticks on their heads."[15] John Stands in Timber, another witness to the Massaum ceremony conducted in 1911, did not remember the elk imitators but recalled that deer imitators wore caps with leather cutouts representing the antlers.[16]

Overall, a Lakota origin for the petroglyphs is most likely. First, the trapezoidal shape of the elk imitators' masks (especially the one on the left in fig. 4.11) matches historic Lakota images of Elk Dreamers' masks. Verbal descriptions of the Cheyenne ceremony make no reference to face masks. The occurrence of two Elk Dreamers together on the petroglyph panel also suggests Lakota tradition. In his illustrations of the Elk Dreamers dance and the Sun Dance, Standing Bear showed paired elk imitators in each instance.[17] Bad Heart Bull's drawing of the Deer Dreamers ceremony also seems to show paired dancers: two elk imitators with leafy wands; two pairs of black-tailed deer; two dancers with spotted body paint and what appear to be pronghorn antlers; and two additional elk imitators with square mirrors, one holding a cedar courting flute.[18] This pairing may reflect the duality of the deer spirits in Lakota tradition. For example, deer were thought to be capable of taking on human form in order to lure men to them. Such men went crazy or died as a result of the encounter.[19] The double deer or elk symbolized the dual characteristics of deer or elk power. It could be either beneficial or harmful, depending on how it was invoked and used.

The remaining petroglyphs in the rockshelter are too deteriorated to be clearly seen. Perhaps they illustrated other parts of the Elk Dreamers ceremony or other parts of a vision requiring its enactment. Pictures of ceremonies are rare in northern plains rock art, but depictions of vision experiences seem to be found in all parts of the region. The secluded location of this rock art was appropriate for vision seeking. Here, in the forested island of the Cave Hills, a vision seeker prayed for the special powers of the elk and perhaps fulfilled the vision by depicting the Elk Dreamers ceremony.

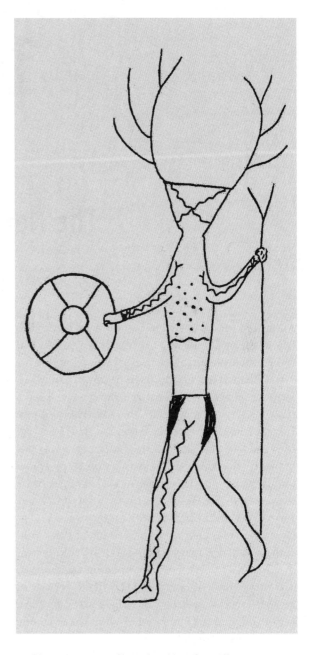

Figure 14.14. Lakota drawing of an Elk Dreamer wearing a trapezoidal mask, a breechcloth, and body paint and holding a branched stick and a hoop with mirror. (Courtesy American Museum of Natural History.)

The Newcomers

An incised rock art panel in the southern Black Hills tells of the beginning of a new era. It is a sketchy but recognizable picture of a horse-drawn wagon (see fig. 2.4). Perhaps it records the first time some Lakotas saw a trader's wagon—an event remembered in Lakota tribal history as taking place in 1830. The southern Lakotas called this year "When they saw their first wagons" and said that "Red Lake, a trader, brought goods in them."[1] Red Lake was Thomas Leston Sarpy, whose middle name sounded similar to the Lakota word *ble shan,* or red lake. To escape from a hasty marriage, Sarpy came west in 1827 to work for the American Fur Company. He established a post east of the Black Hills at the mouth of Rapid Creek in about 1830. Known as the Ogallala Trading Post, the building was burned, and Sarpy killed, in January 1832, when he or one of his traders accidentally knocked a lighted candle into a keg of gunpowder. Thus ended his short career among the southern Lakotas.

The relatively peaceful fur trade era soon gave way to open conflict between Indians and whites in the Black Hills country (fig. 15.1). A new kind of white man entered Indian territory—not to trade but to take. Gold, minerals, grazing land, even the bones from the old buffalo jumps were all objects of his desire. Treaties were forgotten in the mania of the 1875–76 Black Hills gold rush. The Lakotas and Cheyennes proved formidable enemies, as Custer, Fetterman, and Grattan were to learn the hard way. These Indians defeated the U.S. Army in fight after fight, but in the long run the unseen enemies—starvation and disease—would prove unconquerable.

When non-native people entered the Black Hills country, they, too, began to leave marks on the rocks. These are easily distinguished from the Indian rock art. Most are names and dates. The few pictures are different from the Indian designs. Whereas the Indian art was concerned primarily with religious matters, the non-Indian inscriptions are nearly all secular. Like modern graffiti, these inscriptions and paintings are essentially egocentric and disconnected from any sense of awe, beauty, or reverence for place. They seem to express an attitude of dominance over place that is lacking in most Indian rock art, and they seem to reflect a childish desire to make one's mark on the environment and thereby, in some sense, to claim

Figure 15.1. This petroglyph illustrates one form of Indian-white conflict—Indians raiding the horses of whites entering their territories. This lightly incised rock art from the Cave Hills shows a warrior riding a branded horse (site 39FA49). Indian ledger drawings from this era include brands to indicate horses or mules stolen from U.S. Cavalry herds.

ownership of it. In earlier times, the belief that the rock had its own living spirit prevented people from thoughtlessly changing its appearance. In traditional Plains Indian culture, supernatural power was believed to be diffused throughout all of creation, including plants, animals, rocks, and sky. In this tradition, one interacts with the rock as being to being. As a product of this interaction, rock art embodies a communication between living things. Western civilization brought a different attitude to the environment, considering it lifeless raw material to be used and subdued as human enterprise dictated.

The first and most famous of the historic inscriptions are from the Black Hills expedition of 1874. One is near the town of Custer, South Dakota, and another is on top of Inyan Kara Mountain in Wyoming. These are chiseled into granite and are generally agreed to be authentic. One is George Armstrong Custer's name, and the other his initials. Apparently he had them carved merely to mark his passage into territory that had not previously been explored by white men—at least not any who survived to tell about it. At Ludlow Cave, several members of the expedition carved their names or initials into the soft sandstone; at least one such inscription survives today (fig. 15.2).

In Red Canyon, along the main trail leading into the Black Hills from the south, are reminders of the

Figure 15.2. This inscription was made near Ludlow Cave by a member of Custer's 1874 Black Hills expedition. Several members of the expedition had the initials *J. T.* (Photo by Phil Henry; reproduced with permission.)

some of the earliest non-native travel routes and set-tlements. Along the old Deadwood-Cheyenne stage line are carved several names and dates from the two years, 1876–77, during which the stagecoach used this trail. The Red Canyon trail was soon abandoned for a more easily defended route. The Black Hills were still Lakota and Cheyenne territory at this time, and the lumbering stage coach was an easy target for warriors angered at the trespass. A sign at the entrance to the canyon read, "Look to your rifles well, For this is the Canyon of Hell, the Red Canyon."[2] A small army post was established at the mouth of the canyon to protect the stage and freight wagons entering the Red Canyon road.[3] Some of the names and dates in Red Canyon may be those of men stationed at Camp Collier for its short two years of operation (fig. 15.3).

Other historic inscriptions were made to com-memorate the early white settlement of the Black Hills country. A sandstone boulder in the southern Cave Hills is covered with the names of the original settlers in that portion of Harding County. Other early inscriptions are scattered throughout the Black Hills country. Most are merely names or initials and dates. A rock art panel in a southern Black Hills canyon bears a set of cattle brands, including that of the famous XIT Ranch (fig. 15.4). It stands today as a reminder of the region's boom times, when cattle were king on the northern Great Plains.[4]

A few petroglyphs seem to have been made merely to pass the time. A fine carving of a nude woman dancer adorns a high cliff along the Cheyenne River (fig. 15.5). It occurs near, but not over, Indian

Figure 15.3. Although damaged by vandalism, the date on this inscription can still be read as June 16, 1877. It may bear the name of a soldier at Camp Collier or a stagecoach passenger passing along the old Red Canyon route. Neither the day nor the year is correct for the Black Hills expedition. Although the name Ludlow is correct for Custer's chief engineer, William Ludlow, the initial does not appear to be a *W.*

Figure 15.4. This panel of cattle brands in the southern Black Hills occupies a secluded side canyon.

carvings. An elaborate inscription in the northwestern Black Hills appears to have been the special project of an early woman settler there (fig. 15.6).

The main message of non-Indian rock art in the Black Hills country is simply "I was here." One can almost excuse the earliest non-Indian settlers for wanting to record that they had survived the trek to the Black Hills. They were, literally and figuratively, carving out a place for themselves in a new country. Like all invading cultures, they sometimes sought to erase the traces of those whose country they took over. Some perceived the Indian carvings and paintings as signs of a non-Christian, and therefore evil, religious system. They believed it was their religious and patriotic duty to eradicate these, or at least to provide their own signs of Euro-American culture in the new territories. Although most of the postcontact carvings lack the religiosity so integral to the Indian rock art, a few inscriptions contain Christian slogans or symbols. Other settlers may have hoped that friends or family would see their names along the trail and discover in that way news of their journey. Others simply dismissed the Indian rock art as a quaint but irrelevant remnant of a dying culture, not worth preserving. Just as the Indians' pervading religiosity is mutely recorded in the rock art, the white man's desire to put his stamp on nature is recorded in the hundreds of thoughtlessly carved or spray-painted graffiti that mar the rock art sites. Each mirrors the cultural environment in which it was made.

Figure 15.5. This graceful nude on a cliff in the southern Black Hills is easily distinguished from the Indian rock art at the same locale. Its exact age and creator are unknown.

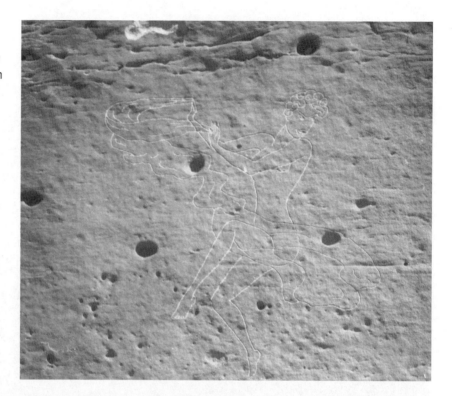

Figure 15.6. This elaborate inscription was the work of an early woman settler in the northern Black Hills.

A Disappearing Treasure

The rock art of the Black Hills country is a fragile and rapidly disappearing record of the past. In the Cave Hills, petroglyphs are carved into soft sandstones that flake away at a finger touch and yield only too easily to the knives of vandals (fig. 16.1). Many of the best examples of rock art are inside rock overhangs. As the soft sediments below the caprock erode away, these natural shelters become undermined and collapse, often taking the petroglyphs with them. For example, the mouth of Ludlow Cave has collapsed at least twice since it was first described in print. The collapse has formed a huge rubble cone in front of the cave. It is unlikely that many of the hundreds of petroglyphs once present in the cave survived the collapse. Although painted rock art was observed in the Cave Hills in the early 1900s,[1] none exists today. Many of the petroglyphs recorded in the 1920s are gone or faded. Cave Hills rock art is literally disappearing before our eyes.

Little can be done about the natural erosion and rock fall that threaten the Cave Hills rock art. An even greater threat, however, is the human one. Vandalism, looting, road construction, and mining all take a toll on the Cave Hills rock art. These preventable activities are actively destroying what remains of the spectacular body of rock art adorning this area. Road construction and mineral exploration on federal portions of the Cave Hills—where most of the rock art is found—are now regulated by laws designed to protect important archaeological resources, including rock art. Vandalism and looting are prohibited by state and federal law, but too many visitors to the area are ignorant or defiant of these regulations. One shield petroglyph was hacked out of a cave wall and carried off. Another was destroyed in the process (fig. 16.1). Numerous others have been worn away by people and cattle brushing against the sandstone surfaces. Even more have been ruined by the impulse to add names, dates, and slogans beside or over the petroglyphs. One South Dakota entrepreneur is now selling reproductions of rock art that he claims are made from actual casts. One can only hope his claims are exaggerated, because few activities are more destructive to petroglyphs than attempting to make casts of them.

Ignorance is little excuse for these behaviors. The U.S. Forest Service has placed signs at the entrance to

Figure 16.1. Vandalized Cave Hills petroglyph panel, site 39FA232.

the Cave Hills and in some of the Black Hills canyons explaining the regulations concerning archaeological remains. The controversial case involving a *Tyrannosaurus rex* fossil from central South Dakota received national media attention and has served as a reminder of laws protecting archaeological and scientific resources on federal land. Disdain for the law, and for the fragile traces of human history represented by the rock art, is the root of the problem.

If this rock art is to be preserved for everyone's enjoyment and enlightenment, law-abiding citizens must teach their friends and children that defacing and stealing rock art are unacceptable. Parents and communities must monitor the activities of young people, whose drinking parties have led to much of the damage seen today. Archaeologists, teachers, and all those who appreciate the value of these rare finds must take time to educate others about their significance. Everyone must learn to visit these places with-

out touching the petroglyphs, covering them with chalk or casting medium, brushing against the surfaces on which they are made, or picking up artifacts. Horses and hiking boots can be especially destructive to the fragile archaeological deposits lying below rock art panels. We all must learn to be circumspect about bringing visitors to unprotected sites. If each one tells two other people about the site, and they in turn tell others, the site location quickly becomes well known. Some of the visitors may have little or no understanding of the importance of rock art and how to avoid damaging it, or they may lack the maturity to make responsible decisions about activities at these places.

In the Black Hills proper, rock art is less directly threatened by natural erosion. In general, the sandstones there are harder and less likely to spall away or collapse. Vandalism is an ongoing threat in the Black Hills, but not as severe a problem as in the Cave Hills. Some sites on private land were heavily damaged by vandalism in the early decades of the twentieth century. Many of the most promising archaeological deposits associated with rock art in the southern Black Hills have been destroyed by unauthorized digging. This has been motivated more by curiosity than by greed. People have just been curious to see what they could find in the dirt below rock art panels. Ironically, the ensuing damage has ensured that many questions about Black Hills rock art will never be answered. Well-designed research motivated by anthropological and scientific curiosity about these sites—from which everyone can benefit—has been thwarted by idle curiosity, from which no one benefits. The same site can either enhance someone's private arrowhead collection—never to be seen or studied—or enhance for all generations our culture's understanding of those who came before.

In the Black Hills, the road to rock art ruin has often been paved with good intentions. Various people have traced over rock art with chalk, hoping to obtain better photographs of it. Unfortunately, the chalk proved difficult or impossible to remove, and the photographs told more about the mind of the chalker than that of the original artist. The most impressive of the three Vertical Series panels in the Black Hills was totally defaced by a well-meaning person. He first chalked the paintings and then attempted, unsuccessfully, to remove the chalk with a scrub brush and water. What remains of the rock art is now obscured by a fog of white chalk and brush marks. Others have attempted to make casts or rubbings of the rock art. These processes remove tiny bits of the surface containing the rock art, thus hastening its destruction. They may also leave unsightly residues of wax or latex on the rock. Any residue—chalk, charcoal pencil, wax, and even the oil from one's fingers—changes the rock chemistry. This may hasten deterioration of the rock surface and may interfere with chemical dating techniques.

Other damage has been the result of sheer ignorance and vanity (fig. 16.2). The story of the destruction

Figure 16.2. Fortunately, most people did not agree that defacing rock art on public lands was a good way to usher in the new millennium. Although a party of six people forever immortalized their ignorance in the southern Black Hills in 2000, only one actually destroyed an ancient petroglyph with his monument to himself.

of the lone Black Hills shell mask petroglyph was related in a previous chapter. Several members of a family carved their names into the impressive red cliffs of a southern Black Hills canyon, forever marring its beauty and destroying an ancient petroglyph in the process. All of these graffiti makers were on federal land and should have known better, even if they did not see the rock art they were destroying. They are now subject to federal prosecution, fines, and imprisonment as the result of their thoughtless act of vanity. Many rock art sites in the Black Hills bear bullet scars. Apparently, some area marksmen take a perverse pride in their ability to hit a large, unmoving target at close range. Perhaps other sportsmen could encourage them to visit a shooting range instead.

Those who enjoy rock art and the natural environment should vow first to do no harm. Taking photographs and making sketches are harmless activities that allow visitors to take the rock art home without harming it. Site visitors simply need to remember not to touch or step on the rock art or to disturb the dirt beneath it. State and federal archaeologists charged with protecting these sites will appreciate receiving copies of photographs, sketches, and notes. Interested individuals can make a real contribution to the study and protection of rock art sites in this way.

Another important contribution is simply to monitor the condition of the sites one stops to visit. Is there evidence of new looting or vandalism? Is the rock art threatened by other kinds of activities or natural erosion? Let the state archaeologist or Forest Service personnel know, so they can take steps to prevent further damage. If the site is on private land, encourage the landowner to keep an eye on it and to bar any visitors who might damage the site. Teach others how to enjoy rock art without damaging it. Finally, don't participate in the sale or purchase of any kind of archaeological remains. Doing so only provides a ready market for items stolen from public land and promotes irreparable destruction of sites.

Archaeological sites are a nonrenewable resource. They are a part of everyone's heritage. Rock art sites are a unique kind of archaeological resource in that they can be immediately experienced, enjoyed, and pondered by those who visit them. They provide a unique bridge across the centuries and across cultures. It is our collective responsibility now to explore and use this fragile bridge while protecting all of its components for future time-travelers.

Tracks in the Stone

What are the lessons of the tracks so many people left behind as rock engravings and paintings on the rocky cliffs and in the caves of the Black Hills country? Even the best tracker cannot read the entire message, but the rock art still has much to tell the careful observer about those who came before. From it, we can learn something about who those people were, how they lived, what they believed in, and how one group interacted with another.

The Black Hills have been recognized as a place apart for many thousands of years. Pecked Realistic rock art literally stamped the southern canyons as places of power for Archaic hunters. Large, complex scenes of the hunt were painstakingly chiseled into the sandstone surfaces of the canyons of the southern Black Hills (fig. 17.1). Although these canyons are deeper now, they would have been impressive passageways into and out of the Black Hills even during the period when sediment piled up to form the surfaces on which the artists stood so many centuries ago. Then, as now, these canyons provided water and browse for deer and other game animals. The hunting scenes apparently continued to be made and refreshed

over several thousand years—making them one of the longest-lived artistic endeavors in history. This Archaic period rock art was made before the bow and arrow came into use in the northern plains and perhaps extends as far back in time as the late Paleo-indian period.

Pecked Realistic rock art in the Black Hills was a hunters' art. Nearly all the recorded panels show either game animals or hunting scenes. The carefully detailed panels illustrate a complex hunting technique using large nets as game traps. Men, women, and children worked together to drive animals into the enclosures, where they could be killed with atlatl, thrusting spear, or club. Other hunting weapons shown in Pecked Realistic rock art include goads, throwing sticks, rabbit snares, and items that cannot be readily identified.

Although Pecked Realistic rock art lacks the strange abstract designs typical of trance-related art, it illustrates spiritual concerns in other ways. The costumed figures that enliven the hunting scenes probably represent people with special powers to lure or control the animals. Lines of elaborately costumed

Figure 17.1. This pecked hunting scene is stranded high above the present surface
at site 39FA681 in the southern Black Hills.

dancers—some in a state of sexual arousal—provide a glimpse of a rich tradition of hunt-related ritual, perhaps involving trance seeking. Two other kinds of figures also suggest that shamanism was interwoven with the hunt. One is exemplified by a panel showing a man apparently flying or floating above a hunting scene. The sensation of flying or rising above one's temporarily lifeless body is a common trance experience. The other kind of shamanic art shows creatures in various stages of transformation between human and deer states. These range from humans with upraised, antlerlike hands and a deer with human feet to a dancing human with a full set of antlers on his head. The transformation between human and animal states is another common trance experience. This experience undoubtedly had special resonance among hunting people, who literally lived by the transformation of animal into human flesh.

Most Pecked Abstract rock art (fig. 17.2) dates later than the Pecked Realistic hunters' art and earlier than the incised and ground rock art found throughout the Black Hills country and northern Great Plains. The dizzying arrays of spirals, waves, concentric circles, and grids that form Pecked Abstract rock art are typical of rock art found throughout much of the American West but largely lacking from the Great Plains. Essentially the same set of abstract designs can be found throughout the world in art related to trance states. These designs depict the phenomena known as phosphenes or entoptics—images perceived by the brain in the absence of visual stimuli. Because such hallucinations are universally experienced by people undergoing trance, art depicting them is frequently associated with trance seeking or other shamanic activity.

The pronounced contrast between Pecked Realistic hunting scenes and Pecked Abstract designs invites speculation about cultural changes. In fact, the reasons for this dramatic shift in art style are unclear. Perhaps the two kinds of art represent two separate groups of people who occupied the area consecutively. Perhaps an older religious tradition developed into or was displaced by a newer one that included trance seeking and production of rock art. It is equally probable that trance seeking was a part of early religious traditions all along, but that rock art did not play a part in this activity until later. Perhaps environmental changes or new hunting techniques led to the abandonment of the carefully orchestrated communal game hunts illustrated in the earlier rock art. Unfortunately, other archaeological data from the area are silent on these questions, and the art traditions are too remote in time to be confidently linked to any historic Indian groups and their customs (fig. 17.3).

Another early rock art style in the Black Hills is even more enigmatic. With just three examples at two sites, the dark red painted designs can indicate only that another rock art tradition occurred between or concurrent with the Pecked Realistic and Pecked Abstract traditions. These painted designs are reminiscent of painted rock art at the Medicine Lodge Creek site in Wyoming's Bighorn basin. The meaning of this tenuous connection is unclear.

The last two millennia witnessed another great blossoming of rock art traditions in the Black Hills country. These included several kinds of rock art made by either incising or painting the rock surface. They express a variety of themes, from warfare and eagle trapping to the continuity of human life.

Little information is available to date the painted designs that occur here and there in the southern Black Hills. A few panels of Painted Realistic rock art clustered in a southern Black Hills canyon resemble art from the Oneota archaeological complex, centered in the upper Mississippi region and extending from Wisconsin to Kansas and as far west as eastern South Dakota. Because the Poncas were the only Oneota-related people known to have traveled as far west as the Black Hills, this rock art may have been made by Poncas periodically revisiting the canyon during treks far from their villages near the Platte-Missouri confluence. So far, area archaeologists have been unable to confirm more exactly the connection between the Poncas and this part of the Black Hills. Whoever created them, these panels appear to have been made during occasional visits to the canyon for religious purposes. The art shows fantastic creatures and a human with upraised hands and no legs. Although their specific meaning can no longer be understood, they seem to express ideas of transformation and power.

Figure 17.2. This Pecked Abstract–style rock art is located in rimrock overlooking a southern Black Hills canyon. Site 39FA680.

Figure 17.3. This pecked rock art from the eastern Black Hills contains both animals and abstract designs. Site 39PN439.

Other painted art widely scattered throughout the southern Black Hills shows animals and weapons. Bears, bison, humans, arrows or darts, spears, and abstract designs are the most common elements of this style (fig. 17.4). Neither the tribal affiliation nor the meaning of this art can be determined from the small sample available for study, but some of it may be related to vision questing or other individual religious activities. Many of the animals are "killed"—impaled by darts or spears—suggesting that some of this art may be related to prayers for success in hunting. But because animals are sometimes used as symbols of spirit powers, it is also possible that a less literal interpretation of this theme is called for. If some of the weapons shown in the art are indeed atlatls and darts, then these paintings are more than 2,000 years old. Perhaps the discovery of more examples—or datable pigments—will one day reveal the age, authorship, and meaning of this art.

Vertical Series art occurs at only three or four sites in the Black Hills (fig. 17.5) but is widely scattered throughout the northwestern plains from southern Alberta to central Montana, northern Wyoming, and western South Dakota. Some of the symbols can be recognized from historic Plains Indian picture writing, but most are indecipherable. This rock art could have been made by any or all of several tribes, including the Blackfeet, Crows, Lakotas, Poncas, and Cheyennes. Lakota oral tradition tells of sites in the Black Hills and Bighorns containing inscriptions that could be interpreted only by religious specialists. Because this kind of rock art occurs in these two areas, perhaps it is the rock art told of long ago. Because the symbols cannot be readily interpreted, as can other kinds of picture writing, it seems most likely that they were intended to take on different meanings at different times. The few symbols that can be interpreted refer to the passage of time, hunting, and success in battle. Some may also refer to more abstract ideas, such as the earth center and the spirit realms above and below the earth's surface.

Throughout the northern plains, three intertwined themes inform most incised rock art dating to the last 2,000 years. These are combat, the renewal of life, and spiritual power. Early warrior art—sometimes referred to as the Ceremonial style—shows warriors with large body shields (fig. 17.6). Some of the warriors have bear paws for feet, and other images have animals near or connected to the warrior. This suggests that the image represents not just the warrior with his distinctive gear but also symbols of the powers given to him by spirit helpers. Later warrior art—sometimes termed biographical art—shows warriors in action. Like much historic ledger art, biographical panels tell the stories of individual warriors' coups. They functioned both to celebrate and publicize brave deeds and to warn away potential intruders.

Women's special status was celebrated in art illustrating a spiritual connection between women of child-bearing age and the buffalo. A constellation of deeply incised and abraded rock art included vulva designs, animal tracks, handprints, footprints, and many hundreds of abraded grooves (fig. 17.7). The grooves may have been produced as girls and women made bone awls and other bone tools needed for the womanly arts. In this way, the groove might have become a symbol of womanhood and the continuity of life, just as the awl itself was.

In traditional Plains Indian culture, both men and women were expected to act for the benefit of the larger group: men by hunting and providing protection from enemies, women by turning the product of the hunt into food and shelter and by producing and nurturing children. Both men and women sought spirit helpers to aid them in these great tasks. This is the context that brings the seemingly diverse incised rock art together into a single artistic tradition.

Figure 17.4. Darts or arrows, atlatls, game animals, and a human are included in this panel of black painted rock art. Site 39FA88, southern Black Hills.

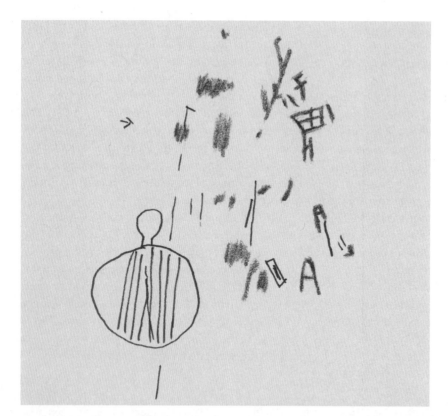

Figure 17.5. The red painted designs that occur with this incised shield-bearing warrior and vulva may be the remains of a Vertical Series panel, but the designs can no longer be clearly seen. Oil Creek, Wyoming, southwestern Black Hills.

Figure 17.6. This lightly incised image of a shield-bearing warrior carefully records the appearance of a precontact-era body shield. Site 39HN199, north Cave Hills.

Figure 17.7. Deeply carved vulvas, female figures, and grooves are tucked inside a tiny rockshelter at site 39FA676 in the southern Black Hills.

With the coming of non-Indians, a new kind of rock marking began. Names, dates, and cattle brands were stamped into the landscape. Rather than a medium for religious expression, the rocky surfaces became message boards on which newcomers recorded their passing.

Not every example of rock art in the Black Hills country fits into these categories. Some, like the strange, swirled faces in Medicine Creek Cave, are unique. Their origin and meaning remain obscure. Other kinds of rock art, such as the handful of dark red geometric figures in the southern Black Hills and the simple pecked heads found at a single site on the Cheyenne River, suggest more extensive early rock art traditions, now mostly erased by erosion. Not all Indian rock art was religiously motivated, and not all non-Indian inscriptions were secular. It is impossible to study this body of rock art without recognizing its great complexity and diversity.

The rock art of the Black Hills country does have one thing in common: virtually all of it was made in response to the natural surroundings. Whether marking or protecting trails, commemorating successful battles, hunts, or vision quests, invoking spiritual aid, or announcing the arrival of explorers or settlers, the rock inscriptions are purposefully located within the larger landscape (fig. 17.8). Some rock art marks places of spiritual power; other rock art denotes areas where game could be easily taken. Some rock art records the successive movement of diverse peoples along the natural passages into and around the Black Hills and Cave Hills. At Ludlow Cave and Medicine Creek Cave, petroglyphs help define a sacred zone related to the renewal of the bison herds and life itself. Warrior art lining natural passes in the Cave Hills perhaps served to warn away potential intruders, whereas names and dates carved along the old stagecoach routes seem to claim the area for a new people.

Figure 17.8. Incised rock art on the ceiling of a small perched rockshelter may record vision experiences. Site 39HN121, north Cave Hills. (Photo by Phil Henry; reproduced with permission.)

Both settlers and Indians were attracted to the Black Hills country for its special resources. To the Indian, it was the source of lodgepoles, deer, shelter in winter, and water in summer. It was the home of powerful spirits. To the whites, it was the source of gold, timber, and an even more valuable resource—prime cattle country. The kind of art each group produced reflects the way it viewed the Black Hills country. For some it was a place to take the deer, elk, and bison on which life depended. For others it was a place to seek out visions and spiritual power. For some it was a treasure house to be jealously guarded. For some it was the object of pilgrimages; for others, of exploration. Some came to give; some came to take away. Many of them left behind the traces of their passing in the form of engravings, paintings, and inscriptions. The story they wrote together is the story of human life in the Black Hills country.

Notes

Chapter 1. The Black Hills Country and Its People

1. Sundstrom, "Sacred Black Hills."

2. Bowers, *Mandan Social and Ceremonial Organization;* Bowers, *Hidatsa Social and Ceremonial Organization;* Sundstrom, *Material Culture of Ludlow Cave;* James H. Howard, *Ponca Tribe.*

3. Turner, *Mammals of the Black Hills;* Froiland, *Natural History of the Black Hills.*

4. Buechel, *Lakota Tales and Texts,* 94–96; DeMallie, *Sixth Grandfather,* 309–10; LaPointe, *Legends of the Lakota,* 17–20; Densmore, *Teton Sioux Music,* 319; Stands in Timber and Liberty, *Cheyenne Memories;* Powell, *Sweet Medicine,* 472–77; Marquis and Limbaugh, *Cheyenne and Sioux,* 30.

5. Turner, *Mammals of the Black Hills,* 20; see also Nicholas Black Elk, quoted in DeMallie, *Sixth Grandfather,* 155.

6. Schell, *History of South Dakota;* Hyde, *Red Cloud's Folk.*

7. Jackson, *Custer's Gold;* Ludlow, *Report of a Reconnaissance.*

8. Sundstrom, *Culture History.*

9. Fiedel, "Older than We Thought"; Eighmy and LaBelle, "Radiocarbon Dating."

10. For reviews of current evidence on the peopling of the Americas, see Fiedel, "Peopling of the New World"; Strauss, "Solutrean Settlement"; Meltzer, "Discovery of Deep Time"; Strauss et al., *Humans at the End of the Ice Age.*

11. Lahren and Bonnichsen, "Bone Foreshafts"; Owsley and Hunt, "Clovis and Early Archaic Period Crania."

12. Hannus, "Lange-Ferguson Site: An Event of Clovis Mammoth Butchery"; Hannus, "Lange-Ferguson Site: A Case for Mammoth Bone Butchering Tools."

13. Frison, *Prehistoric Hunters,* 85.

14. Frison and Stanford, *Agate Basin Site,* 143–56.

15. Donohue, "Progress on the Investigation."

16. Frison and Stanford, *Agate Basin Site;* Agogino and Frankforter, "Brewster Site."

17. Frison and Stanford, *Agate Basin Site.*

18. Hofman and Ingbar, "Folsom Hunting Overlook"; Kornfeld, "Rocky Foolsm Site"; Noisat, *National Register Evaluation of Sixteen Cultural Resources.*

19. Agenbroad, *Hudson-Meng Site;* Todd, "Excavation, Research, and Public Interpretation"; Wheeler, *Preliminary Appraisal;* Hannus, "Report on 1985 Test Excavations"; Frison and Stanford, *Agate Basin Site.*

20. Donohue, "Progress on the Investigation."

21. Sundstrom, *Culture History.*

22. Tratebas, "Black Hills Settlement Patterns."

23. Frison, *Prehistoric Hunters.*

24. Frison, *Prehistoric Hunters,* second edition.

25. For example, see Aaberg, "Plant Macrofossil Record"; Sundstrom, "Moveable Feast."

26. Irwin-Williams, Irwin, and Haynes, "Hell Gap."

27. Antevs, "Great Basin."

28. Sheehan, "Cultural Responses to the Altithermal or Inadequate Sampling?"; Sheehan, "Cultural Responses Reconsidered"; Artz, "Cultural Response or Geological Process?"

29. L. Alex, *Archaeology of Beaver Creek Shelter;* Martin et al., "Beaver Creek Shelter."

30. Vallejo, *Level III Heritage Resources Inventory;* Donohue, Abbott, and Rhodd, "Excavation at Boulder Creek Rock Shelter"; Schneider et al., *Data Recovery Investigations;* Hannus et al., *Archeological Mitigation;* Sundstrom et al., *Blaine Site.*

31. Frison, *Prehistoric Hunters,* second edition; Frison, Wilson, and Wilson, "Fossil Bone and Artifacts."

32. Michael Fosha, South Dakota Archaeological Research Center, personal communication, October 2000.

33. Sundstrom, *Culture History;* Tratebas, "Black Hills Settlement Patterns"; Frison, *Prehistoric Hunters,* second edition.

34. Larson, "Housepits and Mobile Hunter-Gatherers."

35. Wedel, *Prehistoric Man,* 249–55; Husted, *Bighorn Canyon Archeology;* Syms, "McKean Complex"; Benedict and Olson, "Origin of the McKean Complex"; Black, "Archaic Continuity"; Bender and Wright, "High-Altitude Occupations."

36. Sundstrom, *Culture History;* Tratebas, "Black Hills Settlement Patterns"; Frison, *Prehistoric Hunters,* second edition.

37. Frison, *Prehistoric Hunters,* second edition, 188–91.

38. Sundstrom, "Moveable Feast"; Keyser, "Evidence for McKean Complex Plant Utilization."

39. Keyser and Davis, "Lightning Spring"; Mulloy, "McKean Site"; Mulloy, *Preliminary Historical Outline;* Kornfeld, Frison, and Larson, "Keyhole Reservoir Archaeology"; Steege and Paulley, "Lissolo Cave"; Buechler, *Report of Data Retrieval;* Tratebas and Vagstad, *Archaeological Test Excavations;* Noisat and Campbell, *Cultural Resources Inventory;* Donohue, "Progress on the Investigation"; Miller, *National Register Evaluation of 39CU466;* Noisat, *National Register Evaluation of Twelve Cultural Resources.*

40. Hovde, "Hermosa Tipi Ring Site."

41. L. Alex, *Archaeology of Beaver Creek Shelter;* Martin et al., "Beaver Creek Shelter"; Donohue, Abbott, and Rhodd, "Excavation at Boulder Creek Rock Shelter"; Wheeler, *Archeological Remains;* Schneider et al., *Data Recovery Investigations.*

42. Gant and Hurt, "39MD9, The Gant Site"; Reher, "Silver King Mine Survey"; Sundstrom, *Hermosa-Hayward Project.*

43. Tratebas, "Black Hills Settlement Patterns."

44. Carlson et al., "Sidney Burial."

45. Frison, *Prehistoric Hunters,* second edition, 194–99.

46. McKibbin et al., *Archaeological Excavations at 48CA1391;* Hovde, "Hermosa Tipi Ring Site"; Hovde, *Archaeological Investigations of Stone Circle Sites.*

47. Neuman, *Sonota Complex.*

48. Frison, *Prehistoric Hunters,* second edition, 199–211.

49. Schneider et al., *Data Recovery Investigations;* McKibbin, *Archaeological Investigations at 38WE320;* Mulloy, "McKean Site"; Mulloy, *Preliminary Historical Outline;* Kornfeld, Frison, and Larson, "Keyhole Reservoir Archaeology."

50. Frison, *Prehistoric Hunters,* second edition, 211–12.

51. Lehmer, *Introduction;* R. Alex, "Village Sites Off the Missouri River."

52. Haug et al., *Archaeological Excavations in Highway 18 Right-of-Way;* Tratebas, *Archaeological Excavations near Stone Quarry Canyon.*

53. Reher and Frison, *Vore Site.*

54. L. Alex, "39BU2: A Fortified Site"; R. Alex, "Village Sites Off the Missouri River."

55. Tratebas, "Black Hills Settlement Patterns."

56. Sundstrom, *Living on the Edge.*

57. For summaries of tribal movements during the postcontact era, see Reher, "Ethnology and Ethnohistory"; Reher and Frison, *Vore Site;* Greiser, "Late Prehistoric Cultures"; Schlesier, *Plains Indians;* McGinnis, *Counting Coup;* Bamforth, *Ecology and Human Organization on the Great Plains;* Hodge, *Handbook of American Indians North of Mexico.*

58. Grinnell, *Cheyenne Indians,* 1: 31; Mooney, *Calendar History.*

59. Hyde, *Red Cloud's Folk.*

60. McGinnis, *Counting Coup.*

61. Hyde, *Red Cloud's Folk.*

62. Mooney, *Ghost-Dance Religion.*

63. Sundstrom, *Rock Art of the Southern Black Hills: Contextual Approach;* Keyser, "Graphic Example."

64. Buckles, "Analysis of Primitive Rock Art."

Chapter 2. Windows to the Past

1. David Whitley, in *The Art of the Shaman: Rock Art of California,* lists the following elements as definitive of shamanism: individual practitioners believed to maintain direct and personal links with the supernatural world; visionary experiences (trance and vision); belief in supernaturally based healing, sorcery, and control of natural elements such as the weather and animals; belief in spirit worlds above and below the earth's surface; and belief in supernatural ("spirit") helpers that protect and aid individuals.

2. Various rock art dating methods are discussed in Wellmann, *Survey,* 20–24; Watchman, "Potential Methods for Dating Rock Paintings"; Russ, Hyman, and Rowe, "Dating and Chemical Analysis"; Russ et al., "Radiocarbon Dating"; Loy et al., "Accelerator Radiocarbon Dating"; Keyser, *Indian Rock Art of the Columbia Plateau,* 17–20; Sanger and Meighan, *Discovering Prehistoric Rock Art,* 172–79; Roberts et al., "Luminescence Dating"; Dorn, "Change of Perspective"; Dorn, "Chronometric Techniques."

3. For a detailed discussion of the use of context in interpreting art, see chapter 2 in Sundstrom, *Rock Art of the Southern Black Hills: Contextual Approach.*

4. David Lewis-Williams, in *Believing and Seeing: Symbolic Meaning in Southern San Rock Paintings,* provides a classic discussion of the use of metaphor in rock art.

5. For example, see Bement, *Bison Hunting at Cooper Site.*

6. Nagy, "Cheyenne Shields."

Chapter 3. Explorations

1. Krause and Olson, *Prelude to Glory.*

2. Brevet General George Armstrong Custer, US Army, letter to Assistant Adjutant General, Department of Dakota, July 15, 1874; Custer, *Boots and Saddles;* Carroll and Frost, *Private Theodore Ewert's Diary;* Frost, *With Custer in '74,* 30.

3. T. Lewis, "Ancient Rock Inscriptions"; T. Lewis, "Incised Boulders."

4. McLaughlin, *Myths and Legends of the Sioux,* 104–7.

5. Will, "Some Observations."

6. H. Smith, "Archaeological Reconnaissance."

7. Renaud, "Southern Wyoming and Southwestern South Dakota"; Helgevold, *History of South Dakota Archaeology.*

8. L. Buker, "Archaeology of the Southern Black Hills."

9. F. Buker, *Black Hills Archaeology.*

10. Frank Buker, letter to Forest Ranger Beals, Black Hills National Forest, April 12, 1932, photocopy in author's files.

11. Miscellaneous correspondence, Black Hills National Forest, 1932, photocopies in author's files.

12. Meleen and Pruitt, *Preliminary Report.*

13. Site files, South Dakota Archaeological Research Center, Rapid City.

14. Over, "Prehistoric Flint Quarry"; Over, "Archaeology of Ludlow Cave"; see also Over, "Indians Who Lived in Ludlow Cave."

15. Wheeler, *Preliminary Appraisal;* Wheeler, *Archeological Remains;* Hughes, "Investigations."

16. Sigstad and Jolley, *Archaeological Survey;* Haug, *Archaeological Reconnaissance;* Haug, *Cultural Resource Survey in Southern Black Hills;* Haug, *Cultural Resources Survey of Selected Silver King Mine Properties;* Chevance, *Archaeological Survey;* Chevance, *Cultural Resources Survey;* Lippincott, *Report of a Cultural Resources Survey;* Lippincott, *Archaeological Survey.*

17. Ott and Alexander, *Photographic Documentation.*

18. Dalla, *Hay Draw Timber Sale;* Slay and Smith, *Cultural Resources Survey;* Groenfeldt, *Cultural Resources Survey;* Chevance and Haug, *Archaeological Survey.*

19. Miscellaneous files, South Dakota Archaeological Research Center, Rapid City.

20. Correspondence, Black Hills National Forest and South Dakota Historic Preservation Office, photocopies in author's files

21. Sundstrom, *Rock Art of the Southern Black Hills, South Dakota and Wyoming.*

22. Field notes and site forms, South Dakota Archaeological Research Center, Rapid City.

23. Keyser and Sundstrom, *Rock Art of Western South Dakota.*

24. Sundstrom, *Rock Art of the Southern Black Hills: Contextual Approach.*

25. Sundstrom, *Fragile Heritage.*

26. Sundstrom, "Additional Rock Art Sites"; Sundstrom, *South Dakota Rock Art Survey II;* Sundstrom, *Fragile Heritage;* Sundstrom, *Material Culture of Ludlow Cave;* Sundstrom, *North Cave Hills Rock Art Survey 1997;* Sundstrom, *North Cave Hills Archaeological Survey 1998.*

27. Sundstrom, Olson, and Loendorf, *Hulett South Site.*

28. Cowan, *Heritage Resource Survey;* Weathermon, *Level III Heritage Resource Inventory.*

29. Sundstrom, *Draft Management Plan.*

Chapter 4. Plains Indians and Rock Art

1. LaPointe, *Legends of the Lakota,* 52.

2. Ibid., 52–53; Barbeau, *Indian Days,* 208; Stone, *First Encounters,* 26.

3. Poole, *Among the Sioux,* 75.

4. Clark, *Indian Sign Language,* 320.

5. For example, Oscar Howe, the well-known Lakota artist, noted that carved drawings on rocks foretold future events. Quoted in Maurer, *Visions of the People,* 161.

6. Nicholas Black Elk, quoted in DeMallie, *Sixth Grandfather,* 376.

7. Stone, *First Encounters,* 26.

8. John Around Him, quoted in E. Lewis, *Wo'Wakita,* 76. See also South Dakota Writers' Project, *Legends of the Mighty Sioux,* 110.

9. Custer, *Boots and Saddles,* 85; Drips, *Three Years*

among the Indians; Enoe, "Medicine Rock"; Stilgebouer and Stilgebouer, *Gettysburg, South Dakota;* Little, *River of People,* 46–47.

10. McLaughlin, *Myths and Legends of the Sioux,* 104–7.

11. Badhorse, "Petroglyphs"; DeMallie, *Sixth Grandfather,* 198; Neihardt, *Black Elk Speaks,* 111; Lame Deer and Erdoes, *Lame Deer,* 113–14.

12. Libby, *Arikara Narrative,* 79.

13. Hassrick, *The Sioux,* 195; Clark, *Indian Sign Language,* 320.

14. Coues, *History of the Expedition,* 236; Dorsey, *Study of Siouan Cults,* 328–29; Mallery, *Picture-Writing,* 32; Matthews, *Ethnography and Philology,* 50–51; North Dakota Writers' Project, *North Dakota,* 223; Thwaites, *Account of an Expedition,* 57–58; Thwaites, *Travels in the Interior,* 339–40.

15. Dempsey, *Amazing Death of Calf Shirt,* 125.

16. Dorsey, *Study of Siouan Cults,* 446–47; Howard, "Notes on the Ethnogeography."

17. Bray and Bray, *Joseph N. Nicollet,* 72–77, 84; Catlin, *Letters and Notes,* 1: 31, 234, 2: 163–73, 201–2; Clark, *Indian Sign Language,* 303; Gilmore, *Prairie Smoke,* 97; Howard, *Ponca Tribe,* 17; Johnson, *Life of Sitting Bull,* 213; Lynd, "History of the Dakotas"; McGee, *Siouan Indians,* 32; South Dakota Writer's Project, *Legends of the Mighty Sioux,* 45–46.

18. Hungry Wolf, *Blood People,* 290; Reeves and Kennedy, *Kunaitupii,* 164; Barbeau, *Indian Days,* 207–9; Klassen, Keyser, and Loendorf, "Bird Rattle's Petroglyphs."

19. Steinbring and Buchner, "Cathedrals of Prehistory."

20. Chamberlain, "Medicine Rock of Malta"; Grinnell, *Blackfoot Lodge Tales,* 262–63.

21. Ewers, "Medicine Rock of the Marias"; Schultz, *Blackfeet and Buffalo,* 375–76.

22. Park, "Simanton Petroglyph Hill Site."

23. Lame Deer and Erdoes, *Lame Deer,* 113–14; Grinnell, *Cheyenne Indians,* 2: 96; Marquis, *Wooden Leg,* 192.

24. Clark, *Indian Sign Language,* 320.

25. Grinnell, *Cheyenne Indians,* 2: 148.

26. Sundstrom, *Material Culture of Ludlow Cave.*

27. Ibid.

28. Custer, *Boots and Saddles,* 85; Drips, *Three Years among the Indians;* Enoe, "Medicine Rock."

29. Thwaites, *Account of an Expedition,* 57–58; Thwaites, *Travels in the Interior,* 339–40; Mackintosh, Roehrick, and Hunt, *North Dakota Historical Markers,* 110.

30. Lyle Nelson manuscript in 39RO33 site file, South Dakota Archaeological Research Center, Rapid City; Mooney, *Ghost-Dance Religion,* 968, 1022.

31. Amiotte, "Lakota Sun Dance," 86.

32. Chittendon and Richardson, *Life, Letters,* 1378–80.

33. Will, *Archaeology of the Missouri Valley,* 300.

34. Beckwith, *Mandan-Hidatsa Myths,* 305.

35. Pepper and Wilson, *Hidatsa Shrine,* 324; Gilbert Livingstone Wilson, unpublished field notes, 1910–13 (on file at the American Museum of Natural History, New York; the Minnesota Historical Society, St. Paul; and the Midwest Archeological Center, Lincoln, Nebraska; extracts published in Wood, *Origins of the Hidatsa Indians,* 193); Wood, *Papers in Northern Plains Prehistory,* 54.

36. Wormington and Forbis, *Introduction,* 170–71.

37. Klassen, Keyser, and Loendorf, "Bird Rattle's Petroglyphs."

38. T. Lewis, "Ancient Rock Inscriptions"; T. Lewis, "Incised Boulders"; North Dakota Writers' Project, *North Dakota,* 220, 289; Catlin, *Letters and Notes,* 2: 165–66.

39. Stands in Timber and Liberty, *Cheyenne Memories,* 104.

40. Howard, *Ponca Tribe,* 17–18.

41. Battiste Good (Brown Hat), quoted in Mallery, *Picture-Writing,* 289–90.

42. Clark, *Indian Sign Language,* 320; Hungry Wolf, *Blood People,* 290.

43. Hultkrantz, *Belief and Worship,* 35; Barbeau, *Indian Days,* 207–11.

44. Howard, *Ponca Tribe,* 17–18, 71.

45. Crow's Heart, quoted in Beckwith, *Mandan-Hidatsa Myths,* 306–7.

46. Steinbring and Buchner, "Cathedrals of Prehistory"; Sundstrom, *Material Culture of Ludlow Cave.*

47. Steinbring and Buchner, "Cathedrals of Prehistory"; Grinnell, *By Cheyenne Campfires,* 263; Snortland-Coles and Loendorf, "National Register Nomination Form"; Loendorf, "Preliminary Survey," 83; Chamberlain, "Medicine Rock of Malta."

Chapter 5. Ancient Hunters and the Idea of Transformation

1. Tratebas, "Stylistic Chronology."

2. Fiedel, "Older Than We Thought."

3. Dorn, "Change of Perspective"; Dorn, "Chronometric Techniques"; Beck et al., "Ambiguities."

4. Fredlund, "Late Quaternary Geomorphic History."

5. Frison, *Prehistoric Hunters.*

6. Frison et al., "Late Paleoindian Animal Trapping Net."

7. Map data from Wellmann, *Survey;* Mallery, *Picture-Writing;* Gebhard, "Petroglyphs of Wyoming"; Loendorf, "Results of Archeological Survey"; Nissen,

"Record of a Hunting Practice"; Nesbitt, *Stylistic Locales;* Schaafsma, *Rock Art of Utah;* Schaafsma, *Indian Rock Art of the Southwest;* Grant, Baird, and Pringle, *Rock Drawings.*

8. Frison et al., "Late Paleoindian Animal Trapping Net," 354.

9. Turner, *Mammals of the Black Hills,* 133–34.

Chapter 6. Glimpses of an Ancient Art

1. Keyser, "Pictographs at Desrosier Rockshelter."

2. Keyser and Knight, "Rock Art of Western Montana"; Keyser, "Audrey's Overhang"; Conner and Conner, *Rock Art;* Keyser, "Central Montana Rock Art Style."

Chapter 7. Archaic Seekers

1. Oster, "Phosphenes"; Knoll, Kugler, and Lawder, "Effects of Chemical Stimulation"; Kellogg, Knoll, and Kugler, "Form Similarity"; Lewis-Williams and Dowson, "Signs of All Times."

2. Kellogg, Knoll, and Kugler, "Form Similarity"; Riechel-Dolmatoff, "Drug-Induced Optical Sensations"; Lewis-Williams and Dowson, "Signs of All Times."

3. Riechel-Dolmatoff, "Drug-Induced Optical Sensations"; Riechel-Dolmatoff, *Beyond the Milky Way;* Furst, "Hallucinogens"; Whitley, "Ethnography and Rock Art."

4. Blackburn, "Biopsychological Aspects"; Hudson and Lee, "Function and Symbolism"; Hedges, "Phosphenes"; Hedges, "Shamanic Origins of Rock Art"; Whitley, "Ethnography and Rock Art"; Whitley, *Art of the Shaman.*

5. Wilbert, "Two Rock Art Sites"; Furst, "Shamanism"; Vastokas and Vastokas, *Sacred Art;* Hedges, "Patterned Body Anthropomorphs"; Hudson and Lee, "Function and Symbolism."

6. Compare Conkey, "Boundedness in Art and Society."

7. Map data from Mallery, *Picture-Writing;* Wellmann, *Survey;* Schaafsma, *Rock Art of Utah;* Schaafsma, *Indian Rock Art of the Southwest;* Grant, Baird, and Pringle, *Rock Drawings;* Cole, *Legacy on Stone.*

Chapter 8. Themes of Life and Renewal

1. Schlesier, *Plains Indians.*

2. Lehmer, *Introduction;* Zimmerman, *Peoples;* Winham and Lueck, "Cultures of the Middle Missouri."

3. Winham and Lueck, "Cultures of the Middle Missouri."

4. Michlovic, "Problem of the Teton Migration."

5. Wood, *Redbird Focus.*

6. Libby, *Arikara Narrative,* 163–64.

7. Krause and Olson, *Prelude to Glory,* 155, 160–63; Custer to Assistant Adjutant General; Custer, *Boots and Saddles,* 299; Carroll and Frost, *Private Theodore Ewert's Diary,* 17–20; Frost, *With Custer in '74,* 30; Libby, *Arikara Narrative,* 163–65.

8. Will, *Archaeology of the Missouri Valley,* 300; see also Bowers, *Hidatsa Social and Ceremonial Organization,* 369, 436.

9. Hoebel, *Cheyennes,* 89; Kroeber, *Arapaho,* plate 29; Linderman, *Plenty-Coups,* 61–64.

10. This petroglyph has sometimes been identified as a domesticated Brahma cow or bull, because of its unusual hump and horns. Such an identification can be ruled out for several reasons. First, Brahma cattle were not introduced into North America until 1849, and there were none outside of Texas, Louisiana, and the Deep South before 1906—long after the petroglyph was made. Second, American Brahma and Zebu cattle have very short, straight or slightly curved horns, not the lyre-shaped horns of the petroglyph, and they all have pedulous ears (drooping down along the sides of the face) and huge dewflaps—features missing from the petroglyph. Pictures of cattle appear in Plains Indian art from the postcontact period, but these bear little resemblance to the petroglyph. Instead, they show the flat-backed, long-horned, spotted Texas cattle that were favorite targets of Kiowa cattle raiders. By the time domesticated cattle reached the northern plains, Indian reservations had been established. Very little such raiding took place north of the Platte River. As in the southern plains, long-horned Texas cattle (which lack the kind of horns and hump shown in the petroglyph) were the standard in the northern plains. Since these would have contrasted with bison in their lack of a dorsal hump, it seems unlikely that Indian observers would have depicted them with a pronounced hump. For historic Plains Indian drawings of domestic cattle, see Merrill et al., *Guide to the Kiowa Collections,* and Berlo, *Plains Indian Drawings,* 23.

11. Mallery, *Picture-Writing,* plate 31; Winchell, *Aborigines of Minnesota,* 560–68; Conway and Conway, *Spirits on Stone,* 24; Secrist, *Pictographs,* 7; Richards and Richards, "Petroglyphs of the Russell Site," 18; O'Neill, *Kansas Rock Art,* 12.

12. See McHugh, *Time of the Buffalo.*

13. Bowers, *Hidatsa Social and Ceremonial Organization,* 445–49; Bowers, *Mandan Social and Ceremonial Organization,* 206–52.

14. Irwin, *Dream Seekers,* 216–17; Nicholas Black Elk, quoted in DeMallie, *Sixth Grandfather,* 241; Black Elk, *Sacred Pipe,* 122–25.

15. Nicholas Black Elk, quoted in DeMallie, *Sixth Grandfather,* 284.

16. Lame Deer and Erdoes, *Lame Deer,* 255.

17. Irwin, *Dream Seekers,* 217; Nicholas Black Elk, quoted in DeMallie, *Sixth Grandfather,* 379, 398; Black Elk, *Sacred Pipe,* 7, 122–26; Rice, *Ella Deloria's Iron Hawk,* 161–68; Lyford, *Quill and Beadwork,* 86.

18. Walker, *Lakota Belief,* 109–12; Black Elk, *Sacred Pipe,* 3–9; Standing Bear, *Land of the Spotted Eagle,* 220–22; DeMallie, *Sixth Grandfather,* 283–85; South Dakota Writer's Project, *Legends of the Mighty Sioux,* 49–51; M. Powers, *Oglala Women,* 43–49; Lame Deer and Erdoes, *Lame Deer,* 251–55.

19. Walker, *Sun Dance,* 79; Hassrick, *The Sioux,* 41–42.

20. Black Elk, *Sacred Pipe,* 116–26; Walker, *Sun Dance,* 79, 146–49; Walker, *Lakota Belief,* 241–55; M. Powers, *Oglala Women,* 66–69.

21. Black Elk, *Sacred Pipe,* 19.

22. W. Powers, "Winter Count."

23. Black Elk, *Sacred Pipe,* 28.

24. Fletcher, "White Buffalo Festival," 260–75, 271–72.

25. Black Elk, *Sacred Pipe,* 85.

26. Ibid., 134–35.

27. Ibid., 127–38; D. Smith, *Red Indian Experiences,* 121.

28. Bowers, *Mandan Social and Ceremonial Organization,* 324–28.

29. Kehoe, "Function of Ceremonial Intercourse."

30. Bowers, *Mandan Social and Ceremonial Organization,* 315–23.

31. Powell, *Sweet Medicine,* xxiii.

32. Bowers, *Hidatsa Social and Ceremonial Organization,* 204–7.

33. Linderman, *Pretty-Shield,* 147.

34. McHugh, *Time of the Buffalo;* C. Taylor, *Plains Indians,* 95; Powell, *Sweet Medicine;* Bowers, *Hidatsa Social and Ceremonial Organization;* Bowers, *Mandan Social and Ceremonial Organization;* Dorsey and Kroeber, *Traditions;* Parks, *Myths and Traditions.*

35. Fletcher and LaFlesche, *Omaha Tribe,* 518.

36. Parks, *Myths and Traditions,* 10.

37. Voget, "Sacred Numerology," 354.

38. Hall, *Archaeology of the Soul,* 188, n. 26.

39. A. Smith, *Shoshone Tales,* 75–76.

40. Wormington and Forbis, *Introduction,* 170–72; Hungry Wolf, *Blood People,* 258.

41. Map data from Wellmann, *Survey;* Mallery, *Picture-Writing;* Darroch, "Hoof, Hand, and Footprint Petroglyph"; Vastokas and Vastokas, *Sacred Art;* Park, "Simanton Petroglyph Hill Site"; Faulkner, *Rock Art of the Eastern Woodlands.*

42. Steward, "Petroglyphs of the United States"; Gifford, *Culture Element Distributions;* McGowan, "Female Fertility Themes"; Fenenga, Dillon, and Whitley, "Unusual Petroglyph"; G. Gough, "Indian Hill Ceremonial Fertility Site."

43. Teit, "Thompson Indians"; Teit, *Salishan Tribes,* 194, 283; Steward, *Petroglyphs of California,* 227; Steward, "Petroglyphs of the United States," 413; Gifford and Kroeber, *Cultural Element Distribution,* 186.

44. Feyhl, "Tool Grooves"; Keyser, "Writing-On-Stone."

45. Spector, *What This Awl Means.*

46. Deloria, *Waterlily,* 159.

47. Sundstrom, *Material Culture of Ludlow Cave.*

48. Wilson, *Waheenee,* 117–18.

49. Over, "Prehistoric Flint Quarry."

50. Loendorf, "Results of Archeological Survey."

51. Steinbring and Buchner, "Cathedrals of Prehistory."

52. Irwin, *Dream Seekers.*

53. Walker, *Lakota Belief,* 79; see also Brown and Brightman, *Orders of the Dreamed,* 140.

54. M. Powers, *Oglala Women,* 73–74; Walker, *Lakota Belief,* 163–66; Irwin, *Dream Seekers,* 214; J. E. Brown, *Animals of the Soul,* 15; St. Pierre and Long Soldier, *Walking in the Sacred Manner,* 53ff.

55. Walker, *Lakota Belief,* 165–66; Wissler, *Societies;* Young Bear and Theisz, *Standing in the Light,* 24–25; Theisz, "Multifaceted Double Woman"; St. Pierre and Long Soldier, *Walking in the Sacred Manner,* 53ff.

56. Thomas Tyon, quoted in Walker, *Lakota Belief,* 165–66; William Bordeaux, quoted in *Sious Falls Argus Leader,* circa 1931, copy in author's possession; Landes, *Mystic Lake Sioux,* 77.

57. St. Pierre and Long Soldier, *Walking in the Sacred Manner,* 53; Lyford, *Quill and Beadwork,* 55; Schneider, "Women's Work," 112.

58. T. Lewis, "Incised Boulders."

59. Riggs, *Dakota Grammar,* 166.

60. Thomas Tyon, quoted in Walker, *Lakota Belief,* 166.

61. Oscar Howe, quoted in Maurer, *Visions of the People,* 161.

62. Landes, *Mystic Lake Sioux,* 77ff.

63. Klein, "Political-Economy of Gender."

64. Weston, "Acculturation"; B. Gough, *Journal of Alexander Henry;* Radisson, *Voyages;* Wood and Theissen, *Early Fur Trade.*

Chapter 9. Brave Deeds and Coup Counts

1. Some women also excelled in these activities, and their accomplishments were as honored as men's. See McGinnis, *Counting Coup,* 68, 135; Ewers, "Women's Roles"; Medicine, "Warrior Women," 204, 250.

2. Grinnell, "Coup and Scalp"; Lowie, *Indians of the Plains,* 104–12.

3. See, for example, Linderman, *Plenty Coups,* 8–9.

4. M. Smith, "War Complex of the Plains Indians"; Secoy, *Changing Military Patterns;* Mallery, *Picture-Writing.*

5. Bad Heart Bull and Blish, *Pictographic History*, 169; Densmore, *Teton Sioux Music*, 361–63; Standing Bear, *My People the Sioux*, 57.

6. Afton, Halaas, and Masich, *Cheyenne Dog Soldiers*; Bad Heart Bull and Blish, *Pictographic History*; Dunn, *1877*; Ewers, *Plains Indian Painting*; Greene, "Women, Bison, and Coup"; Mallery, *Calendar*; Mallery, *Pictographs*; Mallery, *Picture-Writing*; Maurer, *Visions of the People*; Peterson, *Howling Wolf*; Rodee, "Stylistic Development"; Szabo, *Howling Wolf*; Brownstone, "Musée de l'Homme's Foureau Robe."

7. Keyser, "Lexicon."

8. Keyser, "Plains Indian War Complex"; Keyser, "Writing-On-Stone"; Keyser and Sundstrom, *Rock Art of Western South Dakota*.

9. Ewers, "Intertribal Warfare."

10. Keyser, "Writing-On-Stone"; Keyser and Sundstrom, *Rock Art of Western South Dakota*.

11. Loendorf and Conner, "Pectol Shields."

12. Loendorf, "Traditional Archaeological Methods."

13. Keyser and Sundstrom, *Rock Art of Western South Dakota*, 17.

14. Sundstrom and Keyser, "Tribal Affiliation."

15. Maurer, *Visions of the People*, 236–38; Mallery, *Picture-Writing*, 711–12.

16. Mallery, *Picture-Writing*, 447–60.

17. Ibid., 599.

18. M. Powers, *Oglala Women*, 71–72; Michelson, "Narrative," esp. 4–5 and n. 1.

19. C. Taylor, *Plains Indians*, 186–93.

20. D. Smith, *Indian Experiences*, 104.

21. Bad Heart Bull and Blish, *Pictographic History*, 104–16; Berlo, *Plains Indian Drawings*, 110, 118, 148; Afton, Halaas, and Masich, *Cheyenne Dog Soldiers*; Maurer, *Visions of the People*, 223.

22. Keyser, "Shoshonean Origin"; Wormington, *Reappraisal*; Schaafsma, *Rock Art of Utah*; Aikins, *Fremont-Promontory-Plains Relationships*; Loendorf and Conner, "Pectol Shields."

23. Sundstrom and Keyser, "Tribal Affiliation."

24. Map data from Keyser, "Writing-On-Stone"; Conner and Conner, *Rock Art*; Wellmann, *Survey*; O'Neill, *Kansas Rock Art*.

25. Brownstone, "Musée de l'Homme's Foureau Robe."

26. Badhorse, "Petroglyphs"; Powell, *Sweet Medicine*.

27. Beckwith, *Mandan-Hidatsa Myths*, 306; J. Taylor, *Sketches of Frontier and Indian Life*, 130; North Dakota Writers' Project, *North Dakota*, 210–11; McGee, *Siouan Indians*, 169; Hyde, *Life of George Bent*, 54; Grinnell, *By Cheyenne Campfires*, 31–34.

Chapter 10. Eagle Catchers

1. Wilson, *Hidatsa Eagle Trapping*; Grinnell, *Cheyenne Indians*, 1: 300–307; Schultz, *Blackfeet and*

Buffalo, 150–54; Ewers, *The Blackfeet*, 85; Howard, *Ponca Tribe*, 42.

2. Bowers, *Mandan Social and Ceremonial Organization*, 169–73.

3. Will, "Some Observations."

4. Bowers, *Hidatsa Social and Ceremonial Organization*, 333–38; Bowers, *Mandan Social and Ceremonial Organization*, 197–205.

5. Bowers, *Mandan Social and Ceremonial Organization*, 203.

6. Ibid., 216–27.

7. The Crows also credit the bear with teaching them eagle trapping. In Crow tradition, the Bear Above constellation is visible throughout the eagle-trapping season, from early spring through fall. McCleary, *The Stars We Know*, 22–23.

8. I would like to acknowledge Mike Cowdrey for pointing out to me the connections between these petroglyphs and Mandan-Hidatsa eagle trapping traditions.

9. Bowers, *Hidatsa Social and Ceremonial Organization*, 446.

10. Bowers, *Mandan Social and Ceremonial Organization*, 105, 255; Wilson, *Hidatsa Eagle Trapping*.

11. Gilman and Schneider, *Way to Independence*, 13, 99; Wilson, *Waheenee*, 25; see also George Catlin's paintings of Mandan villages in, for example, McCracken, *George Catlin and the Old Frontier*.

12. Gilman and Schneider, *Way to Independence*, 192.

13. Bowers, *Hidatsa Social and Ceremonial Organization*, 312–16.

14. Ibid., 349–52.

15. Bowers, *Mandan Social and Ceremonial Organization*, 216–23.

16. "Lion Boy" ledger drawings from the estate of Miguel Covarrubias, Sotheby's Auction House Catalog, New York, for June 1997.

17. Bowers, *Mandan Social and Ceremonial Organization*, 200–205; Bowers, *Hidatsa Social and Ceremonial Organization*, 333–38.

18. Snake-With-Legs petroglyphs are reported from Crow country in south-central Montana. See Conner and Conner, *Rock Art*, 30–31. The Crow tribes were offshoots of the Hidatsas.

Chapter 11. A Place Apart

1. Bouchet-Bert, "From Spiritual and Biographic."

2. For example, see W. Powers, *Sacred Language*, and Voget, "Sacred Numerology."

3. Lower left and center in figure 11.7, Stiles Tablet no. 2 and Stiles Tablet no. 10, from the Bastian Site, 13CK28, Iowa, adapted from Bray, "Southern Cult Motifs." Lower right, drawing of stone pipe from the Anker Site, Illinois, adapted from the cover of *Chicago*

Area Archaeology (Illinois Archaeological Survey Bulletin 3, 1961, University of Illinois, Urbana).

4. Wood, *Redbird Focus.*

5. Ibid.

6. Howard, *Ponca Tribe.*

7. Libby, *Arikara Narrative,* 163–64.

8. Buckles, "Analysis of Primitive Rock Art."

9. Use of pine boughs for fasting beds is recorded for the Crow and Blackfeet peoples; see Nabokov, *Two Leggings,* 62, and Medicine Crow, *From the Heart of Crow Country,* 334. Other vision-seekers used sage or cedar to make fasting beds; see Linderman, *Plenty-Coups,* 35, 59; Grinnell, *Cheyenne Indians,* 1: 81; J. E. Brown, *Sacred Pipe,* 57; Densmore, *Teton Sioux Music,* 274; Stone, *First Encounters,* 25.

10. Walker, *Lakota Belief.*

11. For example, Densmore, *Mandan and Hidatsa Music,* 108–15.

12. Saltzer, "Preliminary Report"; Diaz-Granados Duncan, "Petroglyphs and Pictographs of Missouri."

13. Ahler, Thiessen, and Trimble, *People of the Willows.*

14. Hall, *Archaeology of the Soul.*

15. Saltzer, "Preliminary Report."

16. Hall, *Archaeology of the Soul.*

Chapter 12. Below Sacred Mountains

1. Bourke, unpublished diary, 1872–96, 1: 1555-16, 26: 44; Clark, *Indian Sign Language,* 104; Grinnell, *Cheyenne Indians,* 1: 201, 2: 368; Grinnell, "Some Early Cheyenne Tales," 189; Grinnell, *By Cheyenne Campfires,* 263; Hyde, *Life of George Bent,* 53, 242; Looking Horse, "Sacred Pipe in Modern Life"; Odell, *Mato Paha;* Powell, *Sweet Medicine,* 18–19; Schlesier, *Wolves of Heaven;* Stands in Timber and Liberty, *Cheyenne Memories,* 35–43, 89–90; Tallbull, Deaver, and LaPoint, "New Way," 125.

2. McAllister, "Kiowa-Apache Social Organization," 162; McAllister, "Four Quartz Rock Medicine Bundle," 215; Mooney, *Calendar History,* 426; Nye, *Bad Medicine and Good,* 49.

3. Deloria, translations of Bushotter texts; Kadlecek and Kadlecek, *To Kill an Eagle,* 146; LaPointe, *Legends of the Lakota,* 38–41; Mails, *Fools Crow,* 154; Neihardt, *When the Tree Flowered,* 178; Odell, *Mato Paha;* South Dakota Writer's Project, *Legends of the Mighty Sioux,* 110–12.

4. Bourke unpublished diary, 1872–96, 1: 1555–56; Boyd, *Kiowa Voices,* 2: 5, 11–12, 89–93; Goodman, *Lakota Star Knowledge,* 55; Harrington, "Kiowa Memories," 165–76; Looking Horse, "Sacred Pipe in Modern Life"; Marriott and Rachlin, *Plains Indian Mythology,* 39–41; Momaday, *Way to Rainy Mountain,* 8; Mooney, *Calendar History,* 160; Nye, *Bad Medicine*

and Good, vii; Parks, *Myths and Traditions,* 146–52, 247–352; Parks and Wedel, "Pawnee Geography," 169–70; Parsons, *Kiowa Tales,* 9–11; Powell, *Sweet Medicine,* 472–77; Price, *Black Hills,* 35; Schlesier, *Wolves of Heaven,* 50–51; South Dakota Writer's Project, *Legends of the Mighty Sioux,* 115–16; Stone, "Legend of Devils Tower."

5. Alexander, *World's Rim,* 43; Bad Heart Bull and Blish, *Pictographic History,* 289–90; Bourke, unpublished diary, 1872–96, 1: 1555–56; Dodge, *Black Hills Journals,* 189; Goodman, *Lakota Star Knowledge,* 13; Warren, "Preliminary Report," 157.

6. Crook County Historical Society, *Pioneers of Crook County,* 42–43; Urbanek, *Wyoming Place Names;* Wyoming Writer's Project, *Wyoming,* 375.

7. Neihardt, *Black Elk Speaks.*

8. Kadlecek and Kadlecek, *To Kill an Eagle,* 90, 118, 146; DeMallie, *Sixth Grandfather,* 157–59; Parkman, *Oregon Trail,* 156.

9. Mallery, *Picture-Writing,* 289–90.

10. Scott, "Notes on the Kado"; Battey, *Life and Adventures,* 15; Mooney, *Calendar History,* 242–44.

11. Mooney, *Calendar History,* 240–42, 324; Scott, "Notes on the Kado."

12. Scott, "Notes on the Kado," plate 25; McCoy, "James Mooney's Fieldwork," 69.

13. James Mooney, original field notes on Kiowa shields, Smithsonian Institution, Washington, DC.

14. Lowie, *Myths and Traditions,* 83–85, 92–93, 96–98; Bowers, *Hidatsa Social and Ceremonial Organization,* 308–23.

15. Cowdrey, "Spring Boy."

16. Ibid.

17. Walker, *Sun Dance,* 93.

18. Densmore, *Teton Sioux Music,* 88–89, 149.

19. Ibid., 251.

20. Wildschut and Ewers, *Crow Indian Medicine Bundles,* 66; Linderman, *Plenty Coups,* 83, 280–81;

21. Skinner, *Societies,* 769.

22. Mooney, *Calendar History,* 240.

23. Scott, "Notes on the Kado," 348; Mooney, *Calendar History,* 155–56.

24. Marriott and Rachlin, *Plains Indian Mythology,* 39–41; Momaday, *Way to Rainy Mountain,* 8; Mooney, *Calendar History,* 160; Nye, *Bad Medicine and Good,* vii; Boyd, *Kiowa Voices,* 2: 5, 11–12, 89–93.

25. Sundstrom, "Mirror of Heaven."

26. DeVoto, *Journals of Lewis and Clark,* 81–82.

27. Dorsey, *Study of Siouan Cults,* 328–29; Mallery, *Picture-Writing,* 32; Matthews, *Ethnography and Philology,* 50–51; McGee, *Siouan Indians,* 32; North Dakota Writers' Project, *North Dakota,* 223; Thwaites, *Account of an Expedition,* 57–58; Thwaites, *Travels in the Interior,* 339–40.

28. Beckwith, *Mandan-Hidatsa Myths*, 29–130, 239–40; Bowers, *Hidatsa Social and Ceremonial Organization*, 12, 233, 435–37; Will, *Archaeology of the Missouri Valley*, 305.

29. Schaafsma, *Indian Rock Art of the Southwest*.

30. Bray and Bray, *Joseph N. Nicollet*, 72–77, 84; Catlin, *Letters and Notes*, 1: 31, 234, 2: 163–73, 201–2; Clark, *Indian Sign Language*, 303; Gilmore, *Prairie Smoke*, 97; Howard, *Ponca Tribe*, 17; Johnson, *Life of Sitting Bull*, 213; Lynd, "History of the Dakotas"; McGee, *Siouan Indians*, 32; South Dakota Writer's Project, *Legends of the Mighty Sioux*, 45–46.

31. Alexander, *World's Rim*, 53; T. Lewis, "Ancient Rock Inscriptions"; T. Lewis, "Incised Boulders."

32. Loendorf, "Traditional Archaeological Methods."

33. Hultkrantz, *Shoshones*, 18; Hultkrantz, *Belief and Worship*, 35.

Chapter 13. The Face in the Rock

1. For examples, see Phillips and Brown, *Pre-Columbian Shell Engravings*.

2. Pohorecky, "Faces Carved on Boulders."

3. Howard, "Southern Cult."

4. For examples, see Berlo, *Plains Indian Drawings*, 190–91; D. Smith, *Red Indian Experiences*.

5. I would like to acknowledge Mike Cowdrey, who first pointed out to me this possible identity for the horned face petroglyph.

6. Schlesier, *Wolves of Heaven*, 93; Grinnell, *Cheyenne Indians*, 2: 293. A photograph of a ceremonial tipi with this image was mislabeled as a depiction of a bison head; see Powell, *Sweet Medicine*, 303.

7. Hoebel, *Cheyennes*, 89.

8. Collins, "Shell Mask Gorget"; Fosha, "Campers Unmask Rare Find"; Fosha, "Shell Mask Finds."

9. Howard, "Southern Cult."

10. Waring and Holder, "Prehistoric Ceremonial Complex"; Muller, "Southern Cult"; Smith and Smith, "Engraved Shell Masks"; Kneberg, "Engraved Shell Gorgets."

11. Muller, "Southern Cult"; Smith and Smith, "Engraved Shell Masks," 9.

12. Fosha, "Shell Mask Finds."

13. Smith and Smith, "Engraved Shell Masks."

14. Howard, "Persistence of Southern Cult Gorgets."

15. Collins, "Shell Mask Gorget."

16. Howard, "Southern Cult."

17. Wedel, *Prehistoric Man*, 223.

18. Fosha, "Shell Mask Finds."

19. Kneberg, "Engraved Shell Gorgets."

20. Waring and Holder, "Prehistoric Ceremonial Complex"; Howard, *Southeastern Ceremonial Complex*; Hudson, *Southeastern Indians*; J. Brown, "Mississippian Period."

21. Smith and Smith, "Engraved Shell Masks," 15.

22. Ibid., 16.

23. Ibid.

24. Skinner, *Societies*.

25. Collins, "Shell Mask Gorget"; Hall, *Archaeology of the Soul*.

26. Hall, *Archaeology of the Soul*.

27. Ibid.

28. Black Elk, *Sacred Pipe*, 101–55; Walker, *Lakota Belief*, 193–241; Thomas, "Sioux Medicine Bundle."

29. Fosha, "Shell Mask Finds."

30. Wheeler, *Archeological Remains*, 59–63; site records, South Dakota Archaeological Research Center, Rapid City.

31. Smith and Smith, "Engraved Shell Masks."

32. Hall, *Archaeology of the Soul*.

33. Grinnell, *Cheyenne Indians*, 1: 164, 175, 222, 292; Moore, *Cheyenne Nation*, 109.

34. Ludlow, *Report of a Reconnaissance*, 12.

Chapter 14. Visions and Oracles

1. Conner and Conner, *Rock Art*, 27.

2. Site files, South Dakota Archaeological Research Center, Rapid City.

3. Mallery, *Picture-Writing*, 654.

4. Black Elk, *Sacred Pipe*, 76.

5. For historic vision drawings combining animal and lightning images, see Berlo, *Plains Indian Drawings*, 190–91; D. Smith, *Red Indian Experiences*; also see American Horse winter count, quoted in Mallery, *Picture-Writing*, 462–64.

6. Women, too, might experience visions of elk, but they expressed their dream powers during the Two Women (Double Woman) dance, rather than during the Elk Dreamers dance. See Lowie, *Dance Associations*, 118–19. For the Elk Dreamers themselves, see Fletcher, *Elk Mystery*; Densmore, *Teton Sioux Music*, 176–79, 293–98; Wissler, *Societies*, 85–88; Lowie, *Dance Associations*, 117–18; Bad Heart Bull and Blish, *Pictographic History*, 200; W. Powers, *Oglala Religion*, 57–58; Powell, "Sacrifice," 84–85; Ewers, Magelsdorf, and Wierzbowski, *Images*, 25, 43, 48.

7. Vestal, *Warpath*, 93–94; Wissler, *Societies*, 85–88; Fletcher, *Elk Mystery*, 276–79, 282; Bad Heart Bull and Blish, *Pictographic History*, 200–201, 279; Irwin, *Dream Seekers*, 34–35; Densmore, *Teton Sioux Music*, 176–79; Walker, *Lakota Belief*, 135.

8. Bad Heart Bull and Blish, 274.

9. Wissler, *Societies*, 88; Lowie, *Dance Associations*, 117.

10. Ewers, Magelsdorf, and Wierzbowski, *Images*, 25, 48; Powell, "Sacrifice," 89.

11. Lowie, *Dance Associations*, 117–18.

12. Grinnell, *Cheyenne Indians*, 2: 285–336; Schlesier, *Wolves of Heaven*.

13. Grinnell, 328.

14. Aadland, *Women and Warriors,* 166 (first two figures from left in the background).

15. Wesley Whiteman, quoted in Schwartz, *Last Contrary,* 69.

16. Stands in Timber and Liberty, *Cheyenne Memories,* 101.

17. Powell, "Sacrifice," 86, 89.

18. Bad Heart Bull and Blish, *Pictographic History,* 274.

19. Walker, *Lakota Belief,* 166–67.

Chapter 15. The Newcomers

1. American Horse winter count, quoted in Mallery, *Picture-Writing,* 568.

2. Curley, *Curley's Guide,* 44.

3. Spring, *Cheyenne and Black Hills Stage and Express Routes,* 124–25.

4. Lee and Williams, *Last Grass Frontier.*

Chapter 16. A Disappearing Treasure

1. Will, "Some Observations."

References

Aadland, Dan. *Women and Warriors of the Plains: The Pioneer Photography of Julia E. Tuell.* Macmillan, New York, 1996.

Aaberg, Steve. The Plant Macrofossil Record from Barton Gulch (24MA171): A Case for Systematic Plant Exploitation and Preparation during the Paleoindian Period in Montana. *Fiftieth Annual Plains Anthropological Conference Program and Abstracts,* 1992, 23.

Afton, Jean, David Fridtjof Halaas, and Andrew E. Masich. *Cheyenne Dog Soldiers: A Ledgerbook History of Coups and Combat.* University Press of Colorado, Niwot, Colorado, 1997.

Agenbroad, Larry D. *The Hudson-Meng Site: An Alberta Bison Kill in the Nebraska High Plains.* University Press of America, Washington, D.C., 1978.

Agogino, George A., and W. D. Frankforter. The Brewster Site: An Agate Basin-Folsom Multiple Component Site in Eastern Wyoming. *Masterkey* 34 (1960): 102–7.

Ahler, Stanley A., Thomas D. Thiessen, and Michael K. Trimble. *People of the Willows: The Prehistory and Early History of the Hidatsa Indians.* University of North Dakota Press, Grand Forks, 1991.

Aikins, C. Melvin. *Fremont-Promontory-Plains Relationships.* University of Utah Anthropological Paper 82. Salt Lake City, 1966.

Alex, Lynn M. *The Archaeology of the Beaver Creek Shelter (39CU779): A Preliminary Statement.* National Park Service, Rocky Mountain Region, Selections from the Division of Cultural Resources, no. 3, 1991.

———. 39BU2: A Fortified Site in Western South Dakota. *South Dakota Archaeological Society Newsletter* 9 (1979): 3–7.

Alex, Robert A. Village Sites Off the Missouri River. In *The Future of South Dakota's Past,* edited by Larry J. Zimmerman and Lucille C. Stewart, pp. 39–45. South Dakota Archaeological Society Special Publication 2, 1981.

Alexander, Hartley Burr. *The World's Rim: Great Mysteries of the North American Indian.* University of Nebraska Press, Lincoln, 1967.

Amiotte, Arthur. The Lakota Sun Dance: Historical and Contemporary Perspectives. In *Sioux Indian Religion: Tradition and Innovation,* edited by Raymond J. DeMallie and Douglas R. Parks, pp. 75–96. University of Oklahoma Press, Norman, 1987.

Antevs, Ernst. The Great Basin, with Emphasis on Glacial and Post-glacial Times. *University of Utah Bulletin* 38 (1948): 168–91.

Artz, Joe Alan. Cultural Response or Geological Process? A Comment on Sheehan. *Plains Anthropologist* 41 (1996): 383–93.

Bad Heart Bull, Amos, and Helen H. Blish. *A Pictographic History of the Oglala Sioux.* University of Nebraska Press, Lincoln, 1967.

Badhorse, Beverly. Petroglyphs: Possible Religious Significance of Some. *Wyoming Archaeologist* 23 (1979): 27–28.

Bamforth, Douglas B. *Ecology and Human Organization on the Great Plains.* Plenum, New York, 1988.

Barbeau, Marius. *Indian Days on the Western Prairies.* National Museum of Canada Bulletin 163. Ottawa, 1960.

Battey, Thomas C. *The Life and Adventures of a Quaker among the Indians.* Boston, 1891.

Beck, W., D. J. Donahue, A. J. T. Jull, and G. Burr. Ambiguities in Direct Dating of Rock Surfaces Using Radiocarbon Measurements. *Science* 280 (1998): 2132–39.

Beckwith, Martha Warren. *Mandan-Hidatsa Myths and Ceremonies.* Memoirs of the American Folklore Society, vol. 32, 1938. Reprint, 1969, Kraus Reprint, New York.

Bement, Leland C. *Bison Hunting at Cooper Site.* University of Oklahoma Press, Norman, 1999.

Bender, Susan J., and Gary A. Wright. High-Altitude Occupations, Cultural Process, and High Plains Prehistory: Retrospect and Prospect. *American Anthropologist* 90 (1989): 619–39.

Benedict, James B., and Byron L. Olson. Origin of the McKean Complex: Evidence from Timberline. *Plains Anthropologist* 18 (1973): 323–27.

Berlo, Janet Catherine, editor. *Plains Indian Drawings, 1895–1935: Pages from a Visual History.* Harry N. Abrams, New York, 1996.

Black, Kevin D. Archaic Continuity in the Colorado Rockies: The Mountain Tradition. *Plains Anthropologist* 36 (1991): 1–29.

Blackburn, Thomas. Biopsychological Aspects of Chumash Rock Art. *Journal of California Anthropology* 4 (1977): 88–94.

Black Elk, Nicholas. *The Sacred Pipe.* Edited by Joseph Epes Brown. University of Oklahoma Press, Norman, 1953.

Bouchet-Bert, Luc. From Spiritual and Biographic to Boundary-Marking Deterrent Art: A Reinterpretation of Writing-On-Stone. *Plains Anthropologist* 44 (1999): 27–46.

Bourke, John Gregory (Captain, U.S. Army). Unpublished diary, 1872–96. 124 vols. Library of the U.S. Military Academy, West Point, New York.

Bowers, Alfred W. *Hidatsa Social and Ceremonial Organization.* Bureau of American Ethnology, Smithsonian Institution, Bulletin 194. Washington, D.C., 1963. Reprint, 1992, University of Nebraska Press, Lincoln.

———. *Mandan Social and Ceremonial Organization.* University of Chicago Press, Chicago, 1950. Reprint, 1991, University of Idaho Press, Moscow, Idaho.

Boyd, Maurice. *Kiowa Voices: Myths, Legends, and Folktales,* vol. 2. Texas Christian University Press, Fort Worth, Texas, 1983.

Bray, Edmund C., and Martha Coleman Bray, editors. *Joseph N. Nicollet on the Plains and Prairies.* Minnesota Historical Society, St. Paul, 1976.

Bray, Robert T. Southern Cult Motifs from the Utz Oneota Site, Saline County, Missouri, Incorporating Material from Iowa and Nebraska. *Missouri Archaeologist* 25 (1963): 1–40.

Brown, James. The Mississippian Period. In *Ancient Art of the American Woodland Indians,* edited by D. S. Brose, J. A. Brown, and D. W. Penny, pp. 93–146. Detroit Institute of Arts, Detroit, 1985.

Brown, Jennifer S., and Robert Brightman. *The Orders of the Dreamed: George Nelson on Cree and Northern Ojibwa Religion and Myth.* Minnesota Historical Society Press, St. Paul, 1998.

Brown, Joseph Epes. *Animals of the Soul: Sacred Animals of the Oglala Sioux.* Element, Rockport, Massachusetts, 1992.

———. *The Sacred Pipe: Black Elk's Account of the Seven Rites of the Oglala Sioux.* University of Oklahoma Press, Norman, 1953.

Brownstone, Arni. The Musée de l'Homme's Foureau Robe and Its Moment in the History of Blackfoot Painting. *Plains Anthropologist* 46 (2001): 249–67.

Buckles, William Gayl. An Analysis of Primitive Rock Art at Medicine Creek Cave, Wyoming, and Its Cultural and Chronological Relationships to the Prehistory of the Plains. M.A. thesis, Department of Anthropology, University of Colorado, 1964.

Buechel, Eugene. *Lakota Tales and Texts.* Edited by Paul Manhart. Red Cloud Indian School, Pine Ridge, South Dakota, 1978.

Buechler, Jeff. *Report of Data Retrieval and Test Excavations at the Deerfield Site (39PN214), Pennington County, South Dakota.* South Dakota State Archaeological Research Center, Contract Investigation Series 106, 1984.

Buker, Frank. *Black Hills Archaeology Re-Write History.* Hills Printing, Hill City, South Dakota, 1955.

Buker, Leon W. Archaeology of the Southern Black Hills. *American Antiquity* 3 (1937): 79–80.

Carlson, Gayle F., John R. Bozell, Terry L. Steinacher, Marjorie Brooks Lovvorn, and George W. Gill. The Sidney Burial: A Middle Plains Archaic Mortuary Site from Western Nebraska. *Plains Anthropologist* 44 (1999): 105–9.

Carroll, John M., and Lawrence A. Frost, editors. *Private*

Theodore Ewert's Diary of the Black Hills Expedition of 1874. CRI Books, Piscatawny, New Jersey, 1976.

Catlin, George. *Letters and Notes on the Manners, Customs, and Condition of the North American Indians.* 2 vols. London, 1844. Reprint, 1973, Dover Publications, New York.

Chamberlain, Lee C. The Medicine Rock of Malta. *Our Public Lands* 22, no. 1 (1972): 8–11. U.S. Department of the Interior, Washington, D.C.

Chevance, Nicholas. *An Archaeological Survey in the Southern Black Hills.* South Dakota Archaeological Research Center, Rapid City, 1978.

———. *Cultural Resources Survey in the Driftwood Canyon and Long Mountain Regions, Fall River County, South Dakota.* South Dakota Archaeological Research Center, Rapid City, 1979.

Chevance, Nicholas, and James K. Haug. *An Archaeological Survey in the Southern Black Hills.* USDA Forest Service Projects C41 and EM50. South Dakota Archaeological Research Center, Rapid City, 1978.

Chittendon, Hiram Martin, and Alfred Talbot Richardson, editors. *Life, Letters and Travels of Father Pierre-John DeSmet, 1801–1873.* 4 vols. New York, 1905.

Clark, William Philo. *The Indian Sign Language.* Hammersly and Company, 1885. Reprint, 1982, University of Nebraska Press, Lincoln.

Cole, Sally J. *Legacy on Stone: Rock Art of the Colorado Plateau and Four Corners Region.* Johnson Books, Boulder, Colorado, 1990.

Collins, James M. A Shell Mask Gorget from Allamakee County, Iowa. *Plains Anthropologist* 40 (1995): 251–60.

Conkey, Margaret W. Boundedness in Art and Society. In *Symbolic and Structural Archaeology,* edited by Ian Hodder, pp. 115–28. Cambridge University Press, Cambridge, 1982.

Conner, Stuart W., and BettyLu Conner. *Rock Art of the Montana High Plains.* Art Galleries of the University of California, Santa Barbara, 1965.

Conway, Thor, and Julie Conway. *Spirits on Stone: The Agawa Pictographs.* Heritage Discoveries, San Luis Obispo, California, 1990.

Coues, Elliot, editor. *History of the Expedition under the Command of Lewis and Clark: A New Edition, Original Manuscript Journals and Field Notebooks of the Explorers.* Francis P. Harper, New York, 1893.

Cowan, Tim. *Heritage Resource Survey of the Proposed Dalton/Piedmont Planning Units: Environmental Assessment in Lawrence, Mead and Pennington Counties, South Dakota. Project S-02-97, Northern Hills Ranger District, Black Hills National Forest.*

Black Hills National Forest, Custer, South Dakota, 1997.

Cowdrey, Mike. Spring Boy Rides the Moon: Celestial Patterns in Crow Shield Design. Unpublished manuscript in author's possession, 1996.

Crook County Historical Society. *Pioneers of Crook County.* Sundance, Wyoming, 1981.

Curley, Edwin A. *Curley's Guide to the Black Hills.* Rand McNally, Chicago, 1877. Reprint, 1973, Dakota Wesleyan University Press, Mitchell, South Dakota.

Custer, Elizabeth Bacon. *Boots and Saddles, or Life in Dakota with General Custer.* Harper and Brothers, New York, 1885.

Dalla, Rowena. *Hay Draw Timber Sale, Custer District, Black Hills National Forest (C-16-78).* Black Hills National Forest, Custer, South Dakota, 1978.

Darroch, John I. A Hoof, Hand, and Footprint Petroglyph Boulder Recovery from Valley County. *Archaeology in Montana* 17 (1976): 19–28.

Deloria, Ella Cara. Translations of George Bushotter texts made circa 1937, X8C.3, Boas Collection, American Philosophical Society Library, Philadelphia. Microfilm no. 372, Reel 32.

———. *Waterlily.* University of Nebraska Press, Lincoln, 1988.

DeMallie, Raymond J., editor. *The Sixth Grandfather: Black Elk's Teachings Given to John G. Neihardt.* University of Nebraska Press, Lincoln, 1984.

Dempsey, Hugh. *The Amazing Death of Calf Shirt and Other Blackfoot Stories.* University of Oklahoma Press, Norman, 1994.

Densmore, Frances. *Mandan and Hidatsa Music.* Bureau of American Ethnology Bulletin 80. Washington, D.C., 1923.

———. *Teton Sioux Music.* Bureau of American Ethnology, Smithsonian Institution, Bulletin 61. Washington, D.C., 1918. Reprint, 1992, University of Nebraska Press, Lincoln, under the title *Teton Sioux Music and Culture.*

DeVoto, Bernard, editor. *The Journals of Lewis and Clark.* Houghton Mifflin, Boston, 1953.

Diaz-Granados Duncan, Carol. The Petroglyphs and Pictographs of Missouri: A Distributional, Stylistic, Contextual, Temporal, and Functional Analysis of the State's Rock Graphics. Ph.D. dissertation, Department of Anthropology, Washington University, St. Louis, 1993.

Dodge, Richard Irving. *The Black Hills Journals of Colonel Richard Irving Dodge.* Edited by Wayne R. Kime. University of Oklahoma Press, Norman, 1996.

Donohue, James A. Progress on the Investigation of the Jim Pitts Stratified Paleoindian Site: Geoarchaeology, Continuing Excavation, and

Artifact Assemblage Processing. *Fifty-third Annual Plains Anthropological Conference Program and Abstracts,* 1995, 72.

Donohue, James A., Jane Abbott, and Ben Rhodd. Excavation at the Boulder Creek Rock Shelter. *South Dakota Archaeological Society Newsletter* 25, no. 1–2 (1995): 1–10.

Dorn, Ronald I. A Change of Perspective. *La Pintura* 23, no. 2 (1996): 10–11.

———. Chronometric Techniques: Engravings. In *Handbook of Rock Art Research,* edited by David S. Whitley, pp. 167–89. Altamira Press, Walnut Creek, California, 2001.

Dorsey, George A., and Alfred L. Kroeber. *Traditions of the Arapaho.* Field Columbian Museum, Chicago, 1903.

Dorsey, James Owen. *A Study of Siouan Cults.* Bureau of American Ethnology Annual Report 11. Washington, D.C., 1894.

Drips, J. H. *Three Years among the Indians in Dakota.* Brulé Index, Kimball, South Dakota, 1894. Reprint, 1974, Sol Lewis, New York.

Dunn, Dorothy *1877: Plains Indian Sketch Books of Zo-Tom and Howling Wolf.* Northland Press, Flagstaff, Arizona, 1969.

Eighmy, Jeffrey L., and Jason M. LaBelle. Radiocarbon Dating of Twenty-Seven Plains Complexes and Phases. *Plains Anthropologist* 41 (1996): 53–69.

Enoe, H. D. Medicine Rock. *Monthly South Dakotan* 6 (1903): 162.

Ewers, John C. *The Blackfeet.* University of Oklahoma Press, Norman, 1958.

———. Intertribal Warfare as the Precursor of Indian-White Warfare on the Northern Great Plains. *Western Historical Quarterly* 6, no. 5 (1975): 397–410.

———. The Medicine Rock of the Marias: A Blackfoot Shrine beside the Whoop-up Trail. *Montana: Magazine of Western History* 2, no. 3 (1952): 45–56.

———. *Plains Indian Painting: A Description of an Aboriginal American Art.* Stanford University Press, Palo Alto, California, 1939.

———. Women's Roles in Plains Indian Warfare. In *Skeletal Biology in the Great Plains,* edited by Douglas W. Owsley and Richard L. Jantz, pp. 325–32. Smithsonian Institution Press, Washington, D.C., 1994.

Ewers, John C., Helen M. Magelsdorf, and William S. Wierzbowski. *Images of a Vanished Life: Plains Indian Drawings from the Collection of the Pennsylvania Academy of the Fine Arts.* Pennsylvania Academy of the Fine Arts, Philadelphia, 1985.

Faulkner, Charles, editor. *Rock Art of the Eastern Woodlands.* American Rock Art Research Association Occasional Paper 2. San Miguel, California, 1996.

Fenenga, Franklin, Brian D. Dillon, and David S. Whitley. An Unusual Petroglyph from Horse Creek, Tulare, California. *Journal of New World Archaeology* 6 (1984): 52–58.

Feyhl, Kenneth J. Tool Grooves: A Challenge. *Archaeology in Montana* 21 (1980): 1–31.

Fiedel, Stuart J. Older than We Thought: Implications of Corrected Dates for Paleoindians. *American Antiquity* 64 (1999): 95–115.

———. The Peopling of the New World: Present Evidence, New Theories, and Future Directions. *Journal of Archaeological Research* 8 (2000): 39–103.

Fletcher, Alice C. The Elk Mystery or Festival, Ogalalla Sioux. *Peabody Museum Annual Reports* 16–17, vol. 3, no. 3–4 (1884): 276–88. Cambridge, Massachusetts.

———. The White Buffalo Festival of the Uncpapas. *Peabody Museum Annual Reports* 16–17, vol. 3, no. 3–4 (1884): 260–75.

Fletcher, Alice C., and Francis LaFlesche. *The Omaha Tribe* Bureau of American Ethnology Annual Report 27. Washington, D.C., 1911. Reprint, 1970, Johnson Reprint, New York.

Fosha, Michael. Campers Unmask Rare Find. *South Dakota Archaeological Society Newsletter* 22 (1992): 4.

———. Shell Mask Finds in South Dakota. *South Dakota Archaeological Society Newsletter* 25 (1995): 10–13.

Fredlund, Glen G. Late Quaternary Geomorphic History of Lower Highland Creek, Wind Cave National Park, South Dakota. *Physical Geography* 17 (1996): 446–64.

Frison, George C. *Prehistoric Hunters of the High Plains.* Academic Press, New York, 1978.

———. *Prehistoric Hunters of the High Plains,* 2d edition. Academic Press, New York, 1991.

Frison, George C., R. L. Andrews, R. C. Carlisle, and Robert Edgar. A Late Paleoindian Animal Trapping Net from Northern Wyoming. *American Antiquity* 51 (1986): 352–61.

Frison, George C., and Dennis J. Stanford. *The Agate Basin Site: A Record of the Paleoindian Occupation of the Northwestern High Plains.* Academic Press, New York, 1982.

Frison, George C., Michael Wilson, and Diane J. Wilson. Fossil Bone and Artifacts from an Early Altithermal Period Arroyo Trap in Wyoming. *American Antiquity* 41 (1976): 28–57.

Froiland, Sven. *Natural History of the Black Hills.* Center for Western Studies, Augustana College, Sioux Falls, South Dakota, 1978.

Frost, Lawrence A., editor. *With Custer in '74: James Calhoun's Diary of the Black Hills Expedition.* Brigham Young University Press, Provo, Utah, 1979.

Furst, Peter T. Hallucinogens in Precolumbian Art. In *Art and Environment in Native America,* edited by Mary Elizabeth King and Idris R. Traylor, pp. 55–102. Texas Tech University Museum Special Publication 7. Lubbock, 1974.

———. Shamanism, the Ecstatic Experience, and Lower Pecos Art: Reflections on Some Transcultural Phenomena. In *Ancient Texans: Rock Art and Lifeways along the Lower Pecos,* edited by Harry J. Shafer, pp. 210–25. Texas Monthly Press, Austin, 1986.

Gant, Robert, and Wesley R. Hurt, Jr. 39MD9, the Gant Site. *Museum News* 26, University of South Dakota Museum, 1965.

Gebhard, David. Petroglyphs of Wyoming: A Preliminary Paper. *El Palacio* 58 (1951): 67–81.

Gifford, E. W. *Culture Element Distributions 12: Apache-Pueblo.* University of California Anthropological Records 4, no. 1. Berkeley, 1940.

Gifford, E. W., and A. L. Kroeber. *Cultural Element Distribution: IV Pomo.* University of California Publications in American Archaeology and Ethnology 37, no. 4. Berkeley, 1937.

Gilman, Carolyn, and Mary Jane Schneider. *The Way to Independence: Memories of a Hidatsa Indian Family, 1840–1920.* Minnesota Historical Society Press, St. Paul, 1987.

Gilmore, Melvin. *Prairie Smoke.* Columbia University Press, New York, 1929. Reprint, 1987, Minnesota Historical Society Press, St. Paul.

Goodman, Ronald. *Lakota Star Knowledge: Studies in Lakota Stellar Theology.* Sinte Gleska University, Rosebud, South Dakota, 1992.

Gough, Barry M. *The Journal of Alexander Henry the Younger, 1799–1814.* Champlain Society, Toronto, 1988.

Gough, Galal R. The Indian Hill Ceremonial Fertility Site Complex. *Rock Art Papers* 5 (1987): 55–60. San Diego Museum Paper 23.

Grant, Campbell, James W. Baird, and J. Kenneth Pringle. *Rock Drawings of the Coso Range.* Maturango Museum, China Lake, California, 1968.

Greene, Candace S. Women, Bison, and Coup: A Structural Analysis of Cheyenne Pictographic Art. Ph.D. dissertation, University of Oklahoma, 1985.

Greiser, Sally T. Late Prehistoric Cultures on the Montana Plains. In *Plains Indians, A.D. 500–1500: The Archaeological Past of Historic Groups,* edited by Karl H. Schlesier, pp. 34–55. University of Oklahoma Press, Norman, 1994.

Grinnell, George Bird. *Blackfoot Lodge Tales.* Charles Scribner's Sons, New York, 1892.

———. *By Cheyenne Campfires.* Yale University Press, New Haven, Connecticut, 1926.

———. *The Cheyenne Indians: Their History and Ways of Life.* 2 vols. Yale University Press, New Haven, Connecticut, 1923. Reprint, 1972, University of Nebraska Press, Lincoln.

———. Coup and Scalp among the Plains Indians. *American Anthropologist* 12 (1910): 296–310.

———. *Life of George Bent.* University of Oklahoma Press, Norman, 1968.

———. Some Early Cheyenne Tales. *Journal of American Folklore* 20 (1907): 169–94.

Groenfeldt, David. *Cultural Resources Survey of the Mayo Timber Sale.* Black Hills National Forest, Custer, South Dakota, 1978.

Hall, Robert L. *An Archaeology of the Soul: North American Indian Belief and Ritual.* University of Illinois Press, Urbana, 1997.

Hannus, L. Adrien. The Lange-Ferguson Site: A Case for Mammoth Bone Butchering Tools. In *Megafauna and Man,* edited by Larry D. Agenbroad, Jim I. Mead, and Lisa W. Nelson, pp. 86–99. Mammoth Site of Hot Springs, South Dakota, and Northern Arizona University, Flagstaff, 1990.

———. The Lange-Ferguson Site: An Event of Clovis Mammoth Butchery with the Associated Bone Tool Technology: The Mammoth and Its Track. Ph.D dissertation, University of Utah, Department of Anthropology, 1985.

———. Report on 1985 Test Excavations at the Ray Long Site (39FA65), Angostura Reservoir, Fall River County, South Dakota. *South Dakota Archaeology* 10 (1986): 48–104.

Hannus, L. Adrien, R. Peter Winham, Timothy V. Gillen, Edward J. Lueck, James Strait, and Kerry Lippincott. *Archeological Mitigation of the Buster Hill Site (39MD145), a Multicomponent Site in the Black Hills, South Dakota.* Archaeology Laboratory of the Center for Western Studies, Augustana College, Sioux Falls, South Dakota, for South Dakota Archaeological Research Center, Rapid City, 1997.

Harrington, John P. Kiowa Memories of the Northland. In *So Live the Works of Men,* edited by Donald D. Brand and Fred E. Harvey, pp. 162–76. University of New Mexico Press, Albuquerque, 1939.

Hassrick, Royal B. *The Sioux: Life and Customs of a Warrior Society.* University of Oklahoma Press, Norman, 1964.

Haug, James K. *Archaeological Reconnaissance in the Vicinity of Red and Craven Canyons, Fall River County, South Dakota.* South Dakota Archaeological Research Center, Rapid City, 1976.

———. *Cultural Resource Survey in the Southern Black Hills, South Dakota.* South Dakota Archaeological Research Center, Rapid City, 1978.

———. *Cultural Resources Survey of Selected Silver King Mine Properties in Custer and Fall River Counties, South Dakota.* South Dakota Archaeological Research Center, Rapid City, 1978.

Haug, James K., Jeanette E. Buehrig, John A. Moore, and James A. Sartain. *Archaeological Excavations in the Highway 18 Right-of-Way, Fall River County, South Dakota, 1978–1979.* South Dakota State Archaeological Research Center, Contract Investigation Series 20, 1980.

Hedges, Ken. Patterned Body Anthropomorphs and the Concept of Phosphenes in Rock Art. *Rock Art Papers* 5 (1987): 17–32. San Diego Museum Paper 23.

———. Phosphenes in the Context of Native American Rock Art, *American Indian Rock Art* 7–8 (1982): 1–10. American Rock Art Research Association, El Toro, California.

———. The Shamanic Origins of Rock Art. In *Ancient Images on Stone: Rock Art of the Californias.* edited by Jo Anne Tilburg, pp. 45–59. University of California at Los Angeles, Institute of Archaeology, 1983.

Helgevold, Mary Keepers. *A History of South Dakota Archaeology.* South Dakota Archaeological Society, Sioux Falls, South Dakota, 1981.

Hodge, Frederick W. *Handbook of American Indians North of Mexico.* Bureau of American Ethnology Bulletin 30. Washington, D.C., 1907.

Hoebel, E. Adamson. *The Cheyennes: Indians of the Great Plains,* 2d edition. Holt, Rinehart and Winston, New York, 1987.

Hofman, Jack, and Eric Ingbar. A Folsom Hunting Overlook in Eastern Wyoming. *Plains Anthropologist* 33 (1988): 337–50.

Holmes, William H. *Art in Shell of the Ancient Americans.* Bureau of American Ethnology Annual Report 2 (1880–81). Washington, D.C., 1883.

Hovde, David M. *Archaeological Excavations of Stone Circle Sites on the Southern Black Hills Periphery and Cheyenne River Drainage.* South Dakota Archaeological Research Center, Contract Investigation Series 36a, 1981.

———. The Hermosa Tipi Ring Site (39PN375). In *From Microcosm to Macrocosm: Advances in Tipi Ring Investigation and Interpretation,* edited by Leslie B. Davis, pp. 29–33. Plains Anthropologist Memoirs 19, 1983.

Howard, James H. Notes on the Ethnogeography of the Yankton Dakota. *Plains Anthropologist* 17 (1972): 281–307.

———. The Persistence of Southern Cult Gorgets among the Historic Kansa. *American Antiquity* 21 (1956): 301–2.

———. *The Ponca Tribe.* Bureau of American Ethnology Bulletin 195. Washington, D.C., 1965. Reprint, 1995, University of Nebraska Press, Lincoln.

———. *The Southeastern Ceremonial Complex and Its Interpretation.* Missouri Archaeological Society Memoir 6. Columbia, Missouri, 1968.

———. The Southern Cult in the Northern Plains. *American Antiquity* 19 (1953): 130–38.

Hudson, Charles M., Jr. *The Southeastern Indians.* University of Tennessee Press, Knoxville, 1976.

Hudson, Travis, and Georgia Lee. Function and Symbolism in Chumash Rock Art. *Journal of New World Archaeology* 6 (1984): 26–47.

Hughes, Jack T. Investigations in Western South Dakota and Northeastern Wyoming. *American Antiquity* 14 (1949): 266–77.

Hultkrantz, Åke. *Belief and Worship in Native North America.* Syracuse University Press, Syracuse, New York, 1981.

———. *The Shoshones in the Rocky Mountain Area.* Translated by Arne Magnus. *YMER* 3: 161–87. Stockholm, 1956. Reprint, 1974, Garland Publishing, as pp. 173–214 of *Shoshone Indians.*

Hungry Wolf, Adoph. *The Blood People: A Division of the Blackfoot Confederacy.* Harper and Row, New York, 1977.

Husted, Wilfred M. *Bighorn Canyon Archeology.* Smithsonian Institution River Basin Surveys: Publications in Salvage Archeology 12. National Park Service, Lincoln, Nebraska, 1969.

Hyde, George E. *Life of George Bent.* University of Oklahoma Press, Norman, 1968.

———. *Red Cloud's Folk.* University of Oklahoma Press, Norman, 1937.

Irwin, Lee. *The Dream Seekers: Native American Visionary Traditions of the Great Plains.* University of Oklahoma Press, Norman, 1994.

Irwin-Williams, Cynthia, Henry J. Irwin, and C. Vance Haynes, Jr. Hell Gap: Paleo-Indian Occupation on the High Plains. *Plains Anthropologist* 18 (1973): 40–53.

Jackson, Donald. *Custer's Gold: The United States Cavalry Expedition of 1874.* University of Nebraska Press, Lincoln, 1972. (Reprint of 1966 edition published by Yale University Press.)

Johnson, W. Fletcher. *Life of Sitting Bull and History of the Indian War of 1890–91.* Edgewood Publishing (n.p.), 1891.

Kadlecek, Edward, and Mabell Kadlecek. *To Kill an Eagle: Indian Views on the Last Days of Crazy Horse.* Johnson Books, Boulder, Colorado, 1981.

Kehoe, Alice B. The Function of Ceremonial Sexual Intercourse among the Northern Plains Indians. *Plains Anthropologist* 15 (1970): 99–103.

Kellogg, Rhonda, M. Knoll, and J. Kugler. Form Similarity between Phosphenes of Adults and Preschool Children's Scribblings. *Nature* 2008 (1965): 1129–30.

Keyser, James D. Audrey's Overhang: A Pictographic Maze in Central Montana. *Plains Anthropologist* 22 (1977): 183–88.

———. The Central Montana Rock Art Style. In *CRARA '77: Papers from the Fourth Biennial Conference of the Canadian Rock Art Research Asssociates*. British Columbia Provincial Museum Heritage Record 8. Vancouver, British Columbia, 1979.

———. The Evidence for McKean Complex Plant Utilization. *Plains Anthropologist* 31 (1986): 225–35.

———. A Graphic Example of Petroglyph Superimpositioning in the North Cave Hills. *Archaeology in Montana* 28, no. 2 (1987): 44–56.

———. *Indian Rock Art of the Columbia Plateau*. University of Washington Press, Seattle, 1992.

———. A Lexicon for Historic Plains Indian Rock Art: Increasing Interpretive Potential. *Plains Anthropologist* 32 (1987): 43–71.

———. Pictographs at the Desrosier Rockshelter. *Plains Anthropologist* 26 (1981): 271–76.

———. The Plains Indian War Complex and the Rock Art of Writing-On-Stone, Alberta, Canada. *Journal of Field Archaeology* 6 (1979): 41–48.

———. A Shoshonean Origin for the Plains Shield Bearing Warrior Motif. *Plains Anthropologist* 20 (1975): 207–15.

———. Writing-On-Stone: Rock Art on the Northwestern Plains. *Canadian Journal of Archaeology* 1 (1977): 15–80.

Keyser, James D., and Carl M. Davis. Lightning Spring: Four Thousand Years of Pine Parkland Prehistory. *Archaeology in Montana* 25 (1984): 1–64.

Keyser, James D., and George C. Knight. The Rock Art of Western Montana. *Plains Anthropologist* 21 (1976): 1–12.

Keyser, James D., and Linea Sundstrom. *Rock Art of Western South Dakota*. South Dakota Archaeological Society Special Publication 8, 1984.

Klassen, Michael A., James D. Keyser, and Lawrence L. Loendorf. Bird Rattle's Petroglyphs at Writing-On-Stone: Continuity in the Biographic Rock Art Tradition. *Plains Anthropologist* 45 (2000): 189–201.

Klein, Alan. The Political-Economy of Gender: A Nineteenth-Century Plains Indian Case Study. In *The Hidden Half: Studies of Plains Indian Women*, edited by Patricia Albers and Beatrice Medicine, pp. 143–73. University Press of America, Washington, D.C., 1983.

Kneberg, Madeline. Engraved Shell Gorgets and Their Associations. *Tennessee Archaeologist* 15 (1959): 1–39.

Knoll, M., J. Kugler, and S. D. Lawder. Effects of Chemical Stimulation of Electrically Induced Phosphenes on their Bandwidth, Shape, Number, and Intensity. *Confinia Neurologica* 22 (1963): 201–26.

Kornfeld, Marcel. The Rocky Foolsm Site: A Small Folsom Assemblage from the Northwestern Plains. *North American Archaeologist* 9 (1988): 197–222.

Kornfeld, Marcel, George C. Frison, and Mary Lou Larson, editors. Keyhole Reservoir Archaeology: Glimpses of the Past from Northeast Wyoming. Draft report submitted to the Bureau of Reclamation, U.S. Department of the Interior, Bismarck, North Dakota, 1991.

Krause, Herbert, and Gary D. Olson. *Prelude to Glory*. Brevet Press and Center for Western Studies, Augustana College, Sioux Falls, South Dakota, 1974.

Kroeber, Alfred L. *The Arapaho*. American Museum of Natural History Anthropological Paper 18. New York, 1904.

Lahren, Larry, and Robson Bonnichsen. Bone Foreshafts from a Clovis Burial in Southwestern Montana. *Science* 186 (1974): 147–50.

Lame Deer, John Fire, and Richard Erdoes. *Lame Deer, Seeker of Visions: The Life of a Sioux Medicine Man*. Simon and Schuster, New York, 1972.

Landes, Ruth. *The Mystic Lake Sioux: Sociology of the Mdewakantonwan Santee*. University of Wisconsin Press, Madison, 1968.

LaPointe, James. *Legends of the Lakota*. Indian Historian Press, San Francisco, 1976.

Larson, Mary Lou. Housepits and Mobile Hunter-Gatherers: A Consideration of the Wyoming Evidence. *Plains Anthropologist* 42 (1997): 353–69.

Lee, Bob, and Dick Williams. *Last Grass Frontier: The South Dakota Stockgrower Heritage*. Black Hills Publishers, Sturgis, South Dakota, 1964.

Lehmer, Donald J. *Introduction to Middle Missouri Archeology*. National Park Service Midwest Archeological Center, Anthropological Paper 1. U.S. Government Printing Office, 1971.

Lewis, Emily H. *Wo'Wakita: Reservation Recollections*. Center for Western Studies, Augustana College, Sioux Falls, South Dakota, 1980.

Lewis, Theodore Haynes. Ancient Rock Inscriptions in Eastern Dakota. *American Naturalist* 20 (1886): 423–25.

————. Incised Boulders in the Upper Minnesota Valley. *American Naturalist* 21 (1887): 639–42.

Lewis-Williams, J. David. *Believing and Seeing: Symbolic Meaning in Southern San Rock Paintings.* Academic Press, London, 1981.

Lewis-Williams J. David, and T. A. Dowson. The Signs of All Times: Entoptic Phenomena in Upper Paleolithic Art. *Current Anthropology* 29 (1988): 201–45.

Libby, Orin G., editor. *The Arikara Narrative of Custer's Campaign and the Battle of the Little Bighorn.* University of Oklahoma Press, Norman, 1998. (Reprint of 1920 edition, published as vol. 6 of the North Dakota Historical Collections.)

Linderman, Frank B. *Plenty Coups: Chief of the Crows.* University of Nebraska Press, Lincoln, 1962. (Reprint of 1930 edition, titled *American: The Life Story of Great Indian, Plenty-coups, Chief of the Crows.*)

————. *Pretty-Shield: Medicine Woman of the Crows.* University of Nebraska Press, Lincoln, 1972. (Reprint of 1932 edition, titled *Red Mother.*)

Lippincott, Kerry. *An Archaeological Survey of Selected Portions of Fall River and Custer Counties, South Dakota, Niobrara and Weston Counties, Wyoming.* Tennessee Valley Authority, Casper, Wyoming, 1980.

————. *A Report of a Cultural Resources Survey on United States Forest Service Property, Black Hills National Forest, South Dakota.* Tennessee Valley Authority, Casper, Wyoming, 1980.

Little, Paul. *River of People: A Multicultural History of the Cheyenne River Reservation Area.* Eagle Butte Bilingual Program, Eagle Butte Public School, Eagle Butte, South Dakota, 1983.

Loendorf, Lawrence L. A Preliminary Survey of the Clark Fork River, Carbon County, Montana. M.A. thesis, University of Montana, Missoula, 1967.

————. The Results of the Archeological Survey in the Pryor Mountains–Bighorn Canyon Recreation Area: 1969 Field Season. Manuscript on file. National Park Service, Midwest Archaeological Center, Lincoln, Nebraska, 1971.

————. Traditional Archaeological Methods and Their Applications at Rock Art Sites. In *New Light on Old Art: Recent Advances in Hunter-Gatherer Rock Art Research,* edited by David S. Whitley and Lawrence L. Loendorf, pp. 95–103. University of California Institute of Archaeology Monograph 36. Berkeley, 1986.

Loendorf, Lawrence L., and Stuart W. Conner. The Pectol Shields and the Shield-Bearing Warrior Rock Art Motif. *Journal of California and Great Basin Anthropology* 15 (1993): 216–24.

Looking Horse, Arval. The Sacred Pipe in Modern Life. In *Sioux Indian Religion: Tradition and Innovation,* edited by Raymond J. DeMallie and Douglas R. Parks, pp. 67–68. University of Oklahoma Press, Norman, 1987.

Lowie, Robert H. *Dance Associations of the Eastern Dakota.* American Museum of Natural History Anthropological Paper 11, part 2. New York, 1913.

————. *Indians of the Plains.* McGraw-Hill, New York, 1954.

————. *Myths and Traditions of the Crow Indians.* American Museum of Natural History Anthropological Paper 25. New York, 1918.

Loy, T. H., R. Jones, D. E. Nelson, B. Mehan, J. Vogel, J. Southon, and R. Cosgrove. Accelerator Radiocarbon Dating of Human Blood Proteins in Pigments from Late Pleistocene Art Sites in Australia. *Antiquity* 64 (1990): 110–16.

Ludlow, Captain William. *Report of a Reconnaissance of the Black Hills of Dakota, Made in the Summer of 1874.* U.S. Government Printing Office, Washington, D.C., 1875.

Lyford, Carrie A. *Quill and Beadwork of the Western Sioux.* U.S. Department of the Interior, Bureau of Indian Affairs, Division of Education. U.S. Government Printing Office, Washington, D.C., 1940.

Lynd, James W. History of the Dakotas: James W. Lynd's Manuscripts. *Collections of the Minnesota Historical Society* 2, no. 2 (1864): 143–74.

Mackintosh, Donald P., Kaye L. Roehrick, and N. Jane Hunt. *North Dakota Historical Markers and Sites.* Brevet Press, Sioux Falls, South Dakota, 1975.

Mails, Thomas. *Fools Crow.* Doubleday, Garden City, New York, 1979.

Mallery, Garrick. *A Calendar of the Dakota Nation.* U.S. Geological and Geographical Survey Bulletin 3. Washington, D.C., 1877.

————. *Pictographs of the North American Indians.* Bureau of American Ethnology Annual Report 4. Washington, D.C., 1886.

————. *Picture-Writing of the American Indians.* Bureau of American Ethnology Annual Report 10. Washington, D.C., 1893. Reprint, 1972, Dover Publications, New York.

Marquis, Thomas B. *Wooden Leg: A Warrior Who Fought Custer.* University of Nebraska Press, Lincoln, 1931.

Marquis, Thomas B., and Ronald H. Limbaugh. *Cheyenne and Sioux: The Reminiscences of Four Indians and a White Soldier.* Pacific Center for Western Historical Studies, Stockton, California, 1973.

Marriott, Alice, and Carol K. Rachlin. *Plains Indian Mythology.* Thomas Y. Crowell, New York, 1975.

Martin, James E., Robert A. Alex, Lynn Marie Alex, Jane P. Abbott, Rachel C. Benton, and Louise F. Miller. The Beaver Creek Shelter (39CU779): A Holocene Succession in the Black Hills of South Dakota. In *Prehistory and Human Ecology of the Western Prairies and Northern Plains,* edited by Joseph A. Tiffany, pp. 17–36. Plains Anthropologist Memoirs 27, 1993.

Matthews, Washington. *Ethnography and Philology of the Hidatsa Indians.* U.S. Geological and Geographical Survey, Miscellaneous Publication 7. Washington, D.C., 1877.

Maurer, Evan M. *Visions of the People: A Pictorial History of Plains Indian Life.* Minneapolis Institute of Arts, Minneapolis, 1992.

McAllister, J. G. The Four Quartz Rock Medicine Bundle of the Kiowa-Apache. *Ethnology* 4 (1965): 210–24.

———. Kiowa-Apache Social Organization. In *Social Anthropology of the North American Tribes,* edited by Fred Eggan, pp. 99–169. University of Chicago Press, Chicago, 1937.

McCleary, Timothy P. *The Stars We Know: Crow Indian Astronomy and Lifeways.* Waveland Press, Prospect Heights, Illinois, 1997.

McCoy, Ron. James Mooney's Fieldwork among the Kiowa and Kiowa-Apache. *American Indian Art,* Summer 1995: 64–71.

McCracken, Harold. *George Catlin and the Old Frontier.* Bonanza Books, New York, 1959.

McGee, W. J. *The Siouan Indians.* Bureau of American Ethnology Annual Report 15. Washington, D.C., 1897.

McGinnis, Anthony. *Counting Coup and Cutting Horses: Intertribal Warfare on the Northern Plains, 1738–1889.* Cordillera Press, Evergreen, Colorado, 1990.

McGowan, Charlotte. Female Fertility Themes in Rock Art. *Journal of New World Archaeology* 2 (1978): 15–27.

McHugh, Tom. *The Time of the Buffalo.* Alfred A. Knopf, New York, 1994.

McKibbin, Anne. *Archaeological Investigations at 38WE320, Weston County, Wyoming.* Black Hills National Forest, Custer, South Dakota, 1988.

McKibbin, Anne, Kevin D. Black, Ronald J. Rood, Margaret A. Van Ness, and Michael D. Metcalf. *Archaeological Excavations at 48CA1391, Campbell County, Wyoming.* Metcalf Archaeological Consultants, Eagle, Colorado, 1988.

McLaughlin, Marie L. *Myths and Legends of the Sioux.* Bismarck Tribune Company, Bismarck, North Dakota, 1916. Reprint, 1990, University of Nebraska Press, Lincoln.

Medicine, Beatrice. Warrior Women: Sex Role Alternatives for Plains Indian Women. In *The Hidden Half: Studies of Plains Indian Women,* edited by Patricia Albers and Beatrice Medicine, pp. 267–80. University Press of America, Washington D.C., 1983.

Medicine Crow, Joseph. *From the Heart of Crow Country.* University of Nebraska Press, Lincoln, 1992.

Meleen, Elmer E., and J. J. Pruitt. *A Preliminary Report on Rock Shelters in Fall River County, South Dakota.* Archaeological Studies Circular 1, University of South Dakota, Vermillion, 1941.

Meltzer, David J. The Discovery of Deep Time: A History of Views on the Peopling of the Americas. In *Method and Theory for Investigating the Peopling of the Americas,* edited by R. Bonnichsen and D. G. Steele, pp. 7–26. Center for the Study of the First Americans, Oregon State University, Corvallis, 1994.

Merrill, William L., Marian Kaulaity Hansson, Candace S. Greene, and Frederick J. Reuss. *A Guide to the Kiowa Collections at the Smithsonian Institution.* Smithsonian Institution Press, Washington, D.C., 1997.

Michelson, Truman. The Narrative of a Southern Cheyenne Woman. *Smithsonian Miscellaneous Collections* 87, no. 5 (1932): 1–13.

Michlovic, Michael. The Problem of the Teton Migration. In *Archaeology, Ecology, and Ethnohistory of the Prairie-Forest Border Zone of Minnesota and Manitoba,* edited by Janet Spector and Elden Johnson, pp. 131–45. J&L Reprint, Lincoln, Nebraska, 1985.

Miller, Paul V. *National Register of Historic Places Evaluation of 39CU466, 39CU686, 39CU709, and 39PN150, Black Hills National Forest, Elk Mountain District, Custer and Pennington Counties, South Dakota.* Black Hills National Forest, Custer, South Dakota, 1990.

Momaday, N. Scott. *The Way to Rainy Mountain.* University of New Mexico Press, Albuquerque, 1969.

Mooney, James. *Calendar History of the Kiowa Indians.* Bureau of American Ethnology Annual Report 17. Washington, D.C., 1898.

———. *The Ghost Dance Religion and the Sioux Outbreak of 1890.* Bureau of American Ethnology Annual Report for 1892–93. Washington, D.C., 1896. Reprint, 1991, University of Nebraska Press, Lincoln.

Moore, John H. *The Cheyenne Nation: A Social and Demographic History.* University of Nebraska Press, Lincoln, 1987.

Muller, Jon. The Southern Cult. In *The Southeastern Ceremonial Complex: Artifacts and Analysis,* edited by Patricia Galloway, pp. 11–26. University of Nebraska Press, Lincoln, 1989.

Mulloy, William T. The McKean Site in Northeastern Wyoming. *Southwestern Journal of Anthropology* 10 (1954): 432–60.

———. *A Preliminary Historical Outline for the Northwestern Plains.* University of Wyoming Publications in Science 22, no. 1, 1958.

Nabokov, Peter. *Two Leggings: The Making of a Crow Warrior.* Thomas Y. Crowell, New York, 1967.

Nagy, Imre. Cheyenne Shields and Their Cosmological Background. *American Indian Art* 19, no. 3 (1994): 38–104.

Neihardt, John G. *Black Elk Speaks.* William Morrow, New York, 1932. Reprint, 1961, 1988, 2000, University of Nebraska Press, Lincoln.

———. *When the Tree Flowered: The Story of Eagle Voice, a Sioux Indian.* New edition. University of Nebraska Press, Lincoln, 1991.

Nesbitt, Paul Edward. *Stylistic Locales and Ethnographic Groups: Petroglyphs of the Lower Snake River.* Idaho State University Museum Occasional Paper 23. Pocatello, Idaho, 1968.

Neuman, Robert W. *The Sonota Complex and Associated Sites on the Northern Great Plains.* Nebraska State Historical Society Publication in Anthropology 6, 1975.

Nissen, Karen M. The Record of a Hunting Practice at Petroglyph Site NV-LY-1. In *Four Great Basin Petroglyph Studies,* edited by Robert F. Heizer and Thomas R. Hester, pp. 53–81. University of California Press, Berkeley, 1974.

Noisat, Brad. *The National Register of Historic Places Evaluation of Sixteen Cultural Resources in the Black Hills National Forest, Bearlodge Ranger District, Crook County, Wyoming (B-14-90).* Niwot Archaeological Consultants, Niwot, Colorado, for the Black Hills National Forest, Custer, South Dakota, 1990.

———. *The National Register of Historic Places Evaluation of Twelve Cultural Resources in the Black Hills National Forest, Custer Ranger District, Custer and Pennington Counties, South Dakota.* Niwot Archaeological Consultants, Niwot, Colorado, 1992.

Noisat, Brad, and Jeff Campbell. *Cultural Resources Inventory of the McKenna, West, and Spring Timber Sales in the Black Hills National Forest, Elk Mountain Ranger District, Custer County, South Dakota.* Niwot Archaeological Consultants for Black Hills National Forest, Custer, South Dakota, 1986.

North Dakota Writers' Project, Works Project Administration. *North Dakota: A Guide to the Northern Prairie State.* Oxford University Press, Oxford, 1938.

Nye, Wilbur Sturtevant. *Bad Medicine and Good: Tales of the Kiowas.* University of Oklahoma Press, Norman, 1962.

Odell, Thomas E. *Mato Paha: The Story of Bear Butte.* Self-published. Spearfish, South Dakota, 1942.

O'Neill, Brian. *Kansas Rock Art.* Kansas State Historical Society, Topeka, 1981.

Oster, G. Phosphenes. *Scientific American* 222 (1970): 83–87.

Ott, Richard W., and Robert Alexander. *Photographic Documentation of the Craven Canyon Rock Art Panels, Fall River County, South Dakota.* Grand River Consultants, Grand Junction, Colorado, 1980.

Over, W. H. The Archaeology of Ludlow Cave and Its Significance. *American Antiquity* 2 (1936): 126–29.

———. *Indian Picture Writing in South Dakota.* Archaeological Studies Circular 4, University of South Dakota, Vermillion, 1941.

———. The Indians Who Lived in Ludlow Cave. *University of South Dakota Museum News* 7, no. 6 (1946).

———. A Prehistoric Flint Quarry in South Dakota. *Sunshine State Magazine* 5 (1924): 28–29.

Owsley, Douglas W., and David R. Hunt. Clovis and Early Archaic Period Crania from the Anzick Site (24PA506), Park County, Montana. *Plains Anthropologist* 46 (2001): 1–11.

Park, John A. The Simanton Petroglyph Hill Site (24PH2072): A Ceremonial Complex in Northern Montana. *Archaeology in Montana* 31, no. 2 (1990): 41–49.

Parkman, Francis. *The Oregon Trail: Prairie and Rocky Mountain Life in 1848.* Gramercy Books, New York, 1849. Reprint, 1995, Random House, New York.

Parks, Douglas R. *Myths and Traditions of the Arikara Indians.* University of Nebraska Press, Lincoln, 1996.

Parks, Douglas R., and Waldo R. Wedel. Pawnee Geography: Historical and Sacred. *Great Plains Quarterly* 5 (1985): 143–76.

Parsons, Elsie Clews. *Kiowa Tales.* American Folk-Lore Society Memoir 22. New York, 1929.

Pepper, George H., and Gilbert L. Wilson. *An Hidatsa Shrine and the Beliefs Respecting It.* American Anthropological Association Memoir 2, part 4 (1908): 275–328. Reprint, 1974, Kraus Reprints, New York.

Peterson, Karen Daniels. *Howling Wolf: A Cheyenne Warrior's Graphic Interpretation of His People.*

American West Publishing, Palo Alto, California, 1968.

Phillips, Philip, and James A. Brown. *Pre-Columbian Shell Engravings from the Craig Mound at Spiro, Oklahoma.* Peabody Museum Press, Cambridge, Massachusetts, 1978.

Pohorecky, Zenon S. Faces Carved on Boulders in Southern Saskatchewan. Paper presented at the 43d International Congress of Americanists, Vancouver, British Columbia, 1979.

Poole, D. C. *Among the Sioux of Dakota: Eighteen Months' Experience as an Indian Agent, 1869–70.* Minnesota Historical Society Press, St. Paul, 1988. (Reprint of 1881 edition, Van Nostrand, New York.)

Powell, Peter J., S.J. Sacrifice Transformed into Victory: Standing Bear Portrays Sitting Bull's Sun Dance and the Final Summer of Lakota Freedom. In *Visions of the People: A Pictorial History of Plains Indian Life,* by Evan M. Mauer, pp. 81–106. Minneapolis Institute of Arts, Minneapolis, Minnesota, 1992.

———. *Sweet Medicine: The Continuing Role of the Sacred Arrows, the Sun Dance, and the Sacred Buffalo Hat in Northern Cheyenne History.* University of Oklahoma Press, Norman, 1969.

Powers, Marla. *Oglala Women.* University of Chicago Press, Chicago, 1986.

Powers, William. *Oglala Religion.* University of Nebraska Press, Lincoln, 1975.

———. *Sacred Language: The Nature of Supernatural Discourse in Lakota.* University of Oklahoma Press, Norman, 1986.

———. A Winter Count of the Oglala. *American Indian Tradition* 52 (1963): 27–37.

Price, S. Goodale. *Black Hills: The Land of Legend.* DeVorss and Company, Los Angeles, n.d.

Radisson, Pierre. *Voyages of Pierre Esprit Radisson.* Boston, 1885.

Reeves, Brian O. K., and Margaret A. Kennedy, editors. *Kunaitupii: Coming Together on Native Sacred Sites.* Archaeological Society of Alberta, Calgary, 1993.

Reher, Charles A. Ethnology and Ethnohistory. In *Archaeology of the Eastern Powder River Basin, Wyoming,* edited by George M. Zeimans and Danny N. Walker, pp. 122–58. Office of the Wyoming State Archaeologist, Laramie, 1977.

———. Silver King Mine Survey and test excavation report. Draft manuscript on file, South Dakota Archaeological Research Center, Rapid City, 1981.

Reher, Charles A., and George C. Frison. *The Vore Site, 48CK302: A Stratified Buffalo Jump in the Wyoming Black Hills.* Plains Anthropologist Memoirs 16, 1980.

Renaud, E. B. Southern Wyoming and Southwestern South Dakota. *University of Denver Archaeological Survey of the High Western Plains, Seventh Report.* Denver, 1936.

Rice, Julian. *Ella Deloria's Iron Hawk.* University of New Mexico Press, Albuquerque, 1993.

Richards, Alex, and Dorothy Richards. Petroglyphs of the Russell Site. *Science of Man* 1 (1960): 18–21.

Riechel-Dolmatoff, G. *Beyond the Milky Way: Hallucinatory Imagery of the Tukano Indians.* University of California at Los Angeles, Latin American Center, 1978.

———. Drug-Induced Optical Sensations and Their Relationship to Applied Art among Some Columbian Indians. In *Art and Society: Studies in Style, Culture, and Aesthetics,* edited by Michael Greenhalgh and Vincent Megaw, pp. 289–304. Duckworth, London, 1978.

Riggs, Stephen Return. *Dakota Grammar, Texts, and Ethnography.* U.S. Geological Survey of the Rocky Mountain Region. U.S. Government Printing Office, Washington, D.C., 1893.

Roberts, Richard, Grahame Walsh, Andrew Murray, Jon Olley, Rhys Jones, Michael Morwood, Claudio Tuniz, Ewan Lawson, Michael Macphail, Dorren Bowdery, and Ian Naumann. Luminescence Dating of Rock Art and Past Environments Using Mud-Wasp Nests in North Australia. *Nature* 387 (1997): 696–99.

Rodee, Howard D. The Stylistic Development of Plains Indian Painting and Its Relationship to Ledger Drawings. *Plains Anthropologist* 10 (1965): 218–32.

Russ, Jon, Marian Hyman, and Marvin W. Rowe. Dating and Chemical Analysis of Pecos River Style Pictographs. *American Indian Rock Art* 18 (1992): 35–42.

Russ, Jon, Marian Hyman, Harry J. Shafer, and Marvin W. Rowe. Radiocarbon Dating of Prehistoric Rock Paintings by Selective Oxidation of Organic Carbon. *Nature* 348 (1990): 710–11.

Saltzer, Robert J. Preliminary Report on the Gottschall Site (47LA80). *Wisconsin Archaeologist* 68 (1987): 419–72.

Sanger, Kay Kenady, and Clement W. Meighan. *Discovering Prehistoric Rock Art: A Recording Manual.* Wormwood Press, Calabasas, California, 1990.

Schaafsma, Polly. *Indian Rock Art of the Southwest.* University of New Mexico Press, Albuquerque, 1980.

———. *The Rock Art of Utah.* University of Utah Press, Salt Lake City, 1994.

Schell, Herbert S. *History of South Dakota.* University of Nebraska Press, Lincoln, 1975.

Schlesier, Karl H. *The Wolves of Heaven: Cheyenne Shamanism, Ceremonies, and Prehistoric Origins.* University of Oklahoma Press, Norman, 1987.

———, editor. *Plains Indians, A.D. 500–1500: The Archaeological Past of Historic Groups.* University of Oklahoma Press, Norman, 1994.

Schneider, Edward A., Bruce R. McClelland, William E. Batterman, William M. Harding, William W. Martin, Darryl W. Newton, Thomas P. Reust, and Craig S. Smith. *Data Recovery Investigations along State Highway 24: The Red Canyon Rockshelter and Other Sites in the Bear Lodge Mountains of Wyoming.* TRC Mariah Associates, Laramie, for Wyoming Department of Transportation, Cheyenne, 1997.

Schneider, Mary Jane. Women's Work: An Examination of Women's Roles in Plains Indian Arts and Crafts. In *The Hidden Half: Studies of Plains Indian Women,* edited by Patricia Albers and Beatrice Medicine, pp. 101–21. University Press of America, Washington, D.C., 1983.

Schultz, James Willard. *Blackfeet and Buffalo: Memories of Life among the Indians.* University of Oklahoma Press, Norman, 1962.

Schwartz, Warren E. *The Last Contrary: The Story of Wesley Whiteman (Black Bear).* Center for Western Studies, Augustana College, Sioux Falls, South Dakota, 1988.

Scott, Hugh Lenox. Notes on the Kado, or Sun Dance, of the Kiowa. *American Anthropologist* 13 (1911): 345–79.

Secoy, Frank Raymond. *Changing Military Patterns on the Great Plains.* American Ethnological Society Monograph 21. New York, 1953.

Secrist, Kenneth G. *Pictographs in Central Montana, Part 1: Fergus County.* Montana State University Anthropology and Sociology Paper 20. Bozeman, Montana, 1960.

Sheehan, Michael S. Cultural Responses to the Altithermal or Inadequate Sampling? *Plains Anthropologist* 40 (1995): 261–70.

———. Cultural Responses to the Altithermal or Inadequate Sampling Reconsidered. *Plains Anthropologist* 41 (1996): 395–97.

Sigstad, John S., and Roger Jolley. *An Archaeological Survey of Portions of Fall River and Custer Counties, South Dakota.* South Dakota Archaeological Research Center, Rapid City, 1975.

Skinner, Alanson. *Societies of the Iowa, Kansa, and Ponca Indians.* American Museum of Natural History Anthropological Paper 11, part 9. New York, 1915.

Slay, John S., and Linda Sue Smith. *Cultural Resources Survey of the Roger's Spring Timber Sale (E-14-78).* Black Hills National Forest, Custer, South Dakota, 1979.

Smith, Anne M. *Shoshone Tales.* University of Utah Press, Salt Lake City, 1993.

Smith, DeCost. *Indian Experiences.* Caxton Printers, Caldwell, Idaho, 1943.

———. *Red Indian Experiences.* George Allen and Unwin, London, 1949.

Smith, Harlan I. An Archaeological Reconnaissance in Wyoming. *Journal of the American Museum of Natural History* 8 (1908): 23–26, 106–10.

Smith, Marian W. The War Complex of the Plains Indians. *Proceedings of the American Philosophical Society* 78 (1937): 425–61.

Smith, Marvin T., and Julie Barnes Smith. Engraved Shell Masks in North America. *Southeastern Archaeology* 8 (1989): 9–18.

Snortland-Coles, Signe, and Lawrence L. Loendorf. National Register of Historic Places Nomination Form for the Medicine Rock State Historic Site, North Dakota. Manuscript on file, North Dakota Historic Preservation Office, Bismarck, 1986.

South Dakota Writers' Project. *Legends of the Mighty Sioux.* Work Projects Administration, 1941. Reprint, 1987, Badlands Natural History Association, Interior, South Dakota.

Spector, Janet D. *What This Awl Means: Feminist Archaeology at a Wahpeton Dakota Village.* Minnesota Historical Society Press, St. Paul, 1993.

Spring, Agnes W. *The Cheyenne and Black Hills Stage and Express Routes.* University of Nebraska Press, Lincoln, 1948.

Standing Bear, Luther. *Land of the Spotted Eagle.* University of Nebraska Press, Lincoln, 1933.

———. *My People the Sioux.* Houghton Mifflin, New York, 1928.

Stands in Timber, John, and Margot Liberty. *Cheyenne Memories.* University of Nebraska Press, Lincoln, 1967.

Steege, L. C., and D. G. Paulley. Lissolo Cave. *Wyoming Archaeologist* 7 (1964): 25–33.

Steinbring, Jack, and Anthony P. Buchner. Cathedrals of Prehistory: Rock Art Sites of the Northern Plains. *American Indian Rock Art* 23 (1997): 73–84.

Steward, Julian H. *Petroglyphs of California and Adjoining States.* University of California Publications in American Archaeology and Ethnology 24, no. 2. Berkeley, 1929.

———. Petroglyphs of the United States. *Smithsonian Institution Annual Report for 1936,* pp. 404–25. Washington, D.C., 1937.

Stilgebouer, Cece, and Ruth Stilgebouer. *Gettysburg, South Dakota, Seventy-fifth Anniversary, July 11–12,*

1958: Through 75 Years. State Publishing, Pierre, South Dakota, 1958.

Stone, Richard. *First Encounters: Indian Legends of Devils Tower.* Sand Creek Printing, Belle Fourche, South Dakota, 1982.

———. The Legend of Devils Tower. Pamphlet on file. Devils Tower National Monument, Wyoming, n.d.

St. Pierre, Mark, and Tilda Long Soldier. *Walking in the Sacred Manner: Healers, Dreamers, and Pipe Carriers—Medicine Women of the Plains Indians.* Simon and Schuster, New York, 1995.

Strauss, Lawrence Guy. Solutrean Settlement of North America? A Review of Reality. *American Antiquity* 65 (2000): 219–26.

Strauss, Lawrence Guy, B. V. Eriksen, J. M. Elandson, and D. Yesner, editors. *Humans at the End of the Ice Age: The Archaeology of the Pleistocene-Holocene Transition.* Plenum Press, New York, 1996.

Sundstrom, Linea. Additional Rock Art Sites from the Southern Black Hills. *South Dakota Archaeologist* 13 (1989): 29–54.

———. *Culture History of the Southern Black Hills with Reference to Adjacent Areas of the Northern Great Plains.* J&L Reprint, Lincoln, Nebraska, 1989.

———. *Draft Management Plan for the Craven Canyon Rock Art District, Hell Canyon Ranger District, Black Hills National Forest, Custer, South Dakota.* National Park Service, Midwest Archeological Center, Lincoln, Nebraska, for Black Hills National Forest, Custer, South Dakota, 2003.

———. *Fragile Heritage: Prehistoric Rock Art of South Dakota.* South Dakota Historical Preservation Center, Pierre, South Dakota, 1993.

———. *Hermosa-Hayward Project: Test Excavations in the Eastern Black Hills.* South Dakota State Archaeological Research Center, Contract Investigation Series 34, 1981.

———. *Living on the Edge: Archaeological and Geomorphological Investigations in the Vicinity of Tepee and Hell Canyons, Western Custer County, South Dakota.* Day Star Research, Shorewood, Wisconsin, for South Dakota Historic Preservation Office, Pierre, 1999.

———. The Material Culture of Ludlow Cave, Custer National Forest, Harding County, South Dakota: A NAGPRA Evaluation. Custer National Forest, Billings, Montana, 1996.

———. Mirror of Heaven: Cross-Cultural Transference of the Sacred Geography of the Black Hills. *World Archaeology* 29 (1996): 177–89.

———. A Moveable Feast: 10,000 Years of Food Acquisition in the Black Hills. *South Dakota Archaeology* 19–20 (1995–96): 16–48.

———. *North Cave Hills Archaeological Survey 1998: A Passports in Time Project Sponsored by Custer National Forest.* Custer National Forest, Billings, Montana, 1998.

———. *North Cave Hills Rock Art Survey 1997: A Passports in Time Project Sponsored by Custer National Forest.* Custer National Forest, Billings, Montana, 1997.

———. *Rock Art of the Southern Black Hills: A Contextual Approach.* Garland Publishing, New York, 1990.

———. *Rock Art of the Southern Black Hills, South Dakota and Wyoming.* South Dakota State University Publications in Anthropology 2. Brookings, South Dakota, 1981.

———. The Sacred Black Hills: An Ethnohistorical Review. *Great Plains Quarterly* 17 (1997): 185–212.

———. *South Dakota Rock Art Survey II: Investigations in the South Cave Hills, Harding County, South Dakota.* South Dakota Historical Preservation Center, Pierre, South Dakota, 1993.

Sundstrom, Linea, Ned Hanenberger, James Donohue, Grant Smith, Mike McFaul, Karen Lynn Traugh, Bruce Potter, and Jane Abbott. *The Blaine Site: A Multiple Component Camp in the Red Valley of the Black Hills.* South Dakota Archaeological Research Center, Contract Investigations Series, 1998.

Sundstrom, Linea, and James D. Keyser. Tribal Affiliation of Shield Petroglyphs from the Black Hills and Cave Hills. *Plains Anthropologist* 43 (1998): 225–38.

Sundstrom, Linea, Linda Olson, and Lawrence Loendorf. *Hulett South Site, 48CK1544.* Loendorf and Associates for Wyoming Department of Transportation, Cheyenne, 2001.

Syms, Leigh. The McKean Complex as a Horizon Marker in Manitoba and on the Northern Great Plains. M.A. thesis, Department of Anthropology, University of Manitoba, Winnipeg, 1969.

Szabo, Joyce M. *Howling Wolf and the History of Ledger Art.* University of New Mexico Press, Albuquerque, 1994.

Tallbull, Bill, Sherri Deaver, and Halcyon LaPoint. A New Way to Study Cultural Landscapes: The Blue Earth Hills Assessment. *Landscape and Urban Planning* 36 (1996): 125–33.

Taylor, Colin F. *The Plains Indians.* Salamander Books, London, 1994.

Taylor, Joseph Henry. *Sketches of Frontier and Indian Life on the Upper Missouri and Great Plains.* Self-published. Bismarck, North Dakota, 1897.

Teit, James. The Thompson Indians of British Columbia, Jesup North Pacific Expedition. *Memoirs of the American Museum of Natural History* 2 (1900): 376–86.

————. *The Salishan Tribes of the Western Plateaus.* Bureau of American Ethnology Annual Report 45. Washington, D.C., 1930.

Theisz, R. D. Multifaceted Double Woman: Legend, Song, Dream, and Meaning. *European Review of Native American Studies* 2, no. 2 (1988): 9–16.

Thomas, Sidney J. A Sioux Medicine Bundle. *American Anthropologist* 43 (1941): 605–9.

Thwaites, Reuben Gold, editor. *Account of an Expedition from Pittsburgh to the Rocky Mountains Performed in the Years 1819, 1820, by Order of the Hon. J. C. Calhoun, Secretary of War, under the Command of Major S. H. Long, of the U.S. Top. Engineers: Compiled from the Notes of Major Long, Mr. T. Say, and Other Gentlemen of the Party by Edwin James, Botanist and Geologist of the Expedition,* vol. 2. Arthur H. Clark Company, Cleveland, 1905.

————. *Travels in the Interior of North America by Maximillian, Prince of Wied,* vol. 2. Arthur H. Clark Company, Cleveland, 1906.

Todd, Lawrence C. Excavation, Research, and Public Interpretation at the Hudson-Meng Bison Bone Bed, Sioux County, Nebraska. Paper presented at the 53d annual Plains Anthropological Conference, Laramie, Wyoming, 1995.

Tratebas, Alice M. *Archaeological Excavations near Stone Quarry Canyon, Black Hills National Forest, South Dakota.* South Dakota State Archaeological Research Center, Contract Investigation Series 7, 1979.

————. Black Hills Settlement Patterns: Based on a Functional Approach. Ph.D. dissertation, Indiana University, Bloomington, 1986.

————. Stylistic Chronology versus Absolute Dates for Early Hunting Style Rock Art on the North American Plains. In *Rock Art Studies: The Post-Stylistic Era, or Where Do We Go from Here?* edited by Michel Lorblanchet and Paul G. Bahn, pp. 163–77. Oxbow Books, Oxford, 1993.

Tratebas, Alice M., and Kristi Vagstad. *Archaeological Test Excavations of Four Sites in the Black Hills National Forest, South Dakota.* South Dakota State Archaeological Research Center, Contract Investigation Series 6, 1979.

Turner, Ronald W. *Mammals of the Black Hills of South Dakota and Wyoming.* University of Kansas Museum of Natural History Miscellaneous Publication 60. Lawrence, Kansas, 1974.

Urbanek, Mae. *Wyoming Place Names.* Johnson Books, Boulder, Colorado, 1974.

Vallejo, Robert G. *A Level III Heritage Resources Inventory of the Whisper Timber Sale in Pennington County, S.D.* Black Hills National Forest, Custer, South Dakota, 1993.

Vastokas, Joan M., and Romas K. Vastokas. *Sacred Art of the Algonkians.* Mansard Press, Peterborough, Ontario, 1973.

Vestal, Stanley. *Warpath: The True Story of the Fighting Sioux Told in a Biography of Chief White Bull.* Houghton Mifflin, Boston, 1934.

Voget, Fred W. Sacred Numerology and Management of the Universe by Crow Indians. *Plains Anthropologist* 40 (1995): 353–68.

Walker, James R. *Lakota Belief and Ritual.* Edited by Raymond J. DeMallie and Elaine A. Jahner. University of Nebraska Press, Lincoln, 1980.

————. *The Sun Dance and Other Ceremonies of the Oglala Division of the Teton-Dakota.* American Museum of Natural History Anthropological Paper 16. New York, 1917.

Waring, Antonio J., and Preston Holder. A Prehistoric Ceremonial Complex in the Southeastern United States. *American Anthropologist* 47 (1945): 1–34.

Warren, Lieutenant G. K. Preliminary Report of Explorations in Nebraska and Dakota in 1855–56–57 by Lieut. G. K. Warren, Topographical Engineers, U.S. Army. *South Dakota Historical Collections* 11 (1922): 134–219.

Watchman, Alan. Potential Methods for Dating Rock Paintings. *American Indian Rock Art* 18 (1992): 43–51.

Weathermon, Rick. *Level III Heritage Resource Inventory of the Dougherty and Shanks Planning Areas in Pennington County, South Dakota: Project nos. Ph-10-99, Ph-11-99, Mystic Ranger District, Black Hills National Forest.* Pochteca Archaeology, Laramie, Wyoming, for Black Hills National Forest, Custer, South Dakota, 1999.

Wedel, Waldo R. *Prehistoric Man on the Great Plains.* University of Oklahoma Press, Norman, 1961.

Wellmann, Klaus F. *A Survey of North American Indian Rock Art.* Akademische Druck- und Verlanganstalt, Graz, Austria, 1979.

Weston, Timothy. Acculturation in the Middle Missouri Valley as Reflected in Modified Bone Assemblages. *Plains Anthropologist* 38 (1993): 79–100.

Wheeler, Richard P. *Archeological Remains in the Angostura Reservoir Area, Fall River County, South Dakota, and the Keyhole and Boysen Reservoir Areas, Wyoming.* Smithsonian Institution, River Basin Surveys Reports. Washington, D.C., 1957. Reprint, 1995, J&L Reprints, Lincoln, Nebraska, under the title *Archeological Investigations in Three Reservoir Areas in South Dakota and Wyoming.*

————. *Preliminary Appraisal of the Archeological and Paleontological Resources of Angostura Reservoir, Fall River County, South Dakota.* Smithsonian Institution, River Basin Surveys Reports. Washington, D.C., 1947.

Whitley, David S. *The Art of the Shaman: Rock Art of California.* University of Utah Press, Salt Lake City, 2000.

———. Ethnography and Rock Art in the Far West: Some Archaeological Implications. In *New Light on Old Art: Recent Advances in Hunter-Gatherer Rock Art Research,* edited by David S. Whitley and Lawrence L. Loendorf, pp. 81–93. University of California Institute of Archaeology, Monograph 36. Berkeley, 1994.

Wilbert, Werner. Two Rock Art Sites in Calaveras County. In *Messages from the Past: Studies in California Rock Art,* edited by Clement W. Meighan, pp. 107–22. Institute of Archaeology Monograph 20, University of California at Berkeley, 1981.

Wildschut, William, and John C. Ewers. *Crow Indian Medicine Bundles,* 2d edition. Museum of the American Indian, Heye Foundation, Contribution 17. New York, 1975.

Will, George F. *Archaeology of the Missouri Valley.* Anthropological Papers of the American Museum of Natural History, vol. 22, part 4, 1924.

———. Some Observations Made in Northwestern South Dakota. *American Anthropologist* 11 (1909): 257–65.

Williams, Stephen, and John M. Goggin. The Long-Nosed God Mask in Eastern United States. *Missouri Archaeologist* 18, no. 3 (1956): 4–72.

Wilson, Gilbert L. *Hidatsa Eagle Trapping.* American Museum of Natural History Anthropological Paper 30, no. 4, 1928. Reprint, 1978, J&L Reprint, Lincoln, Nebraska.

———. *Waheenee: An Indian Girl's Story Told by Herself to Gilbert L. Wilson.* Webb Publishing, St. Paul, Minnesota, 1927. Reprint, 1981, University of Nebraska Press, Lincoln.

Winchell, Newton Horace. *Aborigines of Minnesota.* Minnesota Historical Society, St. Paul, 1911.

Winham, R. Peter, and Edward J. Lueck. Cultures of the Middle Missouri. In *Plains Indians, A.D. 500–1500: The Archaeological Past of Historic Groups,* edited by Karl H. Schlesier, pp. 159–69. University of Oklahoma Press, Norman, 1994.

Wissler, Clark. *Societies and Ceremonial Associations in the Oglala Division of the Teton-Dakota.* American Museum of Natural History Anthropological Paper 11, no. 1. New York, 1912.

Wood, W. Raymond. *The Origins of the Hidatsa Indians: A Review of the Ethnohistorical and Traditional Data.* J&L Reprint, Lincoln, Nebraska, 1986.

———. *The Redbird Focus and the Problem of Ponca Prehistory.* Plains Anthropologist Memoir 2, 1965.

———, editor. *Papers in Northern Plains Prehistory and Ethnohistory.* South Dakota Archaeological Society Special Publication 10, Sioux Falls, 1986.

Wood, W. Raymond, and Thomas D. Theissen. *Early Fur Trade on the Northern Plains: Canadian Traders among the Mandan and Hidatsa Indians, 1738–1818.* University of Oklahoma Press, Norman, 1985.

Wormington, H. M. *A Reappraisal of Fremont Culture.* Denver Museum of Natural History Proceedings 1. Denver, 1955.

Wormington, H. M., and Richard G. Forbis. *An Introduction to the Archaeology of Alberta, Canada.* Denver Museum of Natural History Proceedings 11. Denver, 1965.

Wyoming Writer's Project, Works Project Administration. *Wyoming: A Guide to Its History, Highways, and People.* Oxford University Press, New York, 1941.

Young Bear, Severt, and R. D. Theisz. *Standing in the Light: A Lakota Way of Seeing.* University of Nebraska Press, Lincoln, 1994.

Zimmerman, Larry J. *Peoples of Prehistoric South Dakota.* University of Nebraska Press, Lincoln, 1985.

Index

All references to illustrations are in italic type.

234 Index

Ludlow, William, 79, 172, *188*

Ludlow Cave, S.Dak., 32, 34, 43, *46*, 79–83, *80*, 87, 120, 132, 134, 162, 191, 201

Malta Medicine Rock, Mont., 43

Mandan Indians: beliefs concerning rock art, 45–46, 81, 112, 149–53; cultural traditions, 81, 115–24, 132, 149–57; history, 78; rock art possibly affiliated with, 83, 139, 152–53, 173

Maps, elements of illustrated in rock art, 100–101, *102*, 105–106, *106–107*

Marias Medicine Rock, Mont., 43

Maskettes, shell or copper, 137–39, *139*, 165–73

Massaum ceremony, Cheyenne, 184–85

McKenzie Butte, S.Dak., 149

McLaughlin, Marie, 32, *33*

Medicine Creek Cave Site, Wyo., 43, 101–102, 132–40, 144–48, 201

Medicine Deer Rock, Mont. *See* Deer Medicine Rock, Mont.

Medicine Lodge Creek Site, Wyo., 65, *66*, 197

Medicine Pipe Mountain, S.Dak. *See* Bear Butte, S.Dak.

Medicine Rock, Gettysburg, S.Dak., 43

Medicine Rock, N.Dak., 43, 49–57

Men, illustrated in rock art, *47*, 55, *55–62*, *101*, *103–104*, 105–106, *106–109*, *111*

Mi-Ojin-ha-the, 45

Mississippian archaeological complex, 137, 160–62, 169

Missouri River, 45, 179

Missouri River tribes in S.Dak., 181. *See also* Arikara Indians; Hidatsa Indians; Mandan Indians

Myths. *See* Oral tradition of Plains Indians

Naishan Dene Indians: cultural traditions, 141; history, 3, 18; rock art possibly affiliated with, 149

Nets, hunting, *25*, 51–55, *52*, *56–59*, *61*

Niobrara River, 179

Nonoma, Cheyenne thunder spirit being, 162–65, *166*

Offerings, religious, at rock art sites, 41–43, 46, *46*, 85, *92*, 132–33, 152

Ogallala Trading Post, 186